Gender Justice and Human Rights in International Development Assistance

Gender Justice and Human Rights in International Development Assistance provides a critical analysis of how frameworks of gender equality play out in the field of international development assistance (IDA), at theoretical, international legislative and policy levels, donor and national policy levels and programme levels. If current dominant theoretical perspectives are not interrogated, the consequences could be that gender inequalities and injustices are inadequately addressed, or that opportunities are missed to impact on poverty reduction and on transformative gender changes. Through a renewed interpretation of gender equality in IDA, the book aims to show the way towards a more effective response to gender inequalities and injustices faced by women in developing countries.

Drawing on 20 years of experience working with IDA policies and programming across three continents, this book makes an important contribution to the active and dynamic field of critical feminism, and provides practical illustrations on how such critical thinking might contribute to gender transformational changes. *Gender Justice and Human Rights in International Development Assistance* will be important reading for scholars and upper-level students working in the fields of gender equality, human rights, development assistance, foreign affairs, international law and international relations.

Sarah Forti, PhD, is the founder and director of Critical Rights & Gender Consult based in Copenhagen, Denmark, and has more than 20 years of experience in development evaluations, program design and training in the field of human rights, non-discrimination, women's human rights and SGBV (Sexual and Gender-based Violence) across Africa, Latin America and Asia.

Routledge ISS Gender, Sexuality and Development Studies

The *Routledge ISS Gender, Sexuality and Development Studies* series explores the diverse ways in which topics of gender and sexuality relate to international development, both in theory and in practice. The book series aims to publish 'classical' gender, sexuality and development themes – such as the sexual and reproductive rights policy debates on population and sustainable development, adolescence and sex education, and policy on abortion – together with cutting-edge work on embodiment, queer theory and innovative strategies of resistance to hegemonic discourses of sexuality and gender. The book series will pay special attention to the role of intergenerational power relations and how they interact with different gendered understandings of sexuality at diverse stages in the life cycle.

Wendy Harcourt leads the international editorial board with her colleagues from the renowned International Institute of Social Studies of Erasmus University, The Netherlands. The Board welcomes book proposals from researchers working in all geographic areas with special interest in research undertaken from feminist-grounded theory and with marginalized groups in the global South and North.

To find out more about how to submit a book proposal, please contact the Development Studies Editor, Helena Hurd (Helena.Hurd@tandf.co.uk) or Wendy Harcourt (harcourt@iss.nl).

Global Trends in Land Tenure Reform
Gender Impacts
Edited by Caroline S. Archambault and Annelies Zoomers

Gender, Power and Knowledge for Development
Lata Narayanaswamy

Gender Responsive Budgeting in Fragile States
The Case of Timor-Leste
Monica Costa

Gender Justice and Human Rights in International Development Assistance
Transcending Universal Divisions
Sarah Forti

Gender Justice and Human Rights in International Development Assistance

Transcending Universal Divisions

Sarah Forti

Routledge
Taylor & Francis Group
LONDON AND NEW YORK

First published 2019
by Routledge
2 Park Square, Milton Park, Abingdon, Oxon OX14 4RN

and by Routledge
52 Vanderbilt Avenue, New York, NY 10017, USA

First issued in paperback 2020

Routledge is an imprint of the Taylor & Francis Group, an informa business

British Library Cataloguing-in-Publication Data
A catalogue record for this book is available from the British Library

Library of Congress Cataloging-in-Publication Data
A catalog record has been requested for this book

ISBN 13: 978-0-367-66536-4 (pbk)
ISBN 13: 978-1-138-08386-8 (hbk)

Typeset in Goudy
by Apex CoVantage, LLC

To Alma, Carlo and Nicolaj

Contents

Abbreviations and acronyms

CBO	Community-based Organisation
CEDAW	Convention on the Elimination of All Forms of Discrimination Against Women
CGE	Commission on Gender Equality
Cida	Canadian International Development Agency
CSO	Civil Society Organisation
DAC	Development Assistance Committee (OECD)
Danida	Danish International Development Agency
DFID	Department for International Development
DOC	Drivers of Change
DRB	Domestic Relation Bill
EC	European Commission
ECOSOC	United Nations Economic and Social Council
EEC	European Economic Community
EU	European Union
EVD	Evaluation Department in DFID
FEMUM	Federación de Mujeres Municipalistas de América Latina y El Caribe
FGM	Female Genital Mutilation
GAD	Gender and Development
GDP	Gross Domestic Product
GE	Gender Equality
GTZ	German Technical Co-operation
HIV/AIDS	Human Immunodeficiency Virus/Acquired Immunodeficiency Syndrome
HQ	Headquarters
HR	Human Rights
HRBA	Human Rights Based Approach
IDA	International Development Assistance
IDB	Inter-American Development Bank
IDT	International Development Targets
IIDH	International Institute for Human Rights (Central America)
IMF	International Monetary Fund

IOs	International Organisations
MDG	Millennium Development Goals
MTEF	Medium Term Expenditure Framework
NDI	National Democratic Institute
NGO	Non-Governmental Organisation
OECD	Organisation for Economic Cooperation and Development
OPR	Output to Purpose Review
OSW	Office on the Status of Women
PAF	Performance Assessment Framework
PAHO	Pan-American Health Organization
PfA	Platform for Action
PPP	Public Participation Programme
PRA	Participatory Rural Appraisal
PRAM	Participatory Rights Assessment Methodologies
PRS	Poverty Reduction Strategy
PSA	Public Service Agreement
RAP	Regional Assistance Plan
RBA	Rights-based Approach
SDA	Social Development Adviser
SDG	Sustainable Development Goals
SGBV	Sexual and Gender-based Violence
Sida	Swedish International Development Cooperation Agency
STDs	Sexually Transmitted Diseases
SWAp	Sector Wide Approach
SWOT	Strengths, Weaknesses, Opportunities and Threats
TOR	Terms of Reference
TSP	Target Strategy Paper
UK	United Kingdom
UN	United Nations
UTV	Department for Evaluation and Internal Audit
WB	World Bank
WE	Women's Empowerment
WID	Women in Development
WLSA	Women and Law in Southern Africa
WP	White Paper

Acknowledgements

This book owes much of its substance, vision and engagement to the many women and men, met during field missions undertaken in Africa, Latin America and Asia over the last 20 years and to my students at the Danish Fellowship Centre (DFC) in the gender equality and women's human rights training courses – from Burkina Faso, Mali, Niger, Ghana, Liberia, Uganda, Kenya, Tanzania, Zambia, Rwanda, Burundi, Democratic Republic of Congo, Nepal, Bangladesh, Cambodia, Vietnam, Laos, Bhutan, Bolivia, Nicaragua, Costa Rica, Honduras, Ecuador and Guatemala. They have entrusted me with their critical perspectives and personal learning in their struggles and successes with generosity and openness. The book is essentially written for them and in the hope that it may bring some arguments for critical changes to their conditions.

The research could not have been undertaken without the professional support and inspiring working material from the many assignments won over the years and especially those supported by the Danish Ministry of Foreign Affairs and the Swedish Ministry of Foreign Affairs. I am particularly grateful to the non-governmental civil society organisations, their staff and NGO partners in the field whose commitment to the issues of gender justice and HRBA in challenging contexts provided a constant inspiration for bridging community and global solidarity: special thanks must be extended to DFC, KVINFO, DanChurchAid and ICORN. Gratitude is also extended for the most recent and inspiring cooperation with Pauline Stoltz, Associate Professor at the Department of Culture and Global Studies, FREIA Centre for Gender Research at Aalborg University, Denmark.

Amidst the many thought-provoking authors encountered through the reading and studying of their works, I wish to pay a particular tribute to some outstandingly beautiful minds, troublemakers and free thinkers whose works have given me immense sense of joy, inspiration and hope for critical changes to come. These are: Susan Moller Okin, Hilary Charlesworth, Nancy Fraser, Chahdortt Djavann, Elisabeth Badinter, Caroline Fourest, Leila Slimani, Michel Onfray, Kamel Daoud, Marguerite Duras, Christian Bobin, Albert Camus and Charles Baudelaire.

I will remain forever indebted to Wade Mansell, Emeritus Professor at the University of Kent, for remaining the primary source of inspiration since my early days at Kent Law School, for his tireless encouragements and faith in me, which have played a determining part in the achievement of this work. Deepest thanks for their invaluable comments and revisions which have punctuated key parts of the work must be extended to Anna Currado for her invaluable editing, Anne Bottomley and Belinda Meteyard of the University of Kent for providing much inspiration.

I would also like to give my warmest appreciation to mentors that have nurtured my desire for writing and creativity from early days: Dr Britha Mikkelsen, Ms Lucchesi, Italian literature teacher, Ms Maddicott, history teacher at Rye St Antony School, Oxford and Mme Radoulescou, French literature teacher at Notre Dame de Sion, Paris VI ème.

On a personal note, I wish to give special and warmest thanks to my father, Augusto Forti, for providing me with the opportunity to study abroad and for his love, support and firm anchorage in free and critical thinking which have marked my entire education. I would like to thank my mother, Mara Muscetta, for transmitting her precious cultural heritage to me: her love for books, arts and literature. I am very grateful to my dearest family: my brother Enrico and my sister Silvia; to Lisi, Marisa and Rosa as examples of wonderful women; to my loving nieces, nephews and soul sister Laura. Gratitude is also extended to my in-laws Birgit and Kjeld for their invaluable support.

With my deepest love, the book is dedicated to Alma, Carlo and Nicolaj, to whom I would like to transmit much more than the words in this book can ever express.

Introduction

This chapter introduces the reasons that have led to the writing of the book and explains the rationale for selecting a critical perspective to the subject of investigation. It presents the purpose, objectives and structure of the book. The chapter further develops the methodology, including the approach, which consists of a critical approach across multiple disciplines, perspectives and locations. It discusses the analytical framework utilised, the purposive sampling method and concludes with a summary of methods employed for data collection.

Why the need for a critical perspective?

It was the author's hope that much of this book, which was written for a PhD thesis at the University of Kent Law School in 2011, would have become irrelevant by now. At the time, there seemed to be a nascent hope for a (re)legitimisation of human rights, and by ripple effects, a re-emergence of humanist universal values undergirding women's human rights. Some Charlie Hebdo and Bataclan's attacks later and against a backdrop of countless gruesome human rights violations worldwide, instead of a surge for collective solidarity, communitarian and ideological divides were amplified. Slogans such as 'Nous sommes tous Charlie'/'Nous sommes tous Paris' were an attempt at gathering collective solidarity in the face of horror, beyond differences of race, religion, social, economic and political standings, affinities or lifestyles, etc. Behind the massive street gatherings across European cities, countless flowers and candles displays for peace and remembrance, a recurrent rhetoric defending a distinct version of 'multiculturalism' was emerging, known as 'Yes, we condemn these attacks but. . . .' It became increasingly difficult to see that human empathy for such mass violations clearly transcends divides across cultures.

The story of Kamel Daoud, the Algerian journalist and writer, is an emblematic illustration of these paradoxical times. Daoud's debut novel *Mersault, Counter-Investigation*[1] portrays a retelling of Albert Camus' classic *The Stranger* from an Algerian perspective and 'reaped glowing international reviews and literary honours'.[2] Daoud, as a journalist, was amongst the very few to dare publicly voicing concern for women's human rights abuses following what is now known as 'The Cologne New Year Gang assaults' on women. On New Year's Eve 2015, about

80 women reported sexual assaults and muggings by around 1,000 drunk and aggressive young men, mainly from Northern Africa. Daoud wrote an article in *Le Monde*[3] in which he denounced 'the deeply entrenched sexism that exists across the Arab world'. By critically examining the relation to women's bodies and consequently to human life itself, Daoud transcended the particularisms of his culture. Yet, a collective of intellectuals and academics, responding in *Le Monde*[4] to his article accused Daoud of feeding 'Islamophobic fantasies and of fuelling orientalist stereotypes'. Furthermore, Daoud had been victim of a Fatwa (against which he filed a criminal complaint and thereafter won the case in his home country, Algeria). Thus, his humanist discourse was caught between two fires: on the one hand, the surge of religious fundamentalist and cultural totalitarian ideologies and on the other hand, a well-established politically correct left-wing ideology that tended to deny non-Western 'others' the same universal human rights standards as those enjoyed by themselves.[5]

This book contends that this is indeed the paradox in which women's human rights and feminism are caught today. At stake, therefore is our capability of lifting our humanity beyond the self, beyond one's own culture and particularism to reach out and feel at one with the 'other', transcending cultural, social, economic and ideological divides. The current #MeToo campaign, if anything, shows that sexism, violations of women's human rights and sexual and gender-based violence do transcend cultures, religions, social and economic classes and locations, etc. The book's writing is thus driven by a felt need to critically re-examine past ideological hegemonic trends, to try and make sense of a present that is riddled with paradoxes and to provide a critical lens for apprehending the future.

Thus, in the *fin de siècle, l'air du temps* had drifted from the domination of the universal to the domination of identity politics stemming from the increasingly popular postcolonialist ideology. Thus, within a certain left-wing intelligentsia once adhering to and protecting universal human rights, the presumed oppressor became almost inevitably 'the white, heterosexual, middle-class Western man' and the presumed victim, the 'rest' of the world exotified as the 'differently other'. Turning a blind eye on misogynous ideologies, drifting towards a certain complaisance with some forms of violations of women's human rights under the auspice of multiculturalism became increasingly within political elites, academics and NGOs alike. Floating in the air was a revival of communitarian values, highlighting divides and deepening the gaps across cultures and nations, colours and sexes. In the midst of rightfully denouncing Western paternalism, the sway towards the other opposite extreme increasingly offered 'protection' to a variety of human rights violations and injustices. Cultural relativism seemed to have won the hearts and minds of those that once defended its opposite, a common humanity, regardless of race, sex, religious and political affiliation and geographical location. There was a strong presumption that women were 'culturally' more inclined and legitimate to address women's rights issues (as opposed to men or as opposed to other women not belonging to the particular cultural identity group, colour or location) – and thus in a supposedly advantageous and more legitimate position to make a better and more gender-just environment; all they required was to be allowed to participate, be 'included' and 'represented' and transformational changes in the form of equality and justice would ensue.

Questioning, through a critical perspective, whose interests did these premises really serve became the main incentive for turning the author's research thesis into this book. As gender equality, women's human rights and their relevance to a broader, cross-cultural and universal idea of gender justice became the main subject of interest in the author's professional life, the book takes its source of inspiration in a practitioner's perspective. This is reflected through the gender and human rights evaluations, reviews and design of IDA policies and programmes carried out by the author over the last 20 years across Latin America, Northern and Sub-Saharan Africa and Asia. The many years spent living in Sub-Saharan Africa has led to linking the realities of IDA from a field perspective with some of the most striking ideas in Kent Law School within the Introduction to Law course. The connection between the two was obviously 'a critical approach' and the question that immediately followed was, 'But critical to what end and to serve whose interest?'

The critical approach is thus best illustrated in *A Critical Introduction to Law*.[6] The book was the subject of one of the author's first lectures attended at the Kent Law School and it began with an apocryphal story illustrating the central theme of the book, captured in the following fundamental question: 'Who drew the map?'[7] The question in the book applies to the field of law in order to critically reconsider what is usually taken for granted and to question commonsense assumptions about the law.

The same question sparked the approach for this book in relation to the politics of gender equality interpretation in the field of IDA: Who drew the definition of gender equality in IDA and whose interest does it serve? Likewise, this question is raised in relation to gender equality in order to reconsider what is usually taken for granted and to question common assumptions about the meaning of gender equality in IDA.

It was anticipated that a critical approach would lead to further reflection on issues such as the hegemonic ideologies underpinning the interpretations of the concept of gender equality, the interests at play underlying these ideological trends and the extent to which these have addressed (or not) inequalities and injustices faced by women living in poverty in developing countries.

In *A Critical Introduction to Law*, the critical approach undertaken could reveal the following premise: 'Law in the Rule of Law form establishes its identity by excluding ideas of substantive justice, and it does so by equating justice with the idea of rules'.[8]

In other words, Professor Wade Mansell explains that the rule of law version of justice has little to do with distributive social justice and merely ensures equal access to a set of formal procedures which are apparently neutral translations of and are independent from their political and social content.

This leads to the idea that a critical examination of common and recurrent patterns will not merely challenge specific interpretations of a subject, but at a deeper level, will question the adequacy of the theoretical framework which underpins the subject under investigation within a specified field.

Another aspect of Professor Mansell's analysis which relates to post-modern contestations of large and universal ideas[9] is exemplified in the following statement: '[B]etween being dominated by universal answers and being dominated by the fragmented knowledges of the market, there is a third way based on the recognition that the production of knowledge can be a collective and social process'.[10]

Two ideas in this statement have catalysed some of the need to apply a critical analysis at the practitioners' level in the field of IDA. First of all, the paradoxical element that the very critique of hegemonic ideas could become hegemonic itself and thus could succeed in dominating a discourse in a given field with fragmented ideas, thus further isolating local and individual realities. Such post-modern hegemonic critiques of hegemonies are thus as criticisable as the objects of their critiques. More fundamentally for the purpose of this book, they raise the question of the relevance of these standpoints and the politics of identities in relation to addressing gender injustice and inequalities in IDA at all levels but especially in practice, in terms of impacting on poverty reduction. Secondly, together with the rejection of the grand ideas as illegitimate, lies the underlying rejection of universalism and commonalities that would, arguably, possibly legitimise the struggle for women's human rights and gender justice itself – which is being delegitimised as Western postcolonialism.[11]

Ultimately, it is anticipated that such a critique might be useful in formulating a re-envisioned focus underpinning gender equality. Such a focus would be expected to provide, through a renewed interpretation of gender equality in IDA, a more adequate response to women's human rights violations, gender inequalities and injustices faced by women across continents and times.

It is assumed that the implications of not rethinking current dominant theoretical perspectives relating to gender equality in IDA may have serious consequences. At best, the prevailing interpretation of gender equality may inadequately or merely partially address gender inequalities and injustices in practice, essentially being limited to monitoring progress in the quantitative participation of women and fragmented recognition of women's specific needs – further isolating them from one another. At worst, to leave current ideologies intact may miss the opportunity to impact on poverty reduction, since the current framework rarely focuses on substantive social justice for women.

This book has thus been conceived to provide an analysis of how key ideological shifts which underpin the interpretation of gender equality have played out at the theoretical, international legislative and policy level, donor and national policy level and programme level in the field of IDA – and whose interests do they really serve.

Purpose, objectives and structure

The book argues that the inadequacy of IDA's response to substantive socio-economic injustices affecting women living in poverty and facing women's human rights violations has largely been due to how gender equality is defined.

This has coincided with shifts in feminist theory, as divergent schools of thought have promoted competing theories as to how gender equality is best understood and thus defined. This has led to compromises being sought with those whose ideologies show complacency with violations of women's human rights – under the auspice of multiculturalism or those who effectively limit the outcomes of gender equality to quantitative representation of women.

In particular, it is the contention of the book that the interpretation of gender equality in IDA has changed, and now reflects an insufficient focus on redistribution and on universal similarities of violations of women's human rights across differences in cultures. As a consequence, prevailing discourses insufficiently challenge the common patriarchal structures entrenching substantive injustices for women across societies. Furthermore, it is contended that such changes in focus form recurrent patterns. Finally, it is argued that analysing these ideological boundaries and developments not only deepens our understanding of the weak response, but possibly informs a refocus of gender equality in IDA to more adequately address gender inequalities, violations of women's human rights and injustices.

The objectives of the book are thus formulated and structured around three parts as follows:

PART I discusses how the focus of theoretical framing underpinning the concept of gender equality has changed and identifies the key elements that have been displaced, dismissed and eroded in theories, international legislative and policy frameworks.

PART II demonstrates how this change in focus affected the interpretation of gender equality in national politics, donor-level policies and at the programme level.

PART III identifies common and recurrent patterns of changes and possible implications and draws out the key elements of a renewed critical focus to underpin gender equality in IDA, identify pre-conditions to be considered towards the achievement of substantive gender justice and any implications across developed/developing countries particularisms.

The book is thus structured as follows:

Introduction

This chapter introduces the reasons that have led to the writing of the book and explains the rationale for selecting a critical perspective to the subject of investigation. It presents the purpose, objectives and structure of the book. The chapter further develops the methodology including the approach, which consists of a critical approach across multiple disciplines, perspectives and locations. It discusses the analytical framework utilised, the purposive sampling method and concludes with a summary of methods employed for data collection.

Part I

Chapter 1: Breaking the waves

This chapter provides a critical assessment of key theoretical frameworks and ideologies which have posed the most significant challenges to the concept of gender equality in IDA. The chapter proceeds to analyse the implication of these challenges on the key concepts underlying the notion of gender equality such as International Development Assistance (IDA),[12] Women in Development (WID)[13] and Gender and Development (GAD).[14] The chapter thus first discusses how theoretical frameworks and ideologies underpinning gender equality have displaced fundamental notions in the interpretation of gender equality in IDA. In particular, the chapter critically assesses the eclipse of the notion of redistribution and the displacement of the universality[15] of women's human rights violations through the politics of identity's perspective[16] – which essentially focuses on recognition and representation.[17]

The first section of the chapter analyses the implications of the prevailing focus of identity politics in the interpretation of gender equality in the field of IDA. By identifying cultural relativism as one of the most challenging issues for the field, this section assesses the extent to which cultural relativism[18] has found a renaissance through a variety of feminist schools of thoughts from anti-essentialists,[19] to Third Worldists,[20] to postcolonialists[21] and difference feminists.[22] It is argued that this revival has been achieved largely by delegitimising universalism, and with it, the notion of the universality which is inherent to i) fundamental violations of women's human rights such as violence against women and ii) the unequal distribution of power and resources. The chapter focuses on these two aspects as they constitute, amongst other issues, the core problematics faced by women beneficiaries of IDA, as is further evidenced in the first section of Chapter 2. The significance of these developments is further discussed in relation to the very conceptualisation and definition of key concepts and approaches influencing the understanding of gender equality in IDA. These are: IDA itself,[23] the Women in Development approach (WID)[24] and the Gender and Development approach (GAD).[25]

Chapter 2: Wavering across international normative architecture

This chapter analyses the interpretation of gender equality at the international legislative and policy level. It discusses how the concept of gender equality is playing 'hide-and-seek', appearing and disappearing, in a solid or more diluted version through the key international norms and policies. It considers the interpretations of gender equality in key international legal instruments and international policy frameworks. These are the Convention on the Elimination of all Forms of Discrimination Against Women (CEDAW),[26] the Protocol to the African Charter on Human and Peoples' Rights on the Rights of Women in Africa 2003,[27] the key UN Women's World Conferences[28] and contemporary dominant IDA policy frameworks such as the Millennium Development Goals (MDGs),[29] the Paris Declaration on Aid Effectiveness (2005)[30] and the current Sustainable Development

Goals (SDGs). In particular, it provides an analysis of the reservations to gender equality in CEDAW and the omission of violence against women, and of the changing interpretations of gender equality in key IDA international policy frameworks. The chapter concludes with a reflection on the implications of theoretical (re)framings on international normative and policy frameworks.

Part II

Chapter 3: Variations on the politics of gender equality

This chapter analyses the varying political interpretations of gender equality through policy cases illustrating i) both neoliberal and social democratic trends amongst bilateral and multilateral donor policies and ii) the use of political ideologies in interpretations of gender equality at the country policy level. Chapter 3 examines whether and how the changes in focus underpinning the concept of gender equality discussed in Chapter 1 have affected the interpretation of gender equality in donor policies[31] and recipient country policies.[32] As discussed in Chapter 2, following four decades[33] of uneven struggle to recognise gender equality in international law and international policies, several multilateral[34] and bilateral[35] development agencies have formally and explicitly incorporated gender equality into their policies. They have done so either by formulating specific gender equality strategies[36] and/or by recognising gender equality as one of their priorities in their main development policy and strategy documents.

The first section does not purport to present an exhaustive catalogue of latest multilateral and bilateral development agencies' policy documents. Rather, it offers an analysis of a selection of policies from some development agencies that are illustrative of political trends which have been critical during the last 20 years. The second section provides a critical analysis of recipient country policies. It examines how divergent political contexts in IDA recipient countries – from neoliberal to Marxist[37] – can interpret gender equality within a variety of policy instruments such as policies, strategies, political speeches and discourses. These examples seek to illustrate some of the possible implications arising from the use of ldist, neoliberal and Marxist focuses in the interpretations of gender equality at the national policy level.

Chapter 4: Universal nocturnes of injustices

The chapter begins by assessing whether it is possible to distinguish the universal from the particular in key examples of specific violations of women's human rights at the field level. In this way, the chapter seeks to challenge the prevailing assumptions of identity politics perspectives that have tended to promote anti-essentialism through multiculturalism,[38] resulting in the delegitimisation of universalism and with it the claim that women's rights are human rights.[39] If asserting that there are both commonalities and differences in these violations across cultures would be stating the obvious, the first section examines whether it is possible to identify universal patterns whilst avoiding postcolonialist critiques. This section seeks to demonstrate that it is misguided to simply reject universalism altogether.[40] Rather, it is the nature of the approach utilised which needs to be challenged and refined.

Thus, the starting points for this chapter are women's human rights violations concerning violence against women and gender inequalities related to the unequal distribution of resources in Uganda. By extrapolating the related data in Uganda, this section attempts to identify commonalities with other neighbouring countries, regions and continents in order to uncover universal connections with similar patterns of violations of women's human rights and gender inequalities. The approach utilised thus explores the local contexts as a point of departure, as opposed to making abstract and 'ahistorical' generalisations.[41] This chapter further seeks to show that violations of fundamental women's human rights and gender inequalities cannot be defined as if locked within the boundaries of cultural differences and identities. Such an approach ultimately risks the provision of justification and legitimisation of these very same inequalities and violations. In this context, the chapter discusses (mis)representation, (un)recognition and (mal)distribution of power and resources through concrete examples of IDA projects in countries from purposively different continents, respectively in Burkina Faso and Cambodia.

Part III

Chapter 5: Critical reframing of gender equality

Based on a summary of conclusions, Chapter 5 discusses a critical reframing of gender equality towards gender justice. The chapter thus focuses on the main elements which have particular significance for the transformation of the deep structures of inequality and injustice affecting women in the field of IDA and which need to be included in the process of reframing gender equality. These provide a challenge to a certain tendency to find consensus at all costs in conflicting theories[42] and propose instead to take the following stand. In light of Nancy Fraser's tri-dimensional matrix of justice,[43] the section proposes to refocus the interpretation of gender equality around the following: a clear political engagement with gender justice[44] through i) the notion of redistribution[45] and ii) the universality of violations of women's human rights.[46] The re-legitimisation of the universality of women's human rights violations[47] is further discussed in connection with the need for a common political engagement within a wider notion of social responsibility, as defined by Hannah Arendt.[48]

The last section of the chapter concludes with the limitations of this book and an outline of the key elements for further research. It is intended that this section will provide useful elements for decision-makers and practitioners, for their consideration when designing new strategic frameworks, policies and programmes to sharpen outcome and impact on gender justice in IDA.

Methodology

The methodology used for this book is understood to be the methods and approaches that have been used to research through various fields such as the political economy, international relations, political theory, philosophy, geography, development and policy literature, etc. The methodology is situated in the context of IDA and therefore utilises the approach and methods for social scientists. The methods have involved the collection of primary data and evaluation missions carried out in the field over the last ten years, and the consolidation and analysis of the data collected into evaluation reports which have then subsequently been reviewed in light of the book's objectives. Thus, key findings and conclusions from these evaluation reports have been further examined within the book's scope and purpose.

Given the critique provided of prevailing feminist thoughts and ideologies as discussed at length in Chapter 1, feminist methodologies such as feminist standpoint and difference feminism have purposefully not been followed as the key aim of the (self-) critical approach here is less to uncover differences than identify commonalities to possibly and ultimately strengthen feminist discourse towards solidarity.[49] The author does not situate herself solely as a 'neutral' external observer, but also as one of the stakeholders, as a professional independent evaluator in the field of gender equality and human rights in IDA with an interest in seeing IDA achieve transformational changes on gender inequalities and gender injustices. The perspective taken throughout the book is guided by this particular interest. The sections below present and further develop the approach and methods employed.

A critical approach – how to research through multiple disciplines, perspectives and locations

Rather than a general textbook offering an exhaustive overview of all gender justice–related themes in IDA, the book offers a reading grid, profoundly attached to human rights and attempting uncover some of the key paradoxes and contradictions surrounding this field though a critical approach to the multidisciplinary field of research. Whilst remaining conscious of the limits of political and ideological engagement as a social being, the author has adopted both a critical and self-critical approach. The book thus discussed and critically assesses, for instance, both right-wing and left-wing perspectives underpinning the interpretations of gender equality in IDA.

The purpose of book, the advancement of justice for women in developing countries, is inseparable from the origins of the main problem: the injustices faced by women in developing countries. In the author's opinion, the person in the best position to assess whether or not a situation is one of inequality and injustice for women may not always necessarily be the 'victim' herself, as she might perceive her situation to be normal and too natural for it to be at all questionable. Nor is it always necessarily the local community, or NGOs and other (self-proclaimed) Third World women's representatives speaking on so-called Third World Women's behalf.

The approach taken is that by providing comparative data on similar situations of injustices and inequalities across borders, regions and continents, one might lift the problematics from the fragmented isolation and boundaries of socio-cultural identities to draw broader patterns of common and recurrent similarities that may deepen our understanding of otherwise isolated events.

With regard to a critical legal approach, while it is difficult to determine whether an approach as such exists, critical legal theory teaches us to raise critical questions in order to unveil political patterns beneath received ideas across multiple disciplines, locations and time. This is the approach taken throughout the book. A critical approach is thus employed here as a relevant approach across multiple disciplines and locations to challenge unquestioned realities and hegemonic ideological trends.

In so far as the author participated in the field missions of the evaluations presented examples, the approach undertaken has been that of facilitating the critical analytical processes of key stakeholders at the field level. This has been done with a view to enable participants of a workshop, seminar, training, meeting or focus group discussion, key informants and interviewees to place themselves in a critical position vis-à-vis the issues at stake and when possible, participate in the critical analysis of key findings. Whilst collecting data, the author has thus been closer to the role of a facilitator of critical processes rather than someone collecting data and analysing it in isolation from the overall goal of poverty reduction in the field of IDA.

When 'critical participatory' approaches are integrated, they may also have an empowering effect on the participants, when occasionally, for the first time, participants are able to question the socio-culturally received ideas and realities they have been socialised into following without questioning or critically assessing related assumptions. This is of particular relevance when the gender equality impacts of a programme are assessed at the beneficiary level.

It has been found that at the village level, whether in Latin American countries or in Sub-Saharan African countries, such an approach was producing empowering effects on participants, raising self-confidence which almost inevitably affected the quantity and quality of the data collected and the depth of the critical discussions and exchange of ideas – which would have otherwise not been identified.

Analytical framework

In order to analyse such ideological shift, the theoretical and analytical framework followed draws on Nancy Fraser's three-dimensional gender justice model[50] as the most pertinent for analysing gender equality interpretations in the practice of IDA and for drawing out possible ways forward. If other authors such as Martha Nussbaum,[51] Alison Jaggar[52] and Onora O'Neil[53] have all been amongst the many discussing at great length issues related to gender and justice, the main purpose of using gender justice as an analytical framework is to identify the gaps and contradictory ideological trends rather than to offer a comprehensive analysis of different gender justice accounts. Thus, Nancy Fraser offers an analytical model which is anchored in John Rawls' *A Theory of Justice* and is adapted to highlight the gaps and deepen our understanding of the consequences on gender-related concepts in IDA.

This analytical framework is therefore selected as it best matches the contradictions and misplacements occurring in ideological trends underpinning the realities found across three continents. Furthermore, it provides a simple and accessible analytical tool that practitioners and non-academic professionals alike can utilise in the course of their fieldwork, whilst at the same time embracing key complexities. Moreover, such analytical tool, which has been tested since the author's thesis, has proven to be an appropriate one to critique, analyse and categorise the varying interpretations of gender equality and respective underpinning politics throughout the different levels of IDA. Thus, a balanced nucleus between what seem to have become conflicting and at times opposing focuses, namely *representation, recognition and redistribution*, constitute together, the *gender justice* analytical model employed in this book.

Data collection and sampling methods

The rationale for the selection of examples presented in the book is explained as well as a summary of methods employed. Methods are here understood as evidence collection mechanisms for the purpose of research in social science. The methods selected for gathering evidence fall into the following categories of methods for social inquiry: i) demarcation of the field; ii) reviewing literature, articles, conference reports, minutes of meetings and viewing televised news, debates, e-news and e-debates; iii) case studies which consisted in reviewing evaluation reports which have been conducted by the author and have included the following methods: key informant interviews, focus group discussions in workshops and email questionnaires.

Demarcation of the field and purposive sampling

The core environment is primarily situated within the field of international development policy and programmes. The main examples utilised are international development programmes and international development policies at the international, national and donor levels. It is also to some limited extent connected with the legal field in specific instances, namely in the analysis of the interpretation of gender equality in relevant international, regional and national legislative frameworks as they often constitute the normative basis for IDA policies – especially in the case of mainstreaming gender equality in IDA policies and programme. The book therefore does not include case-law, although case-law is relevant for the interpretation of the notion of gender equality at the international and national levels, the purpose of the book is however centred around how IDA through relevant policies and programmes interprets the notion of gender equality and not how gender equality is interpreted by the national and international judicial instances. The subject under investigation, which is the interpretations of the concept of 'gender equality', is thus situated within the development field around which feminist thought, philosophy, politics, law and sociology[54] are influencing and shaping key concepts.

The underpinning focus of the concept of gender equality in IDA is examined through its interpretations by a sample of economically and politically influential agents in the field of IDA. These are donor agencies at the multilateral and bilateral levels such as the World Bank Group (WB) for the multilaterals and Scandinavian and UK bilateral development assistance agencies, part of the Nordic + group[55] at the forefront of integrating gender-related concepts in their works. These agencies by no means represent the entire IDA field, which is also channelled through NGOs,[56] private foundations[57] and other multilateral and bilateral development agencies,[58] but they do constitute an interesting and relevant sample of international development assistance agencies for the purposes of this book. This is therefore a purposive sample of IDA policies and programmes.

As has been verified in IDA evaluations and annual reviews, there are often many gaps and contradictions between IDA policies and the results achieved in their applications by programmes at the field level. Therefore, any in-depth study of IDA could not simply cover the policy level without considering the programme level and further relate it to the theoretical level. This is particularly important as the objective of this book is not a broad, empirical and comprehensive historical and statistical research of gender-related concepts in the IDA field, but instead, an in-depth study to assess the adequacy of interpretations of gender equality in IDA in response to a few but key specific problematics.

The purposive sample of examples selected serve both as illustrations to underpin interpretations of gender equality discussed in Chapter 1 whilst also being instrumental in informing the content of the theoretical framing. Indeed, the theoretical framing is based on the analysis distilled from the examples presented throughout the book.

The purposive samples are critical examples in the sense that they carry strategic importance in relation to the book's main problem. They have thus been selected because they are considered to be either flagship interventions in the field of gender in IDA or negative examples, as these were more likely to provide critical examples and results that could be analysed in the context of the book.

The aim of analysing these examples is to provide an insight into IDA's response to the socio-economic inequalities and injustices of women's situations in developing countries. Understanding this phenomenon may depend on choosing these examples well. Each example has therefore been carefully selected for the purpose of advancing a critical understanding of the issues at stake, their potential for questioning assumptions and outlining the potential implications for future development policies, strategies and programmes.

The selection of a purposive sample from evaluations that were conducted by the author of bilateral international donor agencies' programmes therefore enables an in-depth and qualitative examination of the interpretations of gender equality at IDA policy and programming levels. A variety of international development donor agencies' policies and programmes, which are little if at all concerned with the issues at stake, have been omitted for the purposes of this book. This is not only to focus the field on essential material but also because in the opinion of the author, besides illustrating the limited awareness of the concept at stake, it is unlikely that such examples would contribute in a significant way to the findings and conclusions of this book.

Review of literature and documents and viewing of debates

The following methods involve data collection that is mainly undertaken from the study place as opposed to data collection from the field as follows:

Literature review covers all pertinent literature and includes books, articles of journals, magazines and newspapers on subjects related to the topic such as law, international law, human rights, sociology, politics, international relations, development studies, economics, women's studies, legal anthropology, philosophy, religious studies and any other relevant subjects found in the course of the research process.

Document review consists of reviewing relevant documents and reports related to: i) international development assistance policies, strategy and programme documents and evaluation reports; ii) international legal instruments, regional legal instruments and national legislation; iii) reports stemming from international and national conferences, symposiums and expert meetings; vi) witness reports; and v) statistical data.

Viewing televised debates enabled the author to access other sources by viewing the presentation of new literature in the field, discussion forums and expert analyses on politics, development, philosophy, literature and gender studies as well as the international world news.

Internet browsing is used both as a research engine and for access to relevant websites, documentation and e-debates and to acquire relevant literature.

Minutes of meetings/workshops and conferences reports

In the context of examples at the field level, roundtable meetings and workshops were held with groups of primary and secondary stakeholders from a sample of international development assistance beneficiaries' groups for the provision of primary and secondary evidence.

The author also integrated reports from UN World Conferences that have taken place in the last four decades to ensure the inclusion of analyses of expert opinions and relevant debates around the issues at stake. Workshops in the field of IDA are a common means not only to collect data, but also for 'jointly analysing' data with stakeholders using different participatory methods such as the PARTICIPLAN.[59] This method was widely used to collect data for the examples at the programme and field levels.

Individual semi-structured interviews

Individual semi-structured interviews were carried out with key informants to obtain expert opinions on the issues at stake. Interviews were used to extract both primary and secondary evidence as well as triangulation of facts gathered and analysed. In semi-structured interviews open-ended questions were asked and unexpected issues were also followed up. This method enables more flexibility than questionnaires. Key informants were selected in the context of the evaluation field missions carried out. These include multilateral and bilateral agency officials and programme managers, recipient country government officials and NGO staff. Other key informants, namely experts, were selected to complement and triangulate the evidence collected in the field missions and to extrapolate on the different perspectives of the analysis of the data collected. Such experts are crucial, as the work of the book is intended to fill the gaps and clarify contradictory statements, assumptions and analyses. Experts were selected from different fields of expertise. The interviews with experts were carried out either orally or via email, depending on their availability.

Focus group discussions

Focus group discussions were carried out in the large majority of evaluation field missions undertaken. Focus group discussions were used when the dynamics of the group situation added additional useful insight to the research issues. This method enabled the author to interview a larger proportion of beneficiaries of IDA programmes and at the same time to focus the debates and discussions around specific questions whilst encouraging critical participatory approaches. This ensured that the interviewer facilitated the discussions, whilst leaving participants to determine and prioritise the content of the debates. Particular attention was given to the understanding that the debate should not be dominated by set hierarchies, especially at the community level, but that all participants were able to express their (possibly) critical opinions as freely and independently as possible.

In conclusion, the author has followed a particular tailor-made methodology which is a mix of the above methods. The methods employed for all examples provided at the field level have fully respected issues of confidentiality where required, by not citing any names of persons interviewed.

Notes

1 K Daoud, *Mersault contre enquête* (Actes Sud 2014).
2 D Carvajal, *An Algerian Author Fights Back Against a Fatwa* (New York Times, 4 June 2015).
3 K Daoud, *Cologne Lieu de Fantasmes* (Le Monde, 31 January 2016); Echoing similar problematics see also Goncourt literary prize winner: L Slimani, *Sexe et Mensonges, La vie sexuelle au Maroc* (Les Arènes 2017).
4 Le monde. See Algerian novelist Kamel Daoud sparks Islamophobia row, 7 March 2016 <www.bbc.com/news/world-europe-35653496>
5 See the interview with Zineb El Rhazoui, A Charlie Ebdo Reporter – on BBC NEWS HARDtalk (17 January 2018).
6 W Mansell, B Meteyard and A Thomson, *A Critical Introduction to Law* (3rd edn, Cavendish Publishing 2004). See W Mansell, *A Critical Introduction to Law* (4th edn, Routledge 2015).

7 Ibid 1.
8 Ibid 164.
9 See JF Lyotard, *La Condition postmoderne: Rapport sur le savoir* (Les Éditions de Minuit 1979).
10 Mansell and others 175.
11 Extract of a discussion on the critique of critique of metanarratives, which was never fully developed due to an interruption of the programme on the BBC Radio 3, Producer W Catlin, 'Mr Jenks Jumping Universe' (Loftus Production, London, 11 May 1997), in which interviews between Charles Jenks and several post-modern scientists such as Ilya Prigogine, Stuart Kauffman and Jean-François Lyotard took place. Jenks interpellated Lyotard in the following manner: 'But today we have a new metanarrative, coming from the post-modern sciences of complexity and the new cosmology, the idea of cosmogenesis, the story of the developing universe, the notion that the evolving cosmos is a single, creative, unfolding event that includes life and us in its narrative, one that locates culture in space and time: the universe in four jumps: energy, matter, life and consciousness'. Due to the interruption of the programme Lyotard's much expected response remained unspoken, leaving the conversation ironically 'fragmented'.
12 See R Peet and E Hartwick, *Theories of Development: Contentions, Arguments, Alternatives* (2nd edn, The Guilford Press 2009).
13 See I Tinker, 'The Making of a Field: Advocates, Practitioners and Scholars' in N Visvanathan and others (eds), *The Women, Gender & Development Reader* (Zed Books 1997) 34–36.
14 See K Young, 'Gender and Development' in N Visvanathan and others (eds), *The Women, Gender & Development Reader* (Zed Books 1997) 51–54.
15 See C Jencks, *Critical Modernism: Where Is Post-Modernism Going?* (Wiley-Academy 2007) 23.
16 See N Fraser, *Scales of Justice: Reimagining Political Space in a Globalizing World* (Columbia University Press 2009) 101.
17 See 'Comment on the Universalist-Relativist Debate' in H Steiner, P Alston and R Goodman (eds), *International Human Rights in Context: Law, Politics, Morals* (3rd edn, Oxford University Press 2007) 517. Other examples encompassing the politics of identity, recognition and cultural differences: A Bunting, 'Theorizing Women's Cultural Diversity Feminist International Human Rights Strategies' (1993) 20 (1) *Journal of Law Society* 6; R Kapur, 'A Love Song to Our Mongrel Selves: Hybridity, Sexuality and the Law' (1999) 8(3) *Social and Legal Studies* 353.
18 See E Brems, 'Enemies or Allies-Feminism and Cultural Relativism as Dissident Voices in Human Rights Discourse' (1997) 19(1) *Human Rights Quarterly* 136.
19 See TE Higgins, 'Anti-Essentialism, Relativism and Human Rights' (1996) 19 *Harvard Women's Law Journal* 89 in Steiner, Alston and Goodman (109) 545.
20 See C Mohanty, 'Cartographies of Struggle: Third World Women and the Politics of Feminism' in C Mohanty, A Russo and L Torres (eds), *Third World Women and the Politics of Feminism* (Indiana University Press 1991) 1–51; see also CT Mohanty, 'Under Western Eyes: Feminist Scholarship and Colonial Discourses' in Mohanty, Russo and Torres (eds), *Third World Women and the Politics of Feminism* (Indiana University Press 1991) 51–80.
21 See G Prakesh, 'Subaltern Studies as Postcolonial Criticism' (1994) 99 *American Historical Review* 1475–1490. See also R Kapur, 'The Tragedy of Victimization Rhetoric: Resurrecting the "Native" Subject in International/Post-Colonial Feminist Legal Politics' (2002) 15 *Harvard Human Rights Journal* 2.
22 Examples of difference feminists are illustrated by the following works: A Lorde, 'The Master's Tools Will Never Dismantle the Master's House' in C Morroga and G Anzaldua (eds), *The Bridge Called Me Back: Writings by Radical Women of Color* (Persaphone Press 1981) 98–101; C Gilligan, *In a Different Voice, Psychological Theory and Women's Development* (Harvard University Press 1982); IM Young, *Justice and the Politics of Difference* (Princeton University Press 1990).
23 See Peet and Hartwick.

24 See Tinker.

25 See Young.

26 Convention on the Elimination of All Forms of Discrimination Against Women (adopted 18 December 1979, entered into force 3 September 1981) (1980) 1249 UNTS 13, reprinted in 19 ILM 33 (CEDAW) <www.un.org/womenwatch/daw/cedaw/text/econvention.htm>.

27 Protocol to the African Charter on Human and Peoples' Rights on the Rights of Women in Africa (adopted 11 July 2003, entered into force 25 November 2005) (2003) CAB/LEG/66.6/Rev 1(the Protocol on the Rights of Women in Africa) art 1(J) <www.africa-union.org/home/Welcome.htm.>

28 The main World Conferences on Women have been selected to represent a purposeful example of relevant policy framework underpinning the concept of gender equality at international level. These are: 'First World Conference on Women Held in Mexico City' (19 June to 2 July 1975) <www.un.org/womenwatch/daw/beijing/mexico.html>; 'Second World Conference on Women Held in Copenhagen'(14 to 30 July 1980) <www.un.org/womenwatch/daw/beijing/copenhagen.html>; 'Third World Conference on Women Held in Nairobi' (15 to 26 June 1985) <www.un.org/womenwatch/daw/beijing/nairobi.html>; 'Fourth World Conference on Women Held in Beijing' (4 to 15 September 1995) <www.un.org/womenwatch/daw/beijing/fwcwn.html>.

29 United Nations Millennium Declaration, UNGA Res 55/2 (8 September 2000) UN Doc A/55/L.2 <www.un.org/millennium/declaration/ares552e.htm>.

30 OECD, 'The Paris Declaration on Aid Effectiveness 2005 and the Accra Agenda for Action 2008 (OECD 2005/2008). <www.oecd.org/document/19/0,3746,en_2649_3236398_43554003_1_1_1_1,00.html>.

31 Donor policies are overall frameworks that set the priorities and orientations for IDA of a given agency over a set period of time. They include, amongst others policy papers, strategy papers and action plans.

32 Country policies are national policy frameworks that set the priorities and orientations for poverty reduction. These include poverty strategy action plans, national and sector policy papers as well as orientation speeches.

33 The significant four decades in questions are defined from the 1970s and first World Conference on Women to 2010.

34 Examples of key multilateral IDA agencies are the UN, the WB and the EU.

35 Examples of key bilateral IDA agencies are Swedish International Development Cooperation Agency (Sida), Danish International Development Agency (Danida) and UK Department for International Development (DFID).

36 Gender equality strategies are overall frameworks that provide the definition of gender equality of a particular agency and set the guidelines for mainstreaming gender equality in the IDA sectors and programmes.

37 Marxist interpretation of development is understood in this context as the realisation that: 'Development takes place in class societies in such a way that the material benefits derived from hard work and increased productivity are unequally distributed'. Ibid 16–17.

38 See N Fraser, 'Multiculturalism, Anti-Essentialism, and Radical Democracy: A Genealogy of Current Impasse in Feminist Theory' in N Fraser (ed), *Justice Interruptus: Critical Reflections on the "Postsocialist" Condition* (Routledge 1997) 173–188.

39 See C Bunch, 'Transforming Human Rights from a Feminist Perspective' in J Peters and A Wolper (eds), *Women's Rights Human Rights; International Feminist Perspectives* (Routledge 1995) 11.

40 See H Charlesworth and C Chinkin, *The Boundaries of International Law* (Manchester University Press 2004); H Charlesworth, 'Feminist Methods in International Law' (1999) 93 *American Journal of International Law* 379; PV Sellars, 'Individual' Liability for Collective Sexual Violence' in K Knop (ed), *Gender and Human Rights* (Oxford University Press 2004).

41 The term 'ahistorical' generalisation is cited as a purposefully counter example of the following premise: '. . . the application of the notion of women as a homogeneous category to women in the Third World colonizes and appropriates the pluralities of the simultaneous location of different groups of women in social class and ethnic frameworks; in so doing it robs them of their historical and political agency'. CT Mohanty, *Feminism without Borders: Decolonizing Theory, Practicing Solidarity* (Duke University Press 2003) 39.
42 See BH Lévy, *De la Guerre en Philosophie* (Grasset 2010) 41–47.
43 N Fraser, *Scales of Justice: Reimagining Political Space in a Globalizing World* (Columbia University Press 2009) 16–18.
44 Gender justice is understood within Nancy Fraser's three-dimensional theory of justice. Fraser's understanding of the notion of 'justice' moves beyond that of John Rawls, which can be understood as essentially 'egalitarian liberalist-nationalist denying that norms of egalitarian distributive justice may have any applicability at the global or international level'. See J Rawls, *The Law of Peoples* (Harvard University Press 2001).
45 Fraser 16.
46 Ibid.
47 Political engagement is meant in the sense employed by Bernard-Henry Levy. See Lévy, *De la Guerre* (n 676).
48 H Arendt, *Responsibility and Judgment* (Schocken Books 2003) 158.
49 As sustained for instance by C Wood Sherif, S Harding and DE Smith *Feminism and Methodology*, S Harding (ed), (Open University Press 1987).
50 See N Fraser, *Scales of Justice: Reimagining Political Space in a Globalizing World* (Columbia University Press 2009) 16–18.
51 See M Nussbaum, *Sex and Social Justice* (Oxford University Press 1999).
52 See A Jaggar (ed), *Gender and Global Justice* (Polity Press 2014).
53 See O O'Neill, *Justice Across Boundaries: Whose Obligations?* (Cambridge University Press 2016).
54 'Both sociology and law are concerned with the nature of the legitimate authority, the mechanisms of social control, issues of civil rights, power arrangements, and the relationship between public and private spheres'. R Cotterel, *The Sociology of Law: An Introduction* (2nd edn, Butterworths 1992) 5 citing S Vago, *Law and Society* (2nd edn, Prentice-Hall 1988) 2–3.
55 The Nordic + group is a group of countries in Northern Europe with like-minded thinking on development assistance issues. These include: UK, Denmark, Sweden, Norway, Finland, the Netherlands and Canada.
56 Such as the Norwegian Refugee Council (NRC) and the Danish Refugee Council (DRC).
57 Such as the Nike Foundation.
58 Such as the EU and Europe Aid in particular, other UN agencies such UNDP, UNIFEM, UNICEF, UNFPA, UNHCR and other bilateral agencies such as CIDA, FINNIDA, NORAD, USAID, the Dutch Cooperation.
59 For further details see <www.participlan.com>.

Part I

1 Breaking the waves

This chapter provides a critical assessment of key theoretical frameworks and ideologies which have posed the most significant challenges to the concept of gender equality in IDA. The chapter proceeds to analyse the implication of these challenges on the key concepts underlying the notion of gender equality such as International Development Assistance (IDA),[1] Women in Development (WID)[2] and Gender and Development (GAD).[3]

The chapter thus first discusses how theoretical frameworks and ideologies underpinning gender equality have displaced fundamental notions in the interpretation of gender equality in IDA. In particular, the chapter critically assesses the eclipse of the notion of redistribution and the displacement of the universality[4] of women's human rights violations through the politics of identity's perspective,[5] which essentially focuses on recognition and representation.[6]

The first section of the chapter analyses the implications of the prevailing focus of identity politics in the interpretation of gender equality in the field of IDA. By identifying cultural relativism as one of the most challenging issue for the field, this section assesses the extent to which cultural relativism[7] has found a renaissance through a variety of feminist schools of thought from anti-essentialists[8] to Third Worldists,[9] to postcolonialists[10] and difference feminists.[11] It is argued that this revival has been achieved largely by delegitimising universalism, and with it, the notion of the universality which is inherent to i) fundamental violations of women's human rights such as violence against women and ii) the unequal distribution of power and resources. The chapter focuses on these two aspects as they constitute, amongst other issues, the core problematics faced by women beneficiaries of IDA, as is further evidenced in the first section of Chapter 2.

The significance of these developments is further discussed in relation to the very conceptualisation and definition of key concepts and approaches influencing the understanding of gender equality in IDA. These are: IDA itself,[12] the Women in Development approach (WID)[13] and the Gender and Development approach (GAD).[14]

Wavering framings and ideologies

Theoretical frameworks underpinning the concept of gender equality in the field of IDA have neither reflected a linear process, nor have they resulted in neatly divided, fixed and stable categories. Rather, they have been characterised by a wavering process of interconnected, disconnected and conflicting focuses, critiques and counter-critiques.

This section identifies and discusses the claims of the prevailing focus on the politics of identity and the implications vis-à-vis other fundamental notions underpinning the concept of gender equality. The section shows that one of the main implications of the prevailing focus on identity politics has been the eclipse[15] of two fundamental notions underpinning gender equality of particular significance in the context of IDA. The first fundamental notion underpinning gender equality is the notion of *redistribution*, which essentially encapsulates socio-economic justice,[16] and the second is the notion of the universality of fundamental violations of women's human rights.[17]

The section focuses on these two specific notions as they constitute the core and common problematics faced by women beneficiaries encountered in the field and across diverse socio-cultural settings.[18]

Displacing the notion of redistribution

The relevance of the notion of redistribution as understood in this book relates to Mansell's idea of substantive justice.[19] The notion of justice as redistribution is understood in connection with John Rawls' theory of justice as follows:

> The idea of justice as fairness is to use the notion of pure procedural justice to handle contingencies of particular situations. The social system is to be designed so that the resulting distribution is just however things turn out. To achieve this end, it is necessary to set the social and economic process within the surroundings of suitable political and legal institutions. Without an appropriate scheme of these background institutions the outcome of the distributive process will not be just. . . . It is clear that the justice of distributive shares depends on the background institutions and how they allocate total income, wages and other income plus transfers.[20]

The key problematics discussed by Rawls and which he sums up as follows: 'While some effort is made to secure fair equality of opportunity, it is either insufficient or else ineffective given the disparities in wealth and political influence they permit'[21] carries particular resonance in the field of gender equality in IDA by exposing the deficiencies of focusing solely on the notion of 'fair equality'.

The issue at stake is further problematised by Dworkin as follows:

> So the question of what division of resources is an equal division must to some degree include the question of what powers someone who is assigned a resource thereby gains, and that in turn must include the further question of his right to veto whatever changes in those powers might be threatened through politics.[22]

As the notion of justice is defined as including the notion of distribution, which in turn includes issues of (re)distribution of power and rights, the concept of gender equality in IDA is thus problematised along the same lines. The key questions these reflections on the notion of justice raise for gender equality in IDA are: How has gender equality been interpreted? What did the interpretations provided include? Why did a particular focus prevail, and at what cost?

In seeking to respond to these questions, Nancy Fraser's account offers a relevant and useful explanation of how 'gender equality' has been defined and what has been the changing hegemonic focus underlying its interpretation. Fraser provides a clear illustration and a historical account of the displacement of the notion of socio-economic justice[23] in the interpretation of gender equality as follows:

> If the first phase of post-war feminism sought to 'engender' the socialist imaginary, the second phase stressed the need to 'recognize difference'. 'Recognition', accordingly, became the chief grammar of feminist claims-making in the *fin de siècle*. A venerable category of Hegelian philosophy, resuscitated by political theorists, this notion captured the distinctive character of post-socialist struggles, which often took the form of identity politics, aimed more at valorising difference, than at promoting equality. Whether the question was violence against women or gender disparities in political representation, feminists increasingly resorted to the grammar of recognition to press their claims. Unable to make headway against injustices of political economy, they preferred to target harms resulting from androcentric patterns of cultural values or status hierarchies. The result was a major shift in the feminist imaginary: whereas the previous generation pursued an expanded ideal of social equality, this one invested the bulk of its energies in cultural change. . . . What distinguished the identity politics phase was the relative autonomization of the cultural project – its decoupling from the project of political-economic transformation and distributive justice.[24]

Fraser in this concise statement draws a picture of the wavering ideologies underpinning the notion of gender equality. Her depiction is not within a static theoretical framework but rather portrayed as a succession of fundamental changes in a changing theorising process which characterises the evolution of feminist thought in the last 60 years. It is within this idea of a wavering theorising process that different 'focuses' have emerged. The focuses described by Fraser as 'phases' in feminist thinking are both objects of investigation as well as overall orientations and framing of feminist thinking in a certain period of time. Such description of framing 'in movement', as it were, is particularly relevant and useful when trying to make sense of the succession of ideologies that have informed, shaped and influenced, broadly speaking, the body of gender-related concepts in IDA. The term 'focus' will be used rather than 'phase' as it more closely illustrates the act of concentrating on a particular idea whilst at the same time framing and orienting the discourse within a particular perspective.

Nancy Fraser in her depiction further uses the word 'decoupling' to explain that one underpinning focus was substituted by another as opposed to different focuses coexisting through relevant interconnections in one overall theoretical matrix defined by the notion of justice. She contends that amongst others, the focus on identity politics and cultural difference became the current dominant framing, disconnected from the previous and original focus on distributive justice. It is argued not only that a similar phenomenon is verified in the field of IDA but that it takes the form of an eclipse of the notion of distribution.

Further, by denouncing the consequence of this shift in focus as *displacing* rather than *deepening* the socialist imaginary, Nancy Fraser assesses the implications of the hegemony of identity politics as follows:

> The tendency was to subordinate social struggles to cultural struggles, the politics of redistribution to the politics of recognition. It was assumed, rather, by the proponents of the cultural turn that a feminist politics of identity and difference would synergize with struggles of social equality. But that assumption fell prey to the larger Zeitgeist. In the fin de siècle context, the turn to recognition dovetailed all too neatly with a hegemonic neoliberalism that wanted nothing more than to repress all memory of social egalitarianism. The result was a tragic historical irony. Instead of arriving at a broader, richer paradigm that could encompass both redistribution and recognition, we effectively traded one truncated paradigm for another . . . at precisely the moment when neoliberalism was staging its spectacular comeback.[25]

The irony that Fraser is alluding to reflects well the fact that whilst many proponents of identity politics and especially proponents of Third Worldist and the cultural difference views were critical of Western liberal feminism, which in their view often amounted to neo-colonial imperialism, they fitted 'all too well', through their very anti-liberal critiques, into the neoliberal framework.

If Fraser assumes that identity politics 'fell prey' to the larger zeitgeist, suggesting that it was an unfortunate accident, arguably, the focus on identities may well find more common ground with individualism than with solidarity and collectivism which de facto focuses on commonalities rather than differences and on deepening divides. Thus, the theory of the accidental coincidence is debatable. If good intentions within the Left[26] exist towards the reconciliation of divergent feminist focuses and perspectives into a single and richer paradigm, there is not yet unanimity on the choice of an overall framing for feminist thought or on whether such framework would indeed have any legitimacy. Following the post-modern turn, whereas it is difficult to foresee the return, and unanimous adherence, to a single overall grand feminist framework as in the modernist era, arguably and more realistically the co-existence of diverse focuses might prevail. The idea of attempting to refocus at least one of them in light of its relevance in furthering the overall goal of poverty reduction might be worthwhile.

Whether neoliberalism coincided with identity politics by accident or not, it was also an unfortunate timing for such a coincidence for the broader field of IDA as illustrated by the following implications:

> On the one hand the end of bipolar competition between the Soviets and the West reduced flows of aid to the periphery. On the other hand, US-led dismantling of the Bretton Woods financial regime encouraged the new neoliberal policy structural adjustment, which threatened the post-colonial development state. The result was to greatly reduce the scope for egalitarian redistributive projects in the South. And the response was an enormous surge of identity politics in the post-colony, much of it communalist and authoritarian. Thus, post-colonialist feminist movements, too, were forced to operate without a background political culture that guides popular aspirations into egalitarian channels. Caught between downsized state capacities, on the one hand, and burgeoning communalist chauvinisms, on the other, they too, felt pressure to recast their claims in forms more in keeping with post-socialist Zeitgeist.[27]

Within the IDA field, this 'coincidence of events' – far from being a mere unfortunate theoretical turn – implied at a deeper level that 'development' and 'poverty reduction' could be and would be defined from then on outside the egalitarian paradigm and within a paradigm that ensured the exclusion of the interpretation of inequalities as *maldistribution* of resources and power, which are arguably inherent in the poverty problematics in most developing countries across the three continents visited. This, to a large extent, explains the absence of the term 'redistribution' from IDA policies and programmes of the 1990s and 2000s. The significant implication of this ideological turn is that the concepts of gender equality as well as its immediate and broader context, respectively that of 'poverty reduction' and 'development' could also be robbed of their focus on socio-economic justice.

However, to state that postcolonialist feminist movements were 'forced' to recast their claims within the hegemonic surge of identity politics indicates that at best, postcolonialist feminism at the time had not gained sufficient 'independence'. If it had done so, it surely could not have been 'forced' into adhering to any further hegemonic ideologies. Arguably identity politics must have served the overriding interests of some proponents of feminist postcolonialists at the time. Rather than 'forced', postcolonialist feminists chose identity politics as their overall focus to cast their feminist claims, as it, amongst others, responded to a key underlying concern of the movement: anti-imperialism.

This raises the question of: Who benefitted from disconnecting women's individual experiences from the substantive egalitarian paradigm of social justice? In attempting to answer this question, the book's objective is less to single out potential interest groups than to demonstrate that these manoeuvres have not played out in the interests of women IDA beneficiaries encountered.

Based on Nancy Fraser's work, Shirin Rai also raises concerns regarding the ways in which identity politics has cast a shadow over redistribution (and in turn over social justice) as follows:

> [T]he post-modern turn in social science and gender studies has allowed feminist academics and gender activists to be diverted from the fundamental transformation of social relations.[28]

Rai further emphasises the need to critically re-evaluate the influence of post-modernism with its focus on difference, exclusion and anti-essentialism. As Rai echoes Fraser, she demonstrates that this prevailing focus did not always translate into the redistribution of resources, which implies, in her view, a drawback rather than advancement for the poorest women in developing countries. Thus, without the redistributive notion, it is argued that the concept of gender equality loses a vital focus and overall orientation in the broader field of poverty reduction and IDA. As Fareda Banda illustrates, 'as long as men have primary control over the resources such as land, women will never be able to overcome socio-cultural inequalities',[29] thereby also pointing to the crucial importance of redistribution in the interpretation of the concept of gender equality within the field of IDA.

On this basis, it is obvious that the eclipse of the notion of redistribution has permeated the fundamental theoretical focus underpinning the concept of gender equality. The displacement of the notion of distribution – whether accidental or not – is thus identified as effectively denuding the concept of theoretical grounds with which to address socio-economic injustices within the field of IDA.

Delegitimising and dismissing universalism

Further to displacing the notion of distribution, another central concern has been the trend to isolate injustices and inequalities from each other and from a universal human rights framing.

As Amartya Sen concluded in *The Idea of Justice*:

> [P]eople need not be inescapably doomed to isolated lives without communication and collaboration. It is bad enough that the world in which we live has so much deprivation of one kind or another (from being hungry to being tyrannized), it would be terrible if we were not able to communicate, respond and altercate. When Hobbes referred to the dire state of human beings in having "nasty, brutish and short" lives, he also pointed, in the same sentence, to the disturbing adversity of being "solitary". Escape from isolation may not only be important for the quality of human life, it can also contribute powerfully to understanding and responding to the other deprivations from which human beings suffer.[30]

Sen effectively argues with common sense, for a fourth dimension of justice which, if anything, appeals to a refocus out of the post-modern emphasis on differences and isolations of injustices. On the face of it, certain branches of feminism did not follow that path. On the contrary, some chose to isolate differences in feminist claims.

The politics of identity surged in the fin de siècle and in the postcolonial feminist field, cultural relativism and thus, with it – the isolation of culturally different injustices and inequalities – found a renaissance through the process of delegitimising many forms of 'universalism' that were thought to be *acquis* – including the universality of women's human rights violations.

In the context of gender equality in IDA, the revival of cultural relativism through the politics of identity resulted in

> the notion of subordination of women being thereafter constructed as a problem of culture and thus dissociated from political economy.[31]

The construction of women's subordination as a cultural problem provides a considerably limited theoretical focus for the interpretation of gender equality in IDA as it dissociates the problem not only from political economy, but also from the larger and global matrix of structural inequalities and social justice. This in turn, changes the perspective of how women's subordination is considered and analysed. At best, women's inequality is discussed largely in isolation from broader, global patterns of exploitation and at worst, is potentially justified by reference to differences in cultures, religions and identities. This perspective risks undermining the achievements of many past struggles which had been undertaken to fight cultural and religious patriarchal stereotypes – under the guise of which women's subordination finds a rejuvenating normalisation today.

Nancy Fraser seems to suggest that the abandonment of the egalitarian and social justice paradigm for an inward-looking focus on identity, differences and culture which could justify a return to cultural relativism was unconscious, and the encounter with the broader neoliberal context, accidental. In contrast, Caroline Fourest views this ideological shift as emanating from a more conscious and fundamental political change of paradigm from within the post-socialist Left.

According to Fourest, opposed political standpoints dividing the post-socialist Left are competing for political and theoretical space. In Fourest's view, it would therefore be this competition which is responsible for the shift in feminist theorising rather than an accidental coincidence of identity politics emerging at the wrong time and in the wrong place.

In order to illustrate her point, Fourest takes two examples into consideration: The London European Social Forum of 2004[32] and the Durban World Conference against Xenophobia of 2001.[33] Interestingly Fraser selected the very same examples of global forums to illustrate, in contrast, the appropriate platform to explore a more comprehensive and harmonious common overall framework for a future third phase of feminism.[34] Yet Fourest uses these examples to demonstrate how identity politics, embraced by many advocates of Third Worldist positions, are drifting towards communitarianism and authoritarianism, in conflict with social egalitarian and anti-authoritarian perspectives.

She argues that during both of these events, irreconcilable perspectives amongst the Left were played out. In Durban, according to Fourest, rather than seeing like-minded NGOs combating racism under a united front, the Conference was overshadowed by opposing pro-Islamist and anti-Semitic slogans.[35] At the London European Social Forum, a debate on the hijab was overtaken by some anti-imperialist Left activists and some Third Worldists forging alliances with fundamentalists, paradoxically labelling feminists who perceived the hijab as a symbol of oppression against women as 'racists and Islamophobic'.[36]

Since then, these examples typify a recurring pattern of Third Worldist feminist critiques which are voiced around and against the birth of the slogan 'women's rights are human rights'.[37] Cultural relativist positions thus found a rejuvenating youth in dismantling the grounds for international human rights as summarised in the following statement:

> [T]here is – as a matter of fact, empirically – an impressive diversity. The critiques attached an important consequence to this diversity: that no transcendent or trans-cultural ideas of 'right' could be agreed upon and hence no culture or state was justified in attempting to impose [in an imperialist and neo-colonialist manner] their values on other cultures or states.[38]

Consequently, universal definitions of women's human rights gradually lost their legitimate basis. The result of such theorising was that 'tensions between First and Third World feminists on issues of substance and strategy, became evident and increasingly significant within the IDA arena'[39] and particularly within major World Conferences.

Most postcolonial, cultural relativist and anti-essentialist feminist critiques, despite several nuances and differences in their theories, seem to agree upon the rejection of the 'attempted wholesale application of so-called Western feminist theories on other communities and societies and in particular, the liberal feminist emphasis on the elimination of sex-discrimination'. However, if the original intention was to reject neoliberalism, radical Left and Marxist analyses were also rejected in practice within the same anti-imperialist concern. Recalling Fraser's analysis above, this example illustrates how one hegemonic perspective was replaced by another hegemonic focus on identity and difference in global forums.

Many important feminist thinkers in IDA, such as Naila Kabeer, rallied support for identity politics and the wave of anti-essentialism by defining WID advocates as being primarily First World women who defined the idea of global sisterhood, Third World women and the idea of integration into development processes as being initiated by First World donors or elites in their countries.[40]

This critique led to a clear shift in focus in the context of feminism in IDA. A postcolonialist perspective on the one hand suggested that:

> Third World countries had had little autonomy so far in determining their own development trajectories, as long as power and resources were concentrated in the hands of Western countries. Consequently, most men and

> women were and had always been integrated into development processes but on asymmetrical terms which were determined by the interweaving of relations of class, gender and the international economic order.[41]

Closely interrelated, this discussion raised anti-essentialist concerns about the notion of 'women'. The question was whether the concept of 'women' and in this case 'Third World women' could be said to belong to one category, reflecting Western values, across the globe, transcending culture, sex, ethnicity and class. The perceived imposition of a universal 'sisterhood' amongst women of different cultural backgrounds was now heavily criticised.[42]

One of the most prominent examples of such critique is illustrated by Chandra Talpade Mohanty, who rejects 'the suggestion that women can recognise each other's experiences and problems across cultural, class and ethnic lines',[43] which she argues erases material and ideological power differences within and among women.

The objective of this critique was to challenge the legitimacy of the notion of the universality of women's human rights, focusing on differences and thus challenging the category 'women' as a valid universal analytical category. Mohanty justifies this position by explaining how in her view, Western women have defined Third World women solely in terms of their 'problems' or 'achievements', effectively removing them from history, freezing them in time and space.[44]

Mohanty's critique is not only relevant in showing the entrenchment of feminist cultural relativist perspectives in the universalist versus relativist debate[45] but is of particular significance to the field of IDA as development theory hinges on the analysis of 'problems' and the degree to which 'achievements' can be evidenced. Mohanty's critique not only delegitimises the universality of women's human rights but at the same time the very grounding for IDA and cross-cultural solidarity.

Although in her revised writings she seems to soften her position through a re-discovery of the notion of solidarity, in her earlier analyses both solidarity and commonalities are eclipsed and substituted by cultural differences as the hegemonic focus of her feminist perspective. Indeed, her earlier views can be characterised as prominently based on anti-imperialist and anti-racist theories, as illustrated in her following well-known statement that typifies Mohanty's view of how the notion of Third World difference is produced:

> White western reads progressive/modern, while Third World women are necessarily defined as religious (read: not progressive/backward/traditional), illiterate (read: ignorant), domestic (read: backward) etc.[46]

If her critique has rightly denounced a propensity of 'patronising' attitudes from some Western feminists (read: white/middle class/not well travelled/racist)[47] 'essentialising' the 'rest',[48] one of the most challenging implications is that a wider analysis of women's subordination was also displaced as 'patronising' and replaced by an analysis which focuses solely on differences of cultures and identities – de facto eclipsing the legitimate grounds upon which to defend women's human rights and the struggle against women's subordination. Mohanty, in one sentence, replaced the struggle against what Sen earlier called 'deprivation of one kind for another (from being hungry to being tyrannized)'[49] with the struggle against racism. This effectively collapsed the legitimate claims of women living in poverty, to education, to better employment opportunities, to not be confined to domestic work and child rearing or any other patriarchal cultural gender stereotypes.

Mohanty's statement thus synthesises the major implications of the use of identity politics in the interpretation of gender equality in IDA. It effectively eclipses the legitimacy of women's claims to the right to education, the right to develop a critical perspective vis-à-vis one's conditions and one's socio-economic, cultural and religious environment. By making racist theory the hegemonic framework through which the understanding of gender inequalities is confined, Mohanty erases the validity of claims that are concerned both with the survival and the empowerment of women living in objectively verifiable, unacceptably poor and degrading conditions. By denying the legitimacy of perceiving their conditions as dire – a racist act in Mohanty's view – Mohanty effectively denies poor women living in 'Third World' countries no less than the right to be free from poverty and injustices defining their conditions.[50]

Susan Moller Okin further discusses such critique as follows:

> During the 1980s and the early 1990s, postmodernist scholarship was highly influential in Anglo-American academia; at the same time, African American, lesbian and other critics of earlier feminism were, often rightly, critiquing it [feminism] for ignoring their needs, interests and perspectives. The feminist anti-essentialist critique that often combined the two, was at times carried to the extreme of asserting that no generalizations at all, could or should be made about women, gender, mothering or many other topics that some feminists thought important to be able to discuss. In addition, it was sometimes claimed that whatever the quality of the evidence presented, or the strength of the argument made, the suggestion by any white, middle-class feminist that women and girls in cultures other than our own are disadvantaged or oppressed by elements of their own cultures amounted to offensive cultural imperialism.[51]

Okin makes an important suggestion that difference feminists often used their, albeit challenging differences to build the basis of an 'alternative' theoretical framework. If there is an obvious point for claims of differences to be considered on the basis that they will help building a 'richer paradigm' as Fraser points out, what is the point of difference claims distorting, nullifying and replacing overall frameworks by one which cannot in and of itself address the most pressing problematics of women living in poverty in Third World countries?

Okin provides yet more evidence of Fraser's theory of one paradigm having been traded for the other with the serious implication of losing the achievements of the first, that is a theoretical framework upon which women's rights could be legitimately defended. In an attempt to explain some of the interests at play behind the main Third World critiques against universalism, Okin points out that difference feminist and Third World feminist critiques were directed at:

> Feminists in the academia, who attempted to find anything but differences between women, were as a result, being taken to task for essentialism.[52]

As Okin further points out, anti-essentialist feminists had constructed a 'hardly conducive climate to the framing of women's rights as universal human rights'.[53] Yet at the same time and despite the divergent interests, the Fourth Women's World Conference in Beijing in 1995[54] resulted in an unprecedentedly strong rejection of 'cultural' justifications for violations and abuses of women's human rights.[55]

Nevertheless, some feminists living and pursuing academic careers in the Western world under the label of 'Third World feminists' continued to question universalism in the post-Beijing era, despite the fact that 'patriarchy and the devaluing of women, although manifested differently within different societies, had been clearly demonstrated to be almost universal'.[56]

As Hilary Charlesworth points out:

> [O]ne of the strategies to overcome the hazards of essentialism in feminist work in international law is to focus on problems women appear to face whatever their background.[57]

In the context of IDA, this approach resonates particularly well given the scope of the problematics at hand.[58] It is indeed first of all through the demonstration of the universality of violations of women's human rights that much of universalism's lost legitimacy can be regained.[59] Arguably, cultural relativists and Third Worldists 'cannot criticise Western imperialism and at the same time ignore non-Western states' selective use of the defence of culture in the service of state power'.[60] Thus, it cannot be ignored that the striking proliferation of religious and nationalist regimes in the postcolonial eras – which in certain respects has even defined the postcolonial era – has actually placed women in a situation comparable to that in which they found themselves during colonialism.[61]

To circumvent increased criticism of top-down approaches in the application of international law more specifically, practitioners and researchers in development contexts have taken on board participatory and bottom-up approaches in the application of women's human rights. This is notable in the work of women's non-governmental organisations in Third World countries such as WLSA[62] with their focus on excavating women's rights from customary norms, living law and cultural practices.[63] The idea of digging women's human rights out of their cultural context is, in principle, a very valid one, as a strategy to counter internal resistance and fear of postcolonialism through a wholesale application of so-called Western international human rights standards and values. This has been the subject of much research in the law and development framework, as researchers try to explore a middle way between universalism and relativism.

Academics and field researchers such as Anne Hellum were able to demonstrate that in

> exploring both the general characteristics and the unique features of social and legal relations . . . it is possible to make generalizations concerning women's common values and interests within a limited span of time and places.[64]

The pluralist middle ground between universalism and relativism has thus presented itself as the 'reasonable' compromise, doing away with unfruitful dichotomies by providing a limited version of universalism that would only be applicable in a limited geographical span and time – which de facto de-universalises them.

Arguably, this middle ground leaves a fundamental question without answer: If there are similarities that can be generalised and identified in a certain time and space, why would it not be possible to identify similarities which can be generalised throughout time and space across wider borders?

In contrast, Fareda Banda, points out that,

> Indeed, some of the 'customs' that we cling to as being uniquely African are not so. For example, we were not the first or only people to give bride wealth as a precursor to marriage – other cultures have done it, not least the Germans.[65]

Other examples such as the control of women's sexuality – from chastity belts in European Middle Ages, to clitoridectomy in UK and US, to female genital mutilation (FGM) in Sub-Saharan Africa – all were considered by their defenders to be an affirmation of cultural womanly values and are, paradoxically, found across different cultures in practice.[66]

One can add many other significant examples such as women's quasi-universal lack of control over resources; the exploitation of their domestic household work; women's status as a lesser citizens; and women's timid and often non-existent participation in parliament and public political life.[67] These are all examples which emerge in different societies, whether the formerly colonised or former colonisers, North and South, First and Third World, at different points in history and under infinitely different guises and variants. These are thus anything but single events taking place in a limited span of time and place, in supposedly isolated corners of the world, and least entrenched in cultural specificities, unique historical moments. Thus, arguably less relevant are the theoretical compromises between universalism and relativism, as these essentially produce truncated versions of universalism effectively limiting possibilities of historical, cross-cultural and cross-continental comparisons and still confining women's plight, if not to their individual experience, to a limited time and space frame, as does cultural relativism.

Instead, a collective response to commonly identifiable problems or a 'discursive universalism'[68] – rather than a fragmented and isolated local response – is arguably more likely to bring about social changes in the field of IDA. This is further underlined by Charlesworth, who suggests the concept of 'reflective solidarity'.

Another example is that of Jodi Dean, who has argued for the importance of coming to an agreement about those aspects of our lives affecting us all, and of working within our differences to find norms and practices worthy of the consent of each individual:

> The recognition of difference remains meaningless and useless so long as it is not included as an element of our common life context and incorporated into the struggle to end exclusion and oppression.[69]

Nevertheless, and despite the arguably much-needed legitimate framework to struggle against exclusion, oppression and injustices of all kinds, some Third World feminists such as Mohanty persisted in their views that far from freeing women:

> the application of the notion of 'women' as a homogeneous category to women in the Third World colonizes and appropriates the pluralities of the simultaneous location of different groups of women in social class and ethnic frameworks, in doing so it ultimately robs them of their historical and political agency.[70]

There certainly exists a need to seek some clarity here, and to distinguish between the misguided trend of imposing a particular identity on others with the worthwhile task of identifying common problematics across different identities and different socio-cultural and socio-economic environments. Far from robbing women of political agency, the notion of commonalities across different violations of women's human rights for instance, aims precisely at reinforcing it. Therefore, focusing not on difference in identities but on commonalities and socio-economic injustices across identities ought, if anything, to strengthen women's political agency. Whereas as on the contrary, confining women's socio-economic injustices to their specific locations, cultures and identity may arguably rob women of their agency and the power to challenge the realities in which they live.[71]

Yet, some Third World feminist critiques supported Mohanty's position and took further steps in marking differences in identity politics by advocating a return to 'motherism' and 'womanism'.[72] This return to 'mother nature' shared common ground with the definition of 'woman as mother', similar to that exported by Christian missionaries in the colonial times.

Many Third World feminists[73] have thereafter responded to this call to focus predominantly on identity by concentrating on a variety of compromises which exist in African contexts. Such perspectives have located the negotiation of cultural demands of high fertility and the expectations of motherhood on the one hand, and self-realisation on the other, exclusively within the Sub-Saharan African context. However, this so-called cultural relocation is at the same time evidently reflecting one of the most basic and common dilemmas affecting most women across the globe, regardless of their culture. Surely women's emancipation from subordination is still very much linked, amongst other considerations, to women's ability and opportunity to decide if and when to have children in relation to other activities which also form an integral part of their identity, rather than considering motherhood as the sole and ineluctable culturally defined identity.

In stark contrast to this Third Worldist position are the views of some young women parliamentarians in Benin, for instance. In 1994, they issued warnings to their male counterparts in the political elite specifying that 'unless they were willing to give up some political space, they will instead contribute to the increase of birth rate and thus contribute quite handsomely to the enlargement of poverty!'[74]

Arguably, it is difficult to see how such a theoretical framing can serve justice for women living in poverty. Mohanty has, since her early writing, taken a step back and modified her position by implying that her former analyses had been misread and misunderstood. However, she admits that 20 years ago – a crucial time for consolidating the women's human rights agenda at the global level – she was instead more interested in challenging Eurocentric discourse and was not sufficiently critical of the valorisation of differences over commonalities.[75] Although this may be interpreted as an admission of omission, it falls short of justifying the paradox that in the name of identity politics, the theoretical framings produced by some Third Worldists did more to keep (real) Third World women in poverty and within local injustices by providing justifications for local systems of oppression.

The politics of dismissals and displacements

In order to put the implications of the problematics discussed above into a wider perspective, Caroline Fourest suggests that a key challenge to contemporary feminist theorising is a deep ideological divide, not as could have been anticipated, between the left wing and the neoliberal right wing but within the left-wing intelligentsia itself. This perspective sees opposing identity politics incarnated by recognition movements such as Third Worldists and anti-imperialists on the one hand and anti-totalitarians on the other hand who are attached to fundamental human rights and social justice.[76]

Amidst this dichotomy, Fourest does not see an irreconcilable divide as she explains that one could easily be at once anti-fascist, anti-totalitarian and anti-colonialist, but rather, she argues that having a 'penchant' for one or the other will result in fundamentally different interpretations and readings of world events.[77]

It is argued that this 'fundamental difference' in the interpretation of world events is also reflected in the interpretation of feminist and development theories, with consequences in the interpretations of gender equality in IDA. If 'recognition' of and thus participation in 'cultural differences' becomes essentially a way of silencing or avoiding addressing fundamental violations of women's human rights,[78] then far from coexisting in harmonious albeit complementary analytical frames, Third Worldist priorities and anti-totalitarian concerns are evolving in diametrically opposed theoretical focuses. Competing and contradictory priorities are being developed, out of which some of the most unlikely paradoxes are being produced, complicating and blurring conceptual landmarks even further.

One such paradox may be illustrated by recurrent accusations that feminists defending secularism are neo-colonialists. In contrast, young veiled women in France may be perceived by proponents of the Third Worldist Left as being cutting-edge feminists.[79] This perception would find support at the theoretical level not only in Mohanty's early critiques but also within queer post-feminist movements which find the idea of the subversion of the veil 'hypermodern' because challenging the hegemonic white, middle-class and heterosexual etc. norm.[80] At times, this has resulted in both practical and theoretical paradoxes, with for instance, queer feminist militants demonstrating alongside Islamist homophobic movements, as in the case of the pro-veil in schools demonstrations in Paris in 2005.[81]

In response to the wider implications brought forward by these immediate paradoxes, an association of Algerian and Iranian feminists wrote a letter to the 'so-called Third Worldist feminists' which they put to task as supporting 'the identity politics of exoticism', as follows:

> This message is charged with anger and is addressed to some of our feminist comrades engaged in struggles against racism, to some of Third Worldists and alter-globalists feminists, transcended by a certain colonial and post-colonial guilt. We do not understand, nor can we accept your support to those women that call themselves veiled/Muslim feminists, at the expense of secular Muslim feminism. . . . Is it exoticism or political naivety? Is it an unfortunate alliance between anti-imperialism and American capitalism? Remember other unfortunate liaisons between Islamists and communists in Iran, and what happened when Islamists were back in power. On a daily basis, women were stoned, imprisoned and murdered. Can you hear their cry? Whether we come from Iran, Algeria, Afghanistan or Pakistan today we find each other on secular land in which freedom of conscience is guaranteed by the laws but ironically, it is in this land that such universal values are threatened as we are forced to tolerate intolerance in the name of differences, cultural diversity and anti-essentialism.[82]

This letter points to the implication of identity politics on the extent to which justice will be afforded to (real) Third World women. By showing rather unequivocal examples of politico-religious compromises that have been undertaken at the expenses of secularism and universal human rights, the letter provides evidence of dire consequences of the politics of identity on women.

It ought to have become evident that an understanding of women's injustices and inequalities viewed not in isolation from each other but within broader visions of exploitation and subordination would result in mutually enriching analyses. Instead, some of the most fundamental grounds upon which the fight against oppression could be justified such as the universality of human rights and the notion of solidarity were eroded under the guise of anti-essentialism and in the name of multiculturalism.

In practice, and as Fraser illustrated, Third World feminist critiques drifted towards a focus solely upon national identity and communitarianism on the grounds of anti-imperialism and neo-colonialist struggle, doing away with redistribution – which paradoxically, were the very lens through which exploitation, in all its forms, could be best analysed.

This analysis thus challenges the grounds upon which some theoretical perspectives are sustained and asks the critical question as to whose interests are they really protecting? The sections above have shown that excluding both redistribution and universalism weakens solidarity, robbing women of justice, if anything. Consequently, this challenges the ideological backdrop against which key concepts will be interpreted and understood.

Contended key concepts

This section discusses how ideological wavering above has influenced the interpretations of key concepts related to gender equality in the particular field of IDA. These are the concept of International Development Assistance (IDA) itself, the Women in Development (WID) approach and the Gender and Development (GAD) approach. Definitions and interpretations of WID and GAD are also analysed as the fundamental approaches which have anticipated, produced and defined the concept of gender equality in IDA.

Defocusing international development assistance

The term 'development'[83] within IDA has of course, been underpinned by the same ideological debates discussed above. On the one hand, development may be defined as reflecting a neo-Marxist vision, and on the other hand, it may also be defined as representing a neoliberal economic vision of society, while also containing any other variations within and in between these two paradigms.[84]

As with the change in focus in feminist theorising discussed above, the underpinning focus of IDA under an apparent political neutrality clearly shifted to neoliberalism. This may be exemplified as follows:

> The WB and other major players in the development industry, while appearing to accommodate different views of what should constitute development, give effective support to a particular capitalist-friendly, neoliberal version.[85]

This blurring of the lines by the use of neutral and technical language to mask underlying political inclinations is usually found in most IDA policy documents.[86]

A critical modernist version of the very definition of development would read as follows:

> Development is a complex contradictory phenomenon, one reflective of the best of human aspirations and yet, exactly because great ideas form the basis of power, subject to the most intense manipulation and liable to be used for purposes that reverse its original intent. . . . In its strong sense, development means using the productive resources of society to improve the living conditions of the poorest people. In its weaker sense, development means more of everything for everyone, in the context of a lot more for a few.[87]

This critical definition reflects a less consensual vision of development and arguably a more realistic one, highlighting the gap that exists and is often experienced by development practitioners between definitions of IDA at the theoretical and policy levels and the realities in the field.

In a context in which definitions are riddled with conflicting underlying ideologies, Peet argues that amongst the fiercest and most damaging theoretical critiques of the humanistic project of IDA are those who perceive it as a Western project, defining on behalf of the very beneficiaries the content and orientation of their own development.

In addition to the classic Right/Left divide and reflecting the theoretical changes within the Left discussed in the sections above, one of the most significant challenges to the definition and interpretation of IDA comes from some of the anti-imperialist critiques. Like Mohanty's, these critiques question the Eurocentricism[88] of IDA as follows:

> The real power of the West is not located in its economic muscles and technological might. Rather, it resides in its power to define. The West defines what is, for example, freedom, progress and civil behaviour; law, tradition and community; reason, mathematics and science; what is real and what it means to be human. The non-Western civilisations have simply to accept these definitions or be defined out of existence. . . . As a worldview the West is the dominant outlook of the planet.[89]

Another example is expressed in this conclusion stating that:

> The problem of Eurocentricism and hence the problem of development, is thus the problem of knowledge. It is a problem of discovering 'other' ways of knowing, being and doing. It is a problem of how to be human in ways other than those of Europe. It is also a problem of how the West could liberate its true self from its colonial history and moorings.[90]

Anti-imperialist views have also offered a critique of IDA in terms of power and antagonistic relations between Western developed countries and non-Western developing countries. 'Development' under this particular critique is essentially viewed as meaning 'a standard by which the West measures the non-West'.[91]

As discussed above, this argument has also displaced the notion of redistribution within the definition of IDA:

> If the meaning of development has often been reduced to welfare or poverty alleviation or even free trade and foreign investment, arguably . . . poor people need fundamental changes in power relations to address the very structures that maintain them in these conditions.[92]

If the very theoretical framework that addresses these inequalities and conditions is supplanted by one focusing on representation and recognition, then the necessary structural changes needed to challenge the perpetuation of injustices for both men and women may well be left unaddressed. This is particularly true for women, who constitute over half of the beneficiaries of development assistance and population in postcolonial states:

> Whereas from a masculine perspective, independence ushered in the defining new condition of post-coloniality, for women there was no such break: the struggle continued, now against a patriarchal sphere that no longer required women's support, as independence often involved a transfer of power not to the people of the newly sovereign country but to (male-dominated) local elites who inherited the whole colonial system of the army, the police, the judiciary and the law, government bureaucracy and development agencies.[93]

If such a statement can be verified in most Sub-Saharan countries and some Latin American countries, then it is evident that the Left anti-Eurocentric or postcolonialist theoretical critique in the field of IDA, focused on identity politics and communitarianism, is neither sufficient nor adequate to challenge the main problematics at hand. On the contrary, such ideologies maintain internal situations of social, gender and economic inequalities unchallenged. Consequently, defining IDA without clearly challenging socio-economic inequalities, intra-cultural power relations as well as what La Boétie called voluntary servitude in 1,549[94] runs the risks of maintaining poverty, injustices and inequalities at current levels.

Questioning Women in Development and Gender and Development

This section identifies similarities in ideological patterns mentioned above that also underpin the definitions and understanding of WID and GAD and discusses the implications for the concept of gender equality.

Irrespective of the various nuances[95] in the interpretation of WID, its main contribution to the field of IDA has been generally understood by development practitioners as being the first step to bring women explicitly into the field through specific women's projects that either sought to bring women out of the domestic sphere and into the productive sphere[96] or addressed specific women's problematics.[97] The WID approach thus operated in a field in which women largely occupied the status of invisible recipient of IDA. This is what Tinker called 'the error of omission or failure to acknowledge and utilise women's productive role'[98] in IDA. WID thus mainly focused on the participation of women in a field in which they had been largely excluded.

However, WID did not explicitly seek to alter structural inequalities, power relations and social justice. Rather, it left all social and economic frameworks and structures unchallenged and in practice often resulted in the use of the known to IDA practitioners as the 'add-women-and-stir' approach. As Dixon mentioned, '[T]he real issue which was left behind under WID is that of "who controls the resources?"'[99] Thus, in its application, WID began by prioritising recognition, leaving much of the essential question of redistribution behind.

The WID approach has been further criticised, much in the same ways as was liberal feminism. Arguably though, the underpinning liberal perspectives in WID were not the only limitations. These further coincided 'all too neatly' with the identity politics surge of the 1980s and its hegemonic focus on *representation*[100] and *recognition*[101] at the expenses of *redistribution*.

Consequently, development strategies based on WID were necessarily limited in their ability to bring about transformation of the injustices and socio-economic inequalities women face, since:

> Development in WID was seen as economic growth that could only occur through formally productive activity. Since women's productive role in development countries is mainly operated in informal sectors and women also bear the large majority of the reproductive role and domestic burden, this led to a partial analysis of women's role and relations, thus . . . sidestepping women's subordination and oppression.[102]

Thus, the WID strategy to a large extent failed to redefine the focus and political priorities of IDA. The dissatisfaction of WID translated into the introduction of a new approach towards gender equality in IDA called GAD. Accordingly, the GAD approach focused on analysing much of what had been missed out in WID.[103] This approach further sought to replace the identity-centred notion of 'women' in WID with the broader and more abstract (less 'feminist' connoted) concept of 'gender equality' which in essence focused on closing the gap between women and men. This marked a turning point in the redefinition of gender-related strategies in IDA; by the mid-1990s the concept of 'gender equality' was hailed as the overall goal and the concept of 'gender mainstreaming' was prioritised as the main strategy to achieve this goal across all main sectors of IDA – now no longer confined to marginalised women's projects from the mainstream of development assistance.[104]

As Moser explains, although in practice WID and GAD were used and are still being used interchangeably and/or concurrently[105] in donor agencies' policies and programmes, these approaches differed fundamentally in terms of their focus, with consequent implications in terms of their policies and planning processes:

> The WID approach – despite its change in focus from one of equity to one of efficiency . . ., focuses mainly on women in isolation, promoting measures such as access to credit and employment as the means by which women can be better included into development processes. In contrast, the GAD approach maintains that a focus on women in isolation is to ignore the real problem, which remains their subordinate status to men. In insisting that women cannot be viewed in isolation, GAD emphasized, in principle, a different focus on gender roles and relations.[106]

This shift further opened opportunities for a redefinition of IDA – its focus and priorities as a whole. Thus, beyond gender roles and relations, IDA could in principle, focus on changes in the following aspects: 'systems for organising rights, responsibilities and resources for members in the different social groups'[107] which were keeping women in poverty.

Thus, in principle, IDA could have been transformed to focus on:

> determining . . . how assets are to be distributed between occupants of the different relationships, how authority and status are to be assigned and how labour is allocated.[108]

Indeed, the notion of gender equality in its analytical framework offered greater scope and raised higher hopes for a social justice analysis to refocus IDA's priorities on *redistribution*, as it provided a comparative analytical framework within which allocations of resources, power and opportunities could be weighed and measured. At least in theory, GAD took a step further in questioning underlying social, economic and political structures, calling for and raising hope towards significant structural changes.[109]

However, if this was the potential at a theoretical level, it was rarely made as explicit in practice in development agencies' policy documents and programmes.[110]

Despite all its theoretical premises, many GAD critiques would contend that in practice, the notion of gender equality:

> had been eviscerated of any of its original political intent. Represented to technocrats and policy-makers in the form of tools, frameworks and mechanisms, gender (equality) became a buzzword in development frameworks in the 1990s. In more recent times, it has fallen from favour and has a jaded, dated feel to it. Diluted, denatured, depoliticized, included everywhere as an afterthought, gender (equality) may have become something everyone who works for an aid organisation knows that they are supposed to do something about. But quite what and what would happen if they carried on ignoring it, is rarely pungent or urgent enough to distract the attention of many development bureaucrats and practitioners from business as usual.[111]

If the comments above clearly reflect what many practitioners and gender focal points in IDA agencies have been observing, experiencing and understanding gender in practice, the same feminist ideologies which persisted throughout WID continued to grow in the GAD era. Such ideologies remained concerned with the representation of Third World women in constructing gender-related theory and concepts in the field of IDA.

Third World feminists' ideologies have been, to some extent, useful in emphasising the following series of elements:

> The idea that the subordination of women cannot be divorced from an analysis of the political and economic structures within which women are located; the neglect of systemic interconnections between social processes of capital accumulation, class formation and the changing situation of women; the indifference displayed by WID advocates to the structural asymmetries within and between nations and their faith in the potential to reform market-led development processes.[112]

Arguably, such ideological critiques also contributed together with neoliberalism to shift the underpinning focus of gender equality away from redistribution. Others, such as Tamale, provide an interesting demonstration of this, arguing for a richer paradigm which she calls a comprehensive multi-dimensional feminist theoretical framework in Africa. According to her analysis, this multi-dimensional framework ought to encompass the following elements in a holistic manner: i) elements of indigenous cultures; ii) religion; iii) capitalism; iv) imperialism; and v) postcolonialism. Tamale argues that all five aspects of oppression form an integrated matrix and therefore the dialectic relationship between gender, class, ethnicity, religion, imperialism and postcolonialism is especially pertinent for an analysis of gender relations in the African context.[113] In her view, clearly a framework that would privilege one aspect over the others would offer a truncated analytical framework for women in Africa.

Arguably though, having (mal)distribution on a par with the other dimensions may also offer a truncated perspective of realities in Africa as elsewhere, effectively diluting the overall problematics with other (albeit important) problematics and substantially diminishing the scope and relevance of gender in IDA.

In the views of further critiques, Third World women were still (mis)represented as 'others' whether in the case of GAD and as victims, sex objects or cloistered beings, in the case of WID.[114] Accordingly, critiques perceived WID as 'embedded in neo-colonial/liberal discourse and GAD presenting a disrupted representation of women in the South as an undifferentiated "other"'.[115]

In practice, as the 'add-women-and-stir-approach' persisted from WID to GAD, so did the Third Worldist critiques, drawing parallels between WID and GAD as being both imperialist and colonialist projects – despite the fact that in the IDA practice, often, GAD ended up meaning not much more than an empty shell.[116]

In conclusion, it is clearly demonstrable that recurrent and similar theoretical developments have occurred in the interpretation of IDA, WID and GAD, thus influencing the focus and meaning of fundamental approaches and notions underpinning gender equality in IDA.

The effects of these theoretical shifts have redefined IDA, seriously distancing the field from challenging social inequalities and intra-cultural power relations. Moreover, remaining true to these perspectives runs the risk of maintaining poverty as it is. Shirin Rai[117] echoes this concern about the conflicting feminist ideological trends underpinning GAD discourse and gender equality. She stresses that feminist critiques have been played out in opposition, from a focus on difference (as emancipation from dominant trends of thought and patronising perceptions of otherness) to a focus on the grounds of women's international and universal solidarity, which formed the original basis for international feminist mobilisation.

Finally, the main implication of identity politics edified by Third Worldist critiques, combined with neoliberal trends in IDA, has been the erosion of the meaning and political force behind gender equality and its legitimacy. Identity politics have effectively distorted IDA's original and intended focus on the political struggle for socio-economic justice. This erosion has in turn prevented the concept of gender equality from being supported by a sufficiently solid, coherent and legitimate theoretical framing to adequately address injustices facing women in the context of IDA.

Conclusion

The main change of focus in ideological framing has been the eclipse of the notion of redistribution, which has taken place at various levels. Such misplacement has permeated the fundamental theoretical elements of the framework underpinning the concept of gender equality. The eclipse of the notion of distribution – whether accidental or not – is thus identified as crucial and recurrent within a variety of key elements forming the theoretical underpinning of the concept of gender equality, effectively denuding the concept of theoretical grounds with which to address socio-economic injustices within the field of IDA. Sidelining redistribution thus extends to the definition of IDA, and to the definitions of WID and GAD.

Furthermore, the chapter shows that it ought to have become evident that an understanding of women's injustices and inequalities, viewed not in isolation but within broader visions of exploitation and subordination, including 'voluntary subordination', would result in mutually enriching analyses and theoretical frameworks. Instead of an enriching and solidarity-based theoretical framework underpinning gender equality in IDA, weak critiques of cultural, religious and identity-related oppressions have prevailed under the guise of anti-essentialism and in the name of multiculturalism.

In practice, and as Fraser illustrated, Third World feminist critiques drifted towards a focus solely upon national identity and communitarianism on the grounds of anti-imperialism and neo-colonialist struggle, doing away with redistribution and Marxist analytical tools – which paradoxically were the very lens through which exploitations of all forms could be analysed.

The analysis thus challenges the justification upon which some theoretical perspectives argued that focusing on redistribution and universal women's human rights would have inevitably led to the much-apprehended material neo-colonialist threat of 'robbing women of their historical agency'. On the contrary, the chapter demonstrates that excluding redistribution and universalism leads to a weakening of the solidarity dimension, robbing women of potential grounds for justice claims. This consequently challenges the grounds upon which redistribution and universalism were displaced, dismissed and eroded by the proponents of Third Worldist, anti-essentialist and difference feminism.

Increasingly more relevant is the extent to which postcolonial ruling elites are willing to integrate redistribution and power sharing in their policies, addressing in other words South-South as well as North-South exploitation and inequalities.

It is argued that whilst there are obvious advantages in enriching a socio-economic reading of the gender equality problematics by connecting with other dimensions relevant to exploitation and injustice, the challenge in interpretation lies when dimensions are put on an equal footing. For the choice to date has been wavering between either placing all dimensions on an equal footing resulting in multifocal theoretical frameworks or supplanting socio-economic analysis and universalism with local identities and cultural relativism. In either case, it has been increasingly challenging to frame the interpretation of gender equality within a contemporary theoretical matrix which adequately addresses universal violations of women's human rights and systemic gender inequalities and injustices.

Notes

1 See R Peet and E Hartwick, *Theories of Development: Contentions, Arguments, Alternatives* (2nd edn, The Guilford Press 2009).
2 See I Tinker, 'The Making of a Field: Advocates, Practitioners and Scholars' in N Visvanathan and others (eds), *The Women, Gender & Development Reader* (Zed Books 1997) 34–36.
3 See K Young, 'Gender and Development' in N Visvanathan and others (eds), *The Women, Gender & Development Reader* (Zed Books 1997) 51–54.
4 See C Jencks, *Critical Modernism: Where Is Post-Modernism Going?* (Wiley-Academy 2007) 23.
5 See N Fraser, *Scales of Justice: Reimagining Political Space in a Globalizing World* (Columbia University Press 2009)101.
6 See 'Comment on the Universalist-Relativist Debate' in H Steiner, P Alston and R Goodman (eds), *International Human Rights in Context: Law, Politics, Morals* (3rd edn, Oxford University Press 2007) 517. Other examples encompassing the politics of identity, recognition and cultural differences: A Bunting, 'Theorizing Women's Cultural Diversity Feminist International Human Rights Strategies' (1993) 20 (1) *Journal of Law Society* 6; R Kapur, 'A Love Song to Our Mongrel Selves: Hybridity, Sexuality and the Law' (1999) 8(3) *Social and Legal Studies* 353.
7 See E Brems, 'Enemies or Allies-Feminism and Cultural Relativism as Dissident Voices in Human Rights Discourse' (1997) 19(1) *Human Rights Quarterly* 136.

8 See TE Higgins, 'Anti-Essentialism, Relativism and Human Rights' (1996) 19 *Harvard Women's Law Journal* 89 in Steiner, Alston and Goodman (109) 545.

9 See C Mohanty, 'Cartographies of Struggle: Third World Women and the Politics of Feminism' in C Mohanty, A Russo and L Torres (eds), *Third World Women and the Politics of Feminism* (Indiana University Press 1991) 1–51; see also CT Mohanty, 'Under Western Eyes: Feminist Scholarship and Colonial Discourses' in Mohanty, Russo and Torres (eds), *Third World Women and the Politics of Feminism* (Indiana University Press 1991) 51–80.

10 See G Prakesh, 'Subaltern Studies as Postcolonial Criticism' (1994) 99 *American Historical Review* 1475–1490. See also R Kapur, 'The Tragedy of Victimization Rhetoric: Resurrecting the "Native" Subject in International/Post-colonial Feminist Legal Politics' (2002) 15 *Harvard Human Rights Journal* 2.

11 Examples of difference feminists is understood as illustrated by the following works: A Lorde, 'The Master's Tools Will Never Dismantle the Master's House' in C Morroga and G Anzaldua (eds), *The Bridge Called Me Back: Writings by Radical Women of Color* (Persaphone Press 1981) 98–101; C Gilligan, *In a Different Voice, Psychological Theory and Women's Development* (Harvard University Press 1982); IM Young, *Justice and the Politics of Difference* (Princeton University Press 1990).

12 See Peet and Hartwick.

13 See Tinker.

14 See Young.

15 The term 'eclipse' is understood here and throughout the thesis in its figurative sense, as a loss of significance, power and prominence, ultimately resulting in a loss of focus in the interpretation of gender equality.

16 See J Rawls, *A Theory of Justice* (revised edn, Harvard University Press 1999) and R Dworkin, 'What Is Equality? Part 2: Equality of Resources' (Fall 1981) 10(4) *Philosophy and Public Affairs* 283–345.

17 'Universality' is used throughout the thesis in the sense used by H Charlesworth and C Chinkin, *The Boundaries of International Law* (Manchester University Press 2004) which emphasises the notion of universality of inequalities.

18 This is further evidenced with quantitative and qualitative data in the first section of Chapter 5.

19 W Mansell, B Meteyard and A Thomson, *A Critical Introduction to Law* (3rd edn, Cavendish Publishing 2004) 164.

20 See Rawls 243–244.

21 See Rawls xvi; see also J Rawls, 'Justice as Fairness' (1958) 67 *Philosophical Review*.

22 See Dworkin 283.

23 The term 'displacement' is used as socio-economic equality used to constitute the prevailing focus of socialist thought and in this context it has therefore been 'displaced' out that fundamental position.

24 See Fraser 105.

25 See Fraser 106.

26 The 'Left' is here and hereafter defined as political groups and parties favouring radical, reforming and socialist views.

27 See Fraser 107–108.

28 S Rai, *The Gender Politics of Development* (Zed Books 2008) 2.

29 F Banda, *Women, Law and Human Rights: An African Perspective* (Hart Publishing 2005) 308.

30 A Sen, *The Idea of Justice* (The Belknap Press of Harvard University Press 2009) 415 citing T Hobbes, *Leviathan* (first published 1651).

31 See Fraser 106.

32 The European Social Forum was held in London, UK from 14 to 17 October 2004 see <www.fse-esf.org/spip.php?article58>

33 The World Conference against Racism, Racial Discrimination, Xenophobia and Related Intolerance was held in Durban, South Africa from 31 August to 8 September 2001 see <www.ngo-monitor.org/article/ngo_forum_at_durban_conference_>
34 See Fraser 114–115.
35 C Fourest, *La Tentation Obscurantiste* (Grasset 2005) 50, 135–145. See also on the same topic but related to the First World Conference on Women in 1975, M Snyder, 'Unlikely Godmother: The UN and the Global Women's Movement' in M Marx Ferree and AM Tripp (eds), *Global Feminism: Transnational Women's Activism, Organizing, and Human Rights* (New York University Press 2006) 24–50.
36 See Fourest. See also T Peace, 'L'impact de la 'Participation Musulmane' sur le Mouvement Altermondialiste en Grande-Bretagne et en France' (Été 2008)70 *Cultures & Conflits* 110–128; 'NGO forum at Durban Conference 2001' www.ngo-monitor.org/article/ngo_forum_at_durban_conference_.
37 The slogan was particularly brought forward at the Second World Conference on Women held in Copenhagen from 14 to 30 July 1980.
38 H Steiner and P Alston (eds), *International Human Rights in Context: Law, Politics, Morals* (Oxford University Press 2000) 367. See also M-B Dembour, 'Following the Movement of a Pendulum: Between Universalism and Relativism' in J Cowan, M-B Dembour and R Wilson (eds), *Culture and Rights: Anthropological Perspectives* (Cambridge University Press 2001) 56–79.
39 See Charlesworth and Chinkin 47.
40 N Kabeer, *Reversed Realities, Gender Hierarchies in Development Thought* (Verso 2001) 31–32. Kabeer played a role in influencing feminist theoretical frameworks in IDA and conceptual changes from WID to GAD.
41 For an example of attributing false consciousness to Third World women in the case of female genital mutilation see K Engle, 'Female Subjects of Public International Law: Human Rights and the Exotic Other Female' (1992) 26 *New England Law Review* 1509.
42 For example: 'As white women ignore their built-in privilege of whiteness and define in terms of their own experience alone, then women of Color become "other", the outsider whose experience and tradition is too "alien" to comprehend'. S Mullally, *Human Rights Law Perspective, Gender Culture and Human Rights: Reclaiming Universalism* (Hart Publishing 2006) xxx citing A Lorde, 'Age, Race, Class and Sex: Women Redefining Difference' in A Lorde (ed), *Sister Outsider* (Trumansburg 1984) 117.
43 CT Mohanty, 'Feminist Encounters: Locating the Politics of Experience' in M Barett and A Philips (eds), *Destabilising Theory: Contemporary Feminist Debates* (Stanford University Press 1992) 83.
44 Ibid 84. For an example of Human Rights deconstruction as unidirectional, predictable and arrogant rhetoric see M Mutua, 'Savages, Victims, and Saviors: The Metaphor of Human Rights' (2001) 42 *Harvard International Law Journal* 201.
45 See AA An-Na'im, *Human Rights in Cross-Cultural Perspectives* (University of Pennsylvania Press 1992); D Kennedy, 'The International Human Rights Movement; Part of the Problem?' (2002) 15 *Harvard Human Rights Journal* 127; H Charlesworth, 'A Response to David Kennedy' (2002) 15 *Harvard Law Journal* 127.
46 CT Mohanty, *Feminism without Borders: Decolonising Theory, Practicing Solidarity* (Duke University Press 2003) 40. See also Kapur 2.
47 For an example of an understanding of feminism as a Western notion see U Narayan, *Dislocating Cultures: Identities, Traditions and Third – World Feminism* (Routledge 1997).
48 Other examples supporting this view are: E Spelman, *Inessential Woman: Problems of Exclusion in Feminist Thoughts* (Beacon Press 1980); J Kristeva, 'Women Can Never Be Defined' in Marks and de Courtivron (eds), *New French Feminisms: An Anthology* (Schocken 1981) 137, 140; J Flax, 'Race/Gender and the Ethic of Difference' (1995) 23 (3) *Political Theory* 500; NC Moruzzi, 'A Problem with Headscarves: Complexity of Political and Social Identities' (1994) 22(4) *Political Theory* 653.

49 See Sen.
50 cf de Beauvoir.
51 SM Okin, 'Feminism, Women's Human Rights and Cultural Differences', in U Narayan and S Harding (eds), *Decentering the Center: Philosophy for a Multicultural, Postcolonial, and Feminist World* (Indiana University Press 2000) 36–37.
52 See Okin 38.
53 Ibid.
54 'World Conference on Women Held in Beijing' (4 to 15 September 1995) <www.un.org/womenwatch/daw/beijing/fwcwn.html>
55 See 'Beijing Declaration and Platform for Action' <www.un.org/womenwatch/daw/beijing/fwcwn.html>
56 H Charlesworth, 'What Are Women's International Human Rights?' in R Cook (ed), *Human Rights of Women: National and International Perspectives* (University of Pennsylvania Press1994) 60.
57 Charlesworth and Chinkin 54.
58 As illustrated in Chapter 3.
59 As will be further shown at all levels in Chapters 2, 3 and 4.
60 Steiner and Alston 407.
61 R JC Young, *Postcolonialism: A Very Short Introduction* (Oxford University Press 2003) 99.
62 Women and Law in Southern Africa Research Trust.
63 A Armstrong and others, 'Uncovering Reality: Excavating Women's Rights in African Family Law' (1992) Working Paper N.7 Women and law in Southern Africa.
64 A Hellum, 'Women's Human Rights and African Customary Law: Between Universalism and Relativism – Individualism and Communitarianism' (1999) 10(2) *The European Journal of Development Research* 102.
65 Banda 305.
66 See Y Tamir, 'Hands Off Clitoridectomy' (Summer 1996) 31 *Boston Review* 21; O Koso-Thomas, *The Circumcision of Women: A Strategy for Eradication* (Zed Books 1987).
67 See UNDP, 'Gender Index Statistics' Human Development Reports (2001–2010). See also Chapter 4 for further evidence and statistics.
68 See Charlesworth and Chinkin 55.
69 J Dean, *Solidarity of Strangers: Feminism After Identity Politics* (University of California Press 1996) 174.
70 Mohanty, *Feminism without Borders* 39. See also Kapur, 'A Love Song to Our Mongrel Selves' 353.
71 This is demonstrated throughout the thesis and at all levels of IDA, from the theoretical level in this chapter, to international legal and policy level in Chapter 2, to the donor and national policy level in chapter 3, and finally to the programme and field level in Chapter 4.
72 A Walker, *In Search of Our Mothers' Gardens: Womanist Prose* (Hartcourt Brace & Company 1967). The term ´womanism' was adapted from Pulitzer Prize winning author, Alice Walker. In her book *In Search of Our Mothers' Gardens: Womanist Prose*, Walker used the term to describe the perspectives and experiences of 'women of color'. Although most womanist scholarship centres on African-American women's experience, other non-white theologians identify themselves with this term. This discourse is strongly related to African feminism and postcolonial feminism. Many postcolonial feminists, such as Mills, argue that oppressions relating to the colonial experience, particularly racial, class and ethnic oppressions, have marginalised women in postcolonial societies. Moreover, postcolonial feminists object to the perceived portrayal of women of non-Western societies as passive and voiceless victims, as opposed to the portrayal of Western women as modern, educated and empowered.
73 S Arndt, 'African Gender Trouble and African Womanism: An Interview with Chikwenye Ogunyemi and Wanjira Muthoni' (Spring 2000) *Signs: Journal of Women in Culture and Society* 253.

74 Interviews held with key informants in the context of the gender action plan for the rural transport sector in Benin. The consultancy aimed at the development of a gender action plan to be incorporated in phase II of the road works sector programme supported by Danida in Benin in 2004.

75 Mohanty, *Feminism without Borders* 224. For examples of attempts to identify the middle grounds, a point of dialogue between identity politics in feminism and a focus on commonalities/universalism as mutually enriching discourse see S Benhabib, *Situating the Self: Gender, Community and Postmodernism in Contemporary Ethics* (Polity Press 1992); S Benhabib, *The Claims of Culture: Equality and Diversity in the Global Era* (Princeton University Press 2002).

76 See Fourest, *La Tentation Obscurantiste* 18–21.

77 An example to illustrate the difficulty in bridging such a divide is the death threats received by the Philippe Val, former director of *Charlie Hebdo*, a French satirical newspaper and who won the case for the reproduction of satirical cartoons on the grounds of freedom of expression. Philippe Val is a living example of a visceral anti-totalitarian and anti-fascist.

78 Such examples are also reflected in different reactions and double standards vis-à-vis international events. Fourest points out the contradiction of Third Worldists' reaction, whom she explains whilst most of the time they were ready to denounce (and portray themselves as) the victims of imperialism/colonialism/racism and all forms of identity-based exclusion, they were rather quiet when for example the time came to save Bosnian Muslims from Serbian genocide. She urges to compare this lack of action in the face of such atrocities to that of Bernard Henry Levy, an anti-fascist at heart, and a pupil of Althusser and the biographer of Jean Paul Sartre who did go to Sarajevo to film *Bosna*.

79 See E Macé and N Guénif-Souilams, *Les Féministes et le Garçon Arabe* (Ed. de l'Aube 2004).

80 C Fourest, 'L'intégrisme est-il Queer?' (Automne 2005) 34 *ProChoix* <www.prochoix.org/cgi/blog/index.php/2005/12/14/369-prochoix-n-34-automne-2005>

81 Fourest, *La Tentation Obscurantiste* (n 148) 98. See also I Abraham, 'The Veil and the Closet: Islam and the Production of Queer Space' (2007) *Queer Space: Centers and Peripheries*, UTS, 1–4.

82 C Fourest, *La Dernière Utopie: Menaces sur L'universalisme* (Grasset 2009) 57 citing W Tamzali, 'Féministes, je vous écris d'Alger' *Libération* (Paris, 14 Janvier 2004).

83 'The notion of development stems from the (much criticised, in the age of postmodernism) Enlightenment notion of the use of the modern, scientific mind for improving existence entailing emancipation in two senses – liberation from the vicissitudes of nature through advanced technology and self-emancipation, that is, control over social relations, control over the conditions under which human nature is formed. This entails economic, social and cultural progress as well as refinement of ethical and moral values. Developmentalism, in this school of thought, is the belief in the viability and desirability of such political and economic progress' Peet with Hartwick 1.

84 PF Leeson and M Minogue (eds), *Perspectives on Development: Cross-Disciplinary Themes in Development Studies* (Manchester University Press 1988).

85 U Kothari and M Minogue, *Development Theory and Practice: Critical Perspectives* (Palgrave 2002) 2.

86 This, along with a few exceptions, will be further discussed in detail in Chapter 4, through analysis of multilateral and bilateral donor policy.

87 See Peet with Hartwick, 1–2. See also R Douthwaite, *The Growth Illusion: How Economic Growth Has Enriched the Few, Impoverished the Many and Endangered the Planet* (Lilliput 1992); R Munck, *Politics and Dependency in the Third World: The Case of Latin America* (Zed Books 1984); S Ziauddin, *Postmodernism and the Other: The New Imperialism of Western Culture* (Pluto 1998).

88 See also V Tucker, 'The Myth of Development: A Critique of a Eurocentric Discourse' in R Munch and D O'Hearn (eds), *Critical Development Theory: Contribution to a New Paradigm* (Zed Books 1999)1–27. For a nuanced example locating Africa between the desire to become modern and traditions see KA Appiah, *In My Father's House: Africa in the Philosophy of Culture* (Oxford University Press 1992) 173–193.
89 See Z Sardar, 'Development and the Locations of Eurocentricism' in Munch and O'Hearn (eds), *Critical Development Theory* 44–62.
90 Peet with Hartwick 60. See B Sutcliffe, 'The Place of Development in Theories of Imperialism and Globalization' in Munch and O'Hearn (eds), *Critical Development Theory* 135–154.
91 See Z Sardar, 'Beyond Development: An Islamic Perspective' (1996) 8(2) *European Journal of Development Research* 36; A Michael, *Machines as the Measure of Men: Science, Technology and Ideologies of Western Dominance* (Cornell University Press 1989). See also E Crew and E Harrison, *Whose Development? An Ethnography of Aid* (Zed Books 2002) 25–48, 132–152.
92 S Batliwala, 'The Meaning of Women's Empowerment: New Concepts from Action' in G Sen, A Germain and L Chen (eds), *Population Policies Reconsidered: Health Empowerment and Rights* (Harvard University Press 1994).
93 Young 99.
94 E de La Boétie, *Discourse on Voluntary Servitude or the Against-One, Essay* (1576); E de La Boétie, *Discours de la Servitude Volontaire* (Milles et une nuits 1997).
95 C Moser, *Gender Planning and Development* (Routledge 1993) 56–57. If for the purpose of the thesis the broad and common (albeit less sophisticated) interpretation of WID as understood and used by development practitioners will be considered, it does not exclude the fact as highlighted by Moser that WID was, at least in theory, more nuanced and encompassed the following trends:

> i) The welfare approach 1950–1970, a residual model of social welfare under colonial administration, seeking to bring women into development, as "better mothers"; ii) The 'original' WID equity approach developed in the course of 1975–1985, influenced (amongst other) by the publication of Esther Boserup. The purpose was for women to gain equity in development processes; iii) The second WID approach focused on anti-poverty from the 1970s onwards, toned down the equity approach and was linked to redistribution with growth and basic needs to ensure poor women increased their productivity; iv) The third WID approach focused on efficiency in post-1980s, due to the deterioration of world economy and policies of economic stabilization and adjustment, this approach relied on women's economic contribution to development, to ensure development became more efficient and effective; v) The fourth WID approach focused on women's empowerment from 1975 and was accelerated during 1980s. It arose out of the failure of the equity approach, to empower women through greater self-reliance. Women's subordination was seen not only as a problem in relation to men but also in relation to colonial and neo-colonial oppression.

96 See E Boserup, *Women's Role in Economic Development* (St. Martin's Press 1970). For example, these are specific projects targeting access to micro-credits for women.
97 For example, these are specific projects targeting violence against women, women's sexual and reproductive health projects or the advancement of women's status such as women's empowerment projects, typically awareness raising projects on women's human rights.
98 I Tinker, 'The Adverse Impact of Development on Women' in I Tinker and M Bramson (eds), *Women and Development* (Overseas Development Council 1976).
99 RB Dixon, *Seeing the Invisible Women Farmers in Africa: Improving Research and Data Collection* (University of California 1985) 32.

100 Representation was translated through the participation of women in development projects.
101 Recognition was translated through projects concerned with 'the advancement of women's status'.
102 Peet and Hartwick 182.
103 See the definition of GAD by the research of the Institute for Development Studies at the University of Sussex in K Young, *Planning Development with Women* (St. Martin's Press 1993) 134.
104 See the Platform for Action (PfA) of the Fourth World Conference on Women held in Beijing in September 1995 <www.un.org/womenwatch/daw/beijing/platform/plat1.htm>.
105 This essentially means that the 'add-women-and-stir approach' which oversimplified WID could still be found under GAD, doing away with the transformational potential GAD was assumed to bring forward.
106 See Moser 2.
107 A Whitehead, 'Some Preliminary Notes on the Subordination of Women' (1979) 10(3), *IDS Bulletin*, 10
108 See Kabeer, *Reversed Realities* 58.
109 See EM Rathgeber, 'WID, WAD, GAD: Trends in Research and Practice' (1990) 24 *Journal of Developing Areas* 489–502.
110 As is further examined in Chapters 3 and 4.
111 A Cornwall, E Harrison and A Whitehead, *Feminisms in Development: Contradictions, Contestations and Challenges* (Zed Books 2007) 5–6.
112 Kabeer, *Reversed Realities* 31–32.
113 S Tamale, *When Hens Begin to Crow: Gender and Parliamentary Politics in Uganda* (Fountain Publisher 1999) 3.
114 See Mohanty, 'Under Western Eyes'.
115 Ibid.
116 See Cornwall and others 5–6.
117 See Rai.

2 Wavering across international normative architecture

This chapter analyses the interpretation of gender equality at international legislative and policy level. It discusses how the concept of gender equality is playing 'hide-and-seek', appearing and disappearing, in a solid or more diluted version through the key international norms and policies. It considers the interpretations of gender equality in key international legal instruments and international policy frameworks. These are the Convention on the Elimination of all Forms of Discrimination Against Women (CEDAW),[1] the Protocol to the African Charter on Human and Peoples' Rights on the Rights of Women in Africa 2003,[2] the key UN Women's World Conferences[3] and contemporary dominant IDA policy frameworks such as the Millennium Development Goals (MDGs),[4] the Paris Declaration on Aid Effectiveness (2005)[5] and the current Sustainable Development Goals. In particular, it provides an analysis of the reservations to gender equality in CEDAW and the omission of violence against women, and of the changing interpretations of gender equality in key IDA international policy frameworks. The chapter concludes with a reflection on the implications of theoretical (re)framings on international normative and policy frameworks.

In discussing the costs of compromises in feminist politics in IDA, Andrea Cornwall quotes Prudence Woodford-Berger's remark, as follows:

> Alliances are always made at some costs because they are made with those who share some but not all, political goals; and while many can agree on the need for such alliances, it is much more difficult to agree on the point at which compromises become defeat.[6]

The same could be argued for the theoretical compromises which turned into defeats in the interpretation of gender equality at the international law and policy level. This chapter thus examines whether and how the changes in focus of the theories underpinning the concept of gender equality discussed in Chapter 1 have affected the interpretation of gender equality in international policy and international legislative level.

In the particular context of IDA, if it makes much sense that forging appropriate forms of solidarity across differences has never been more important than in the precarious geo-political realities of today's world, the challenge must be to focus on how to do this without risking the overshadowing of key theoretical elements discussed in chapter 1.

The first section of the chapter discusses gender equality at the international legislative level.[7] The section provides a critical analysis of the reservation process[8] and examines specifically the reservations to CEDAW which were entered by some Member State parties on the grounds of incompatibility with Shari'a law.[9] The section shows that by critically examining the ideology underpinning these reservations, it is possible to challenge the cultural relativist argument upon which these reservations find justification, by excavating universal patriarchal patterns of resistance to the concept of gender equality.

In order to deepen the challenge against a cultural relativist position, the section further contrasts the interpretation of gender equality in CEDAW with the interpretation used in the Protocol to the African Charter on Human and Peoples' Rights on the Rights of Women in Africa 2003. This comparison highlights that whereas violence against women – arguably a key theme for women's human rights together with the definition of gender equality – has been omitted[10] in CEDAW at the international level, it was included in this regional human rights instrument. The section thus examines the reasons given for excluding violence against women at the international level and observes how they were disputed at the regional level. This example is selected as a particularly interesting counter-example to the feminist theories discussed in Chapter 1 which view the universality of human rights as another form of imperialism.[11] This example also seeks to demonstrate that paradoxically, at the regional level (which is a step closer to the expression of cultural difference), that which was omitted on the grounds of 'cultural sensitivity' at the international level could be included without ambiguity and with rare explicitness.

The second section examines how similar patterns discussed in Chapter 1 have played out in international policy frameworks, namely in the UN World Conferences on Women and current IDA international policy frameworks. The second section thus begins by showing the devolution[12] of the meaning of gender equality at the international policy level from the 1970s to 2005 and its reappearance through the SDGs in 2016. The section examines specifically the changes in the interpretation of gender equality in connection to the changes in focus in the underpinning ideologies discussed in chapter 1.

The final section turns to another significant example of the Third Worldist position within the international policy framework of the UN. The section demonstrates how the Vatican, through its position as a permanent observer to the UN through its Mission of the Holy See,[13] has attempted to limit the concept of gender equality using similar key Third Worldist argumentation within UN World Conferences on Women. By critically examining the underpinning ideology behind the Vatican's lobby, which intends to limit the interpretation of gender equality to the notion of gender complementarity,[14] the section challenges the implied defence of cultural relativism. Simultaneously, the section draws parallels with similar attempts to limit the concept of gender equality by those Member States which entered reservations to CEDAW on the grounds of incompatibility with Shari'a law.

The chapter concludes by exploring whether there are common identifiable patterns between the ideological trends resistant to or limiting the concept of gender equality in IDA examined in albeit different socio-cultural and religious contexts. If so, it examines how these may have impacted the weakening of gender equality in the international normative architecture relevant to IDA.

Identity-focused interpretations of gender equality in international legislation

The first sub-section discusses the reservations that were entered by some Member State parties to the Convention on the Elimination of All Forms of Discrimination Against Women (CEDAW)[15] and it explores the particular ideologies underpinning them. The second sub-section contrasts the interpretation of gender equality in CEDAW with the interpretation used in the Protocol to the African Charter on Human and Peoples' Rights on the Rights of Women in Africa 2003.

CEDAW *reservations to gender equality*

CEDAW[16] constitutes the most important international legal instrument for gender equality, providing the key international normative framework through which gender equality can be defined and further interpreted in IDA policies and programmes. CEDAW has been widely used as the main international legal instrument legitimising the promotion of gender equality in IDA donor and national policy and programmes.[17]

Contrary to general assumptions in IDA, CEDAW has been subject to at least a double layer of compromises. In the first instance, there are reservations[18] to particular Articles of the Convention, which Member States were permitted to enter. In the second, there are compromises to the very text of CEDAW which have led to the eclipses of certain interpretations of gender equality. The reservation procedure, whereby governments can reserve the right not to apply a specific part of a treaty and have to declare so when ratifying by 'submitting a reservation' is a process designed to enhance global acceptance of treaty obligations by providing for exceptions to those obligations that governments cannot immediately and fully undertake.

Thus, there are general reservations to CEDAW providing that in the event of a conflict between CEDAW and Shari'a law, Shari'a shall prevail. In this context Reservations to Article 2 or Article 16 of CEDAW on the grounds of incompatibility with Shari'a law were entered by Bahrain, Bangladesh, Egypt, Iraq, Kuwait, Libyan Arab Jamahiriya, Malaysia, Maldives, Morocco, Oman, Saudi Arabia, Singapore, Syrian Arab Republic and United Arab Emirates. Some of the proponents of the reservations claimed that a restricted view of women's political rights is embodied in some interpretations of Shari'a law, in which women are disqualified from holding public office because they cannot be placed in a position of authority over men.

In response, the CEDAW Committee proposed a study into the status of women under Islamic law, but this was rejected by the UN General Assembly in 1987.[19] As of 2007, 77 out of the 185 Member State parties to CEDAW had entered reservations or declarations either addressed to a specific provision or of a general character that embraced the Convention as a whole.[20] The reservation process was intended to promote an inclusive strategy which aimed to ensure that the largest possible number of countries worldwide would be able to ratify CEDAW. Consequently, two-thirds of the world's countries did ratify CEDAW and thus, quantitative inclusion took priority strategically and constituted a success.[21]

This inclusionary strategy of opening the Convention to a broad reservation process sent out a significant signal worldwide, indicating that gender equality and women's rights were generally recognised as being important, but were also de facto negotiable. Moreover, under international human rights law, it showed that differences in standards concerning gender equality were acceptable within varying political, cultural and religious contexts.

Thus, it can be inferred that underpinning the reservation process to CEDAW, the prevailing focus was to reach the largest number of Member States, thus privileging quantitative participation through *representation*. This focus clearly prevailed over the compromised content of CEDAW itself as further analysed below.

It could also be argued that the number of Member States that submitted reservations was an indication both of the universality of gender inequalities and resistance to the concept of equality among different political, cultural and religious contexts.

The reservation process affecting gender equality was accepted as an exception under international law but as discussed below, it scarcely satisfies Article 19 of the Vienna Convention on the Law of Treaties,[22] which stipulates that:

> A State ratifying a treaty may make a reservation unless it is prohibited by the treaty or is incompatible with the object and purpose of the treaty.[23]

However, this provision has proven difficult to apply systematically in general[24] and specifically to CEDAW as demonstrated below.

Article 1 of CEDAW stipulates that:

> For the purposes of the present Convention, the term "discrimination against women" shall mean any distinction, exclusion or restriction made on the basis of sex which has the effect or purpose of impairing or nullifying the recognition, enjoyment or exercise by women, irrespective of their marital status, on the basis of equality of men and women, of human rights and fundamental freedoms in the political, economic, social, cultural, civil or any other field.[25]

And Article 2 of CEDAW stipulates that:

> States Parties condemn discrimination against women in all its forms, agree to pursue by all appropriate means and without delay a policy of eliminating discrimination against women and to this end, undertake: a) to embody the principle of equality of men and women in their national constitutions or other appropriate legislation if not yet incorporated therein and to ensure, through law and other appropriate means, the practical realisation of this principle.[26]

Clearly, therefore, a reservation to Article 1 or 2 of CEDAW seems incompatible with the object and purpose of the CEDAW as per Article 19 of the Vienna Convention mentioned above.

Such incompatible reservations, acceptable under CEDAW, make it more difficult for the CEDAW Committee to hold state parties to account (even on a pro-forma level). This incompatibility is reiterated by the CEDAW Committee in its reporting guidelines.[27] Moreover, it is also problematic for civil society working in the field to invoke gender equality and the non-discrimination principle.[28]

Consequently, the status of CEDAW and of the interpretation of the concept of gender equality is undermined and weakened, as the reservations

> give the impression that the Convention is not as binding as any other international conventions and that these reservations need not be scrutinised against the yardstick of international standards of equality for women because of the sovereignty of cultural and religious ideologies of the subject matter.[29]

At this stage, it is important to further consider and analyse what the underpinning ideologies to these reservations actually entail. For instance, when exploring the positions which prompted the reservations entered by certain Islamic Member States on the grounds of incompatibility with Shari'a law, it is important to consider exactly which principles under Shari'a law are said to be incompatible with Article 2 and the definition of non-discrimination. According to Abdullah Ahmed An-Na'im,[30] the most important (non-exhaustive) general principles of Shari'a law influencing gender equality and women's rights are the notions of *Qawama* and *Al-Hijab*. Both originate in verses of the Holy Qur'an, respectively, verse 4:34 and verses 24:31, 33:33, 33:53 and 33:59.

> Men have *Qawama* [guardianship and authority] over women because of the advantage they have over them and because they spend their assets to support them.[31]

An-Na'im understands that a Shari'a interpretation of verse 4:34 of the Holy Qur'an states that men as a group are the guardians of, and in that sense, have a superior responsibility to women as a group. Likewise, the men of a particular family are the guardians of and have a superior duty to the women of that family.[32]

It is this interpretation which has led to the seeming incompatibility of the Holy Qur'an with the basic principle of gender equality and non-discrimination laid down in Articles 1 and 2 of CEDAW as well as with Articles 7 and 8 of the CEDAW on women's right to participate on an 'equal basis' with men without discrimination in political and public life.[33]

> Shari'a provides that women are disqualified from holding general public office, which involves the exercise of authority over men, because, in keeping with the verse 4:34 of the Holy Qur'an, men are entitled to exercise authority over women and not the reverse.[34]

The other key principle is the notion of *Al-Hijab* (the veil), which has been given paradoxical interpretations in recent years – from being portrayed as a symbol of women's submission and imprisonment, to on the contrary, the allegory of freedom of religion and cultural self-determination.

According to An-Na'im, the notion of *Al-Hijab* reaches far beyond requiring women to cover their bodies and faces in public, for

> Shari'a interpretation of Verses 24:31, 33:33, 33:53 and 33.59 of the Holy Qur'an, specifies that women are supposed to stay at home and not leave it, except when required to, by urgent necessity. When they are permitted to venture beyond home, they must do so with their bodies and faces covered.[35]

Arguably, these underlying principles – although well anchored in socio-cultural and religious specificities – are not merely confined to Islam. These principles can also be found in diverse patriarchal societies which do not allow women to access positions of (political) authority and decision-making roles. There is no better evidence of this than the gender inequalities in parliaments across the world.[36] Only one country, Rwanda, currently has more than 50% of women in parliament and this is still no qualitative evidence of changes in power sharing. It is therefore reasonable to conclude that this underlying rationale for 'acceptable cultural exception' stems from universal characteristics across diverse patriarchal societies.

The notion of *Al-Hijab*, much discussed in contemporary European debates, is hailed as a symbol of discrimination against religion and is further analysed below. In An-Na'im's edifying analysis, *Al-Hijab* is no more and no less than a symbol of control over women's freedom on the ground of what is considered 'virtuous' and 'honourable'. In this consideration, women ought to be modest, discreet and not often seen 'out of the house'. However, the confinement of women's role to the domestic and non-productive sphere – and the 'complementary' opposite privilege, implicitly reserved to men as the presumed breadwinner – is not specific to this religion and culture either, as is evidenced in Chapter 4 below.

One of the most powerful examples illustrating this is discussed by Iranian writer and anthropologist Chahdortt Djavann in her interdisciplinary analysis of the principle of *Al-Hijab*.[37] Exiled in France during the 1990s, she warns against culture becoming the alibi of religion, and then, in turn, becoming an alibi for gender discrimination. Djavann critically examines what the principle of *Al-Hijab* supports and in whose interests. She argues that the hijab (which she defines as a cloth that is supposed to cover the entire body and that therefore cannot be understood as a 'scarf' or a mere form of 'fashion' accessory) has deeper symbolic implications for the construction of both female and male sexuality and identity, not necessarily known to or understood by the person who wears it, whether by free choice, socio-cultural influence or coercion. According to Djavann's analysis, girls under the hijab become the guarantor of their fathers' and brothers' male honour and thus, of part of their identity. The construction of both female and male identities is, she argues, intrinsically linked to the hijab and the related requirements of the expected female modest and obedient behaviour. According to this interpretation, the non-veiled Muslim woman represents a challenge to male honour and indirectly to their respective identity as Muslim men. Women's *Hojb* and *Hayâ* (women's modesty and shame) are respectively guaranteed and protected by the hijab, which becomes the guarantee of Muslim male honour.[38] The veiled woman exists as a *complement* to a full and virtuous masculine identity.

Through using comparative methodology, Djavann draws a parallel between the many 'visible' and 'invisible' non-Muslim veils which are worn today and have been worn across Europe, thereby extracting the practice from the specificity and possibly self-justifying identity, cultural and religious ghetto into a universal symbol of limitation and control over women's personal freedom. 'This veil', she writes, 'goes back to the beginnings of times, a symbol of archaism that was disappearing in the most remote countryside and traditional churches in the old Europe, is now making a rejuvenating come-back, pretending to be what it really isn't'[39] – a symbol of cultural freedom and emancipation.

In this context, so-called cultural differences become a rationale for the pursuit of patriarchal values and violations of fundamental women's human rights. Thus, the reservations entered in the name of cultural differences, when 'excavated' from within their content become nothing more and nothing less than commonly shared expressions of patriarchal hierarchies, which CEDAW was supposed to combat before becoming itself one of its victims.

Furthermore, the reservations entered alone may not have necessarily survived without the post-modern, anti-essentialist and anti-Eurocentric turn in feminism which provided a suitable justification for these reservations and a context-bound interpretation of gender equality.[40]

Interestingly, Charlesworth and Chinkin point out that whereas the Convention on the Elimination of All Forms of Racial Discrimination (1965)[41] benefited from a wide political support in the UN (which was less due to the rejection of discrimination on the grounds of race and more due to the fact that signatories simply failed to accept the existence of racial discrimination as a problem which applied to them), CEDAW 'in contrast, met with the reluctance to confront powerful oil producing states, undermining parallel support for the elimination of gender apartheid as demonstrated by the adverse response within the UN to proposals to tackle the reservations problem'.[42] Indeed, there are no reservations on the article of the race convention that pertains to the very definition of discrimination on the grounds of race.[43] The reservation of significance that led other Member States to enter objections on the grounds of Article 19 of the Vienna Convention[44] was entered by Yemen on Article 5.[45]

On the grounds of this fact, there is a difference in the degree of cultural rejection of the notion of discrimination on the grounds of sex and the quasi-universal acceptance of the notion of discrimination on the grounds of race. This in itself contradicts the anti-essentialist and anti-Eurocentric arguments made against the 'universal' notion of discrimination on the grounds of sex, showing if anything, the limits of the politics of identity as an overall framework. Arguably if the notion of 'discrimination' is criticised as Eurocentric, surely the critique should not be 'à la carte' when convenient to the interest groups conveying such critique. If the notion of discrimination on the grounds of race is easily embraced as 'universal' then all other discriminations, including those challenging patriarchal values such as discrimination on the grounds of sex and sexual orientation ought to be accepted as 'equally' universal.

In conclusion, a full understanding of visible and invisible veils which limit women's freedom and fundamental human rights is only possible through the comparison and questioning of the defence of differences in cultural identities when used as a rationale not to have gender stereotypes challenged. The extrapolation of data 'out of the boundaries of cultural identities', as it were, is particularly relevant if we are to grasp the underpinning ideologies informing the reservation process of some Member States to CEDAW as a significant example of the impact of hegemonic identity politics in international law. The reservations put forward to Articles 1 and 2 of CEDAW are not mere cultural and religious exceptions. Rather, they show the extent to which, the rejection of gender equality and basic women's human rights is being justified least by Member States reservations but justified by the theoretical rationale of identity politics. Clearly here, the compromise in question amounts to defeat of the very purpose of the Convention.

The omission of violence against women as fundamental violation of women's human rights

This section examines the reasons why violence against women was omitted from CEDAW and compares these to the explicit condemnation of it in the Protocol to the African Charter on Human and Peoples' Rights on the Rights of Women in Africa 2003.[46]

In the context of this book, violence against women is another striking example of one of many universal phenomena cutting across race, class, time and location.[47] Furthermore, as 'violence against women is often caused by the structural relationships of power, domination and privilege between men and women . . . often central to maintaining patriarchal hierarchies',[48] it provides a particularly illustrative example of universal patriarchal values.

In spite of such well-known global problematics, in CEDAW,

> the term violence does not appear anywhere in the Convention. The closest the Convention comes to addressing the issue is Art. 6 on exploitation of women (trafficking) – no other forms of violence are mentioned.[49]

Instead, violence against women is only explicitly condemned in the form of 'soft law', not as binding and only in the form of Recommendation 19,[50] which defines gender-based violence as a form of discrimination seriously inhibiting women's ability to enjoy rights and freedoms on a basis of equality with men. Furthermore, Recommendation 19 does not define violence as a fundamental violation of women's human dignity in and of itself. Rather, the notion of violence is inscribed within the non-discrimination egalitarian paradigm. Violence is thus not considered a breach of human rights *per se* and is therefore not recognised as part of the universal subordination of women.

Thus, at the international law level, there are currently no legally binding law instruments defining violence against women in these terms and offering adequate protection. Instead the protection against violence against women is explicitly addressed at the regional level in for example two regional conventions covering both Latin America and Africa,[51] one of which is discussed below. Whereas at the time of writing, Europe and Asia did not yet have conventions explicitly covering violence against women but only soft-law declarations.[52] On these facts, the regional conventions defending women's human rights cannot be accused of Eurocentrism or imperialism. Rather, they show if anything, that regions of so-called Third-World countries are ahead in addressing violence against women explicitly in conventions and that they share much the same features across the continents.

Moreover, both regional instruments were able to overcome all the following obstacles that were brought forward at the international level to justify CEDAW not including explicit provisions on violence against women: i) the conceptual difficulty of compressing a harm characterised as private into the public frame of international law; ii) the fact that violence does not fit into the equality model based on non-discrimination; iii) the felt need for wider ratification of the Convention, which led to compromises on themes considered by some Member States to be 'culturally sensitive'.[53]

Yet the right to liberation from violent and degrading treatment, not only in times of war covered by Security Council Resolution 1325,[54] but especially, in daily private and domestic life, whether in the public or private sphere, ought to have been recognised, as it was subsequently acknowledged, in both regional instruments.

In a sense, this highlights a fundamental contradiction:

> Although the empirical evidence of violence against women is overwhelming and undisputed, it was never adequately reflected in human rights law because it focuses on 'public' actions by the state.[55]

As mentioned, in contrast, both regional instruments covering different continents offer examples of far-reaching, radical and comprehensive definitions of violence against women[56] as illustrated in Article 1(J) of the Protocol to the African Charter on Human and Peoples' Rights on the Rights of Women in Africa 2003[57] (hereafter referred to as 'the Maputo Protocol'), which defines violence against women as follows:

> All acts perpetrated against women which cause or could cause them physical, sexual, psychological, and economic harm, including the threat to take such acts; or to undertake the imposition of arbitrary restrictions on or deprivation of fundamental freedoms in private and public life, in peace time and during situations of armed conflict or of war.

This definition echoes that of Articles 1 and 2 of the Inter-American Convention on the Prevention, Punishment and Eradication of Violence Against Women,[58] which defines violence against women as follows:

> Article 1: For the purposes of this Convention, violence against women shall be understood as any act or conduct, based on gender, which causes death or physical, sexual or psychological harm or suffering to women, whether in the public or the private sphere.
>
> Article 2: Violence against women shall be understood to include physical, sexual and psychological violence: a. that occurs within the family or domestic unit or within any other interpersonal relationship, whether or not the perpetrator shares or has shared the same residence with the woman, including, among others, rape, battery and sexual abuse; b. that occurs in the community and is perpetrated by any person, including, among others, rape, sexual abuse, torture, trafficking in persons, forced prostitution, kidnapping and sexual harassment in the workplace, as well as in educational institutions, health facilities or any other place; and c. that is perpetrated or condoned by the state or its agents regardless of where it occurs.

Furthermore Article 4(2)(a) of the Maputo Protocol[59] under the section related to the rights to life, integrity and security of person stipulates that:

> State Parties shall take appropriate measures to enact and enforce laws to prohibit all forms of violence against women including unwanted or forced sex whether the violence takes place in public or private.

This groundbreaking clause is explicitly calling for a proscription of rape and violence within the private domestic sphere. This is further supported by Article 5 of the Maputo Protocol[60] in the section related to the elimination of harmful practices, targeting female genital mutilation, and Article 6 of the Protocol[61] on forced marriages and Article 14(1) (d) of the Maputo Protocol[62] on the right to self-protection on HIV/AIDS and other Sexually Transmitted Diseases (STDs).

CEDAW was adopted in 1979 by the General Assembly by 130 votes and with 10 abstentions. CEDAW was also pressed to be ready for the presentation to the Second World Conference on Women in Copenhagen the following year and thus compromises on the content ensued. As a result, on 3 September 1981, 30 days after the 20th Member State had ratified it, CEDAW entered into force more rapidly than any previous international human rights treaty.[63]

In contrast, it took a longer time for the Maputo Protocol to come into force;[64] there was a demonstrable will not to compromise fundamental women's human rights. Indeed, for the first time at the African regional level, both the concepts of violence against women and gender equality were addressed in one legal instrument, focusing on violence against women beyond the public sphere. According to Amnesty International, the Maputo Protocol filled a major gap in the regional human rights system.[65] Achieving more than filling gaps at the regional level, the implications of the Maputo Protocol are far-reaching. They challenge the grounds upon which previous inclusionary approaches based on cultural relativism and identity politics led to substantive negotiations and seemingly inevitable compromises.

In conclusion, the Maputo Protocol could explicitly address what CEDAW had omitted and without reservations to gender equality. Thus, the difficulty at the international level is not linked to the impossibility of addressing a private matter such as domestic violence in a public international law instrument, or indeed to the fact that violence does not fit into the egalitarian paradigm. Rather, difficulties in addressing violence against women at the international level are due to the degree of influence of political and religious-based ideologies condoned by identity politics that are at best resistant to the idea of gender equality, and at worst resistant to eradicating violence against women. Clearly the omission of violence against women in CEDAW, as the reservations provide powerful illustrations of the extent of damage the overshadowing of cultural relativism can produce and of the fact that there is little compromise to be made on such fundamental resistance.

Thus, anxiety surrounding the possible exclusion of gender discriminatory Member States from CEDAW on the grounds of 'cultural differences' and religious perspectives resulted in gender equality being overshadowed. The strategy was intended to result in the inclusion of the largest number of countries irrespective of differences surrounding their degree of commitment to the essence of the Convention. By following an inclusionary strategy beyond the point of compromise and ultimately silencing fundamental notions such as violence against women, CEDAW was effectively weakened.

In contrast, the Maputo Protocol of 2003 demonstrates that all the arguments brought forward to legitimise the omission of violence against women in CEDAW and its reservation procedures are seriously questionable at best and invalid at worst. This leads to the conclusion that cultural relativism was prioritised over fundamental women's human rights, both regarding the limited content of CEDAW and in the reservation process surrounding its adherence.

It can be concluded that a universalist analytical grid is useful to uncover the common ideological patterns in patriarchal societies which consider both the struggle against violence against women and gender equality difficult concepts to commit to.

Playing hide-and-seek with international policy frameworks

As discussed above, while the concept of gender equality could not prevent being eroded at the international treaty level, this section investigates whether the policy framework at international level underpinning gender equality was any more consistent and resistant to changing ideologies. It is argued that there have been substantive changes to the interpretation of gender equality at the international policy level between the 1970s and mid-1990s reflecting shifts in theory, as discussed in chapter 1. As noted, there was high international political momentum at the time of the Fourth World Conference on Women in Beijing. However, this period was followed by the gradual evaporation of gender-related concepts within key IDA policy frameworks such as the Millennium Development Goals (MDGs) in 2000 and the 2005 Paris Declaration on Aid Effectiveness, and only lately with the Sustainability Development Goals (SDGs) in 2016 gender equality substantively re-emerged.

As specific reservations put forward by some Member States to CEDAW were examined in the sections above, the sections below, in turn, analyse the influence of the Vatican in relation to the interpretations of gender equality at the international policy level in key UN World Conferences on Women. The last section explores whether parallels can be drawn between the different ideologies underpinning these resistances, and if so, examines the impact on gender equality at the international level.

Evolutions and devolutions in international policy frameworks

This section presents an overview of the changes related to the interpretation of the concept of gender equality which have occurred in various IDA policy frameworks.

The table below illustrates at a glance the changes in gender momentum at the international legal and policy level over the last 50 years.[66] It has been acknowledged that the pace and strength of gender policy development has declined[67] before seemingly rising again through the SDGs. Concerns have been raised about a loss of 'gender momentum' and a narrowing of focus with regard to gender equality objectives[68] in international development assistance.

Chronology of selected key gender-related policies and legal frameworks and international development assistance 1946–2016

1946	Commission on the Status of Women; A first gender perspective on International Bill of Human Rights
1975	First World Conference of the International Women's Year, Mexico City; Adoption of the World Plan of Action for the Implementation of the Objectives of the International Women's Year which called for a Convention on the Elimination of Discrimination Against Women (CEDAW), with effective procedures for its implementation
1979	CEDAW; Adoption of CEDAW. It had been prepared by the Commission on the Status of Women (CSW) in the UN General Secretariat during 1976 and extensive deliberations by the UN General Assembly from 1977 to 1979
1980	Second World Conference on the United Nations Decade for Women: Equality, Development and Peace in Copenhagen. At the special ceremony that took place at the Copenhagen Conference on 17 July 1980, 64 states signed the CEDAW and two states submitted their instruments of ratification
1985	Shift from Women in Development (WID) to Gender and Development (GAD)
1995	Fourth World Conference on Women, Beijing; Adoption of the Platform for Action (PfA) and establishment of Gender Mainstreaming as the main strategy to reach the development goal of Gender Equality
2000	Beijing + 5 Review; Reaffirmation of commitment to the PfA Millennium Declaration, Millennium Development Goals (MDGs) and country-led approaches to development through Poverty Reduction Strategy Papers (PRSPs)
2005	Paris Declaration on Aid Effectiveness, Ownership, Harmonisation, Alignment, Results and Mutual Accountability
2016	Sustainable Development Goals (SDGs), notably SDG 5 on gender equality

Examples of negotiations surrounding the interpretation of the concept of gender equality in key international policies framework are discussed in the following sections.

World Conferences on Women

According to Charlesworth, the four World Conferences are in and of themselves examples of the capacity of women to agree on both shared problems and values which could be the focus of solidarity given their common situation across continents, cultures and races.[69]

The international events described in the examples below demonstrate that women were indeed 'able to use international arenas to negotiate a great range of differences to support both common projects and concerns of particular groups'.[70] Arguably, if they had indeed the opportunity to strengthen the meaning and content of gender equality, the section below shows that on the contrary, reaching consensual common platforms had a cost: Substantively altering the content and the meaning of gender equality at the international policy level changed from a revolutionary perspective to its almost complete evaporation.

In 1975, the Declaration of the First World Conference on Women in Mexico[71] read as follows:

> The World Conference of the International Women's Year, recognizing that women of the entire world, whatever differences exist between them, share the painful experience of receiving or having received unequal treatment, and that as their awareness of this phenomenon increases they will become natural allies in the struggle against any form of oppression, such as is practiced under colonialism, postcolonialism, Zionism, racial discrimination and apartheid, thereby constituting an enormous revolutionary potential for economic and social change in the world today.[72]

Two main points in this statement constitute the cornerstone of the original interpretation of gender equality in the 1970s: i) 'An enormous revolutionary potential for economic and social change'[73] anchors the feminist struggles in IDA, including identity politics within a potentially revolutionary vision of redistributive justice, and within ii) 'women of the entire world, whatever differences exist between them'.[74] Thus, it was applying a universalist perspective as the overall focus, over differences.

The changes which have occurred thereafter and until the recent SDGs in the interpretation of gender equality have not merely altered the meaning of these statements but have substantially weakened their inherent political meaning and strength by substituting the original intended overall focus.

At that point in time, it was believed that the suffering and oppression experienced by women as a universal category, together with many other victims of oppression, could gather the necessary solidarity to create a strong global political movement with 'a revolutionary potential for achieving economic and social changes'.[75]

The initial objective was thus to establish a counter-political power to eradicate all forms of oppression, and to make the world if not a better place, at least a more peaceful one. There were at least two central assumptions in this vision. Firstly, that a politically engaged global feminist movement was about to be established in a united and coherent form and secondly, that it would have a strong influence on IDA policy reforms. Such reforms would result in concrete changes in terms of the structural transformation of societies.

Despite these declarations, the creation of a 'revolutionary' global women's movement did not materialise as the strong and united political force many had hoped for. This was partly due to divergent and conflicting feminist theories and schools of thought,[76] partly due to the negotiations which took place within the UN global policy forum of discussion in question – the World Conferences on Women – as will be explored below. Thus, without the necessary theoretical and political cohesion, the expected influence of the international platforms for gender equality policy-making was weakened from the outset as the focus became building ideological consensus in order to create and agree upon a series of declarations and action plans, punctuating each of the World Conferences on Women. It is partly because of this consensus and partly because of the return on the world scene of diverse conservatisms that there is currently a reluctance to organise a fifth World Conference. Given SDG 5 on gender equality, it is believed that such a conference would run the risk of watering down the gender *acquis*.

The Conferences thus adopted global declarations and plans of action which were intended to serve as global gender policy guidelines both for the international community and national governments and were especially used as background policy frameworks in the context of IDA.

The First World Conference of Women held in Mexico in 1975 negotiated a consensus on equal access for women to resources such as education, employment opportunities, political participation, health services, housing, nutrition and family planning.[77]

By the end of the United Nations Decade for Women in 1985, 127 Member States had responded to this 'consensus' by establishing some form of women's national machinery such as institutions dealing with the promotion of policy, research and programmes aimed at women's advancement and participation in development.

In many developing countries the institutionalisation of women's concerns thus translated in the actual construction of buildings for ministries dealing specifically with women's affairs.[78] At the international level, it tended to materialise in the establishment of women's units within multilateral organisations.[79] Such institutional developments were intended to provide a framework to deal (at a later stage) with the, albeit less consensual substantive issues hinging on impacts as to redistributive justice and poverty reduction.

The second World Conference on Women was held in Copenhagen[80] and culminated in Resolution 35/136,[81] which highlighted amongst other things the following points:

> The maintenance of a global policy framework to deal with the concerns of women; the need for the active participation of women in the achievement of just and lasting world peace and social progress; the establishment of a new international economic order; the complete respect for human rights and fundamental freedoms and the integration of women into the development process so that the equality of men and women could be affirmed, and their situation improved.[82]

In conclusion, the first two World Women's Conferences' interpreted gender equality within a universalist perspective, with (redistributive) justice as an overall goal even though the second World Conference on Women was more evasive about the term 'redistribution'.

However, the definition and underlying ideological vision of gender equality which began in Mexico and Copenhagen and culminated in the Third World Conference on Women held in Nairobi in 1985[83] in its Forward-Looking Strategies for the Advancement of Women[84] and finally in the Platform for Action (PfA)[85] at the Fourth World Conference on Women, held in Beijing in 1995,[86] was substantially altered.

The Fourth World Conference PfA aimed to achieve greater gender equality in participation and opportunities for women in relation to 12 sub-thematic areas[87] and framed the concepts of advancement and empowerment of women within the equality paradigm. Thus, gender equality was reinterpreted within a narrower focus of representation, leaving behind all revolutionary and transformative aspirations. The hegemonic focus of the interpretation of gender equality was then translated as

> women's empowerment and their full participation on the basis of equality in all spheres of society, including participation in the decision-making process and access to power, are fundamental for the achievement of equality, development and peace.[88]

The implication of this new focus was the eclipse of a deeper concept of social justice and the structural changes needed to realise women's empowerment as a goal in and of itself, and wealth 'redistribution'.

The concept of 'structural causes of poverty' was toned down substantially compared to the emphasis it once enjoyed in the 1970s. Moreover, there was no clear strategy about how resources could be better re-allocated to achieve equality amongst women and men. In both the Beijing PfA and Declaration there was no reference to whether and how power would actually shift from the powerful to the powerless, from powerful men to powerless women and from powerful women to powerless women and men. Rather, the more politically neutral and consensual term of 'equal access to resources' was adopted as the standard phrase throughout the PfA.

'Equal access to resources' coupled with 'equal control of resources' was then largely mirrored in development policies, strategies and programme documents[89] without further specification as to whose resources would need to be accessed and controlled more 'equally' and by whom. Without assigning clear and politically stringent responsibilities to the 'praxis' of gender equality, Member States would be more inclined to commit as a gesture of good intention but without feeling a compelling obligation to adhere to commitments in practice.

The inclusion of diverse cultural sensitivities in gender policy-making processes resulted in the reinterpretation of gender equality into a seemingly apolitical and non-militant jargon which paved the way for its substantive weakening. This effectively stripped gender equality of its radicalism, leaving the concept opened to shallow and unclear interpretations.

The Beijing follow-ups, Beijing + 5 in 2000[90] and Beijing + 10 in 2005 and the +5s thereafter,[91] while essentially reaffirming previous commitments in Beijing, witnessed the loss of political momentum gathered in Beijing. Beijing + 5 consisted of a broad assessment of the implementation of the Beijing PfA and Declaration and further actions for implementation.[92]

In its resolution, ECOSOC noted with concern

> the persistent problems in addressing the challenges of poverty eradication, gender inequalities, empowerment and advancement of women and employment as reflected in the outcome documents of the five-year reviews of the Fourth World Conference and the World Summit for Social Development.[93]

Arguably, the weakening of the political potential of the term 'gender equality', at a time in which global trends were not conducive to a more radical interpretation of the term, dovetailed with the narrower interpretation of gender equality by divergent feminist schools of thought.

Millennium Development Goals (MDGs) and the Paris Declaration

The decline of political clout of gender equality and the weakening of the international policy framework characterised by the post-Beijing is best exemplified by the redefinition of gender equality in the Millennium Development Goals (MDGs)[94] in 2000. The MDGs reinterpreted the concept of gender equality (which had already been well predisposed to negotiations, interpretations and malleability as discussed in the sections above) from the 12 critical areas[95] of the Beijing PfA down to two less politically contentious areas, namely girls' education and maternal mortality. Donors and Member States could thus use the concept of gender equality and women's empowerment as the title of MDG 3[96] but actually focus solely on girls' education as being the main indicator against which 'progress' on gender equality was to be measured, together with maternal health in MDG 5.[97]

Whilst the latter is an important health issue in development contexts, it does not necessarily challenge less consensual issues such as women's rights to abortion, unequal power structures and social injustices. Girls' education is another fundamental issue which could achieve easily measurable quantitative equality in terms of school enrolment. Arguably, it needs to be coupled with other less consensual forms of equality such as equality in decision-making and control over resources to have a meaningful and qualitative impact on structural gender inequalities and injustices.

From a much less ambitious interpretation, gender equality culminated in its almost complete evaporation within the OECD/DAC Paris Declaration on Aid Effectiveness of 2005.[98] The policy framework has become virtually gender-blind. Paradoxically, the Organisation for Economic Cooperation and Development/Development Assistance Committee (OECD/DAC) is an organisation which does officially recognise that sustainable development must fully reflect the needs of both women and men as specified in the DAC guidelines on gender equality.[99] Furthermore, in 1995 and 1996, official statements were issued reflecting commitments to the Beijing Platform for Action. DAC's work in the area of gender equality has been primarily carried out through a well-established Network Party on Gender Equality, which provides strategic support to Development Assistance Committee (DAC) Members. Furthermore, a DAC gender strategy was established based on a set of gender guidelines and partnership approaches. The partnership approaches emphasise the following responsibilities for DAC members:

> ensuring the mainstreaming of gender equality considerations in their own processes and products such as analyses, policies, and position papers; and supporting the efforts of partner governments and local actors to promote gender equality – including support to partners' capacity to mainstream equality considerations into policies, strategies, and programmes.[100]

Beyond these policy-level premises, it is interesting to note that the DAC's source book on concepts and approaches linked to gender equality only defines gender equality in relation to culture and does not mention women's human rights.[101] A DAC evaluation of Programme Budget Support indicates that

> it failed to allocate resources to gender mainstreaming processes. The result is that two thirds of OECD/DAC aid focusing on support for gender equality and empowerment of women was for basic education and health (including population and reproductive health) critical to achieving the MDGs 3 and 5 but lacking any further gender strategic perspective.[102]

It is against this internal policy background that the OECD/DAC Paris Declaration on Aid Effectiveness[103] was signed in March 2005 and evolved into the main international policy framework for all key multilateral and bilateral donors at the time. It established global commitments for donors and partner countries to support more 'effective' aid.

Donors and partner countries' interpretation of IDA thus focused on making aid effectiveness a high priority, especially in the following areas:

> i) Strengthening partner countries' national development strategies and associated operational frameworks (e.g., planning, budget and performance assessment frameworks); ii) increasing alignment of aid with partner countries' priorities, systems and procedures and helping to strengthen their capacities; iii) enhancing donors' and partner countries' respective accountability to their citizens and parliaments for their development policies, strategies and performance; iv) eliminating duplication of efforts and rationalising donor activities to make them as cost-effective as possible; v) reforming and simplifying donor policies and procedures to encourage collaborative behaviour and progressive alignment with partner countries' priorities, systems

> and procedures; vi) defining measures and standards of performance and the accountability of partner country systems in public financial management, procurement, fiduciary safeguards and environmental assessments, in line with broadly accepted good practices and their rapid and widespread application.[104]

Beyond those commitments outlined above, which are macro-economic and managerial in nature, the only two socially related aspects which were included at the time and which the declaration defined as critical challenges were HIV/AIDS and corruption. Gender equality or indeed any other gender-related concepts appear to have been sidelined.

Thus, the inclusionary strategies which were used both in the international legislative and policy frameworks and which relied upon 'consensus' to produce international legal instruments and policy documents were aimed at targeting the broadest possible quantitative adherence rather than highest *qualitative impact* and preserving the early 'revolutionary' aspirations of the meaning of gender equality. As discussed, over the past four decades (amongst other things and with some exceptions), the negotiations at the international level have been trading the conceptual meaning of gender equality in order to secure the widest number of ratifying or adhering Member States, as seen in CEDAW. It has thus been argued that the benefits gained from these negotiation processes were secured at the expense of key elements of gender equality being traded off or overshadowed. This was clearly evidenced by the erosion of its political strength, devolution and eventually by its evaporation from key IDA policy frameworks.

Illustrating Nancy Fraser's point made earlier, 'the spectacular comeback of neoliberalism'[105] exemplified as the period when neoliberal macro-economists took over the reins of IDA, 'coincided all too neatly'[106] with the little revolutionary political force left in the interpretation of gender equality at the IDA policy level, to counterbalance these neoliberal visions. The Paris Declaration of 2005 had thus a free terrain and could expediently redefine 'development' from a neoliberal and macro-economic perspective, excluding gender equality interpretations which would relate to the notion of socio-economic justice or the need to reduce structural inequalities, without particularly challenging resistance.

Sustainable Development Goals (SDGs)

Although this is too early stage for any practitioners to provide an evidence-based analysis of possible outcomes from the implementation of SDGs[107] and in particular Goal 5: Achieve gender equality and empower all women and girls, it is nevertheless important to note the undeniable and considerable step forward the SDGs represent compared with their predecessors, the MDGs as discussed above. The SDGs are significantly more ambitious in terms of gender equality as the targets and indicators related to SDG 5 actually cover all three aspects of gender justice as follows:

Representation

Target 5.5 Ensure women's full and effective participation and equal opportunities for leadership at all levels of decision-making in political, economic and public life;

Recognition

Target 5.2 Eliminate all forms of violence against all women and girls in the public and private spheres, including trafficking and sexual and other types of exploitation;
Target 5.3 Eliminate all harmful practices, such as child, early and forced marriage and female genital mutilation;
Target 5.6 Ensure universal access to sexual and reproductive health and reproductive rights;

Redistribution

Target 5.4 Recognize and value unpaid care and domestic work through the provision of public services, infrastructure and social protection policies and the promotion of shared responsibility within the household and the family as nationally appropriate;
Target 5.a Undertake reforms to give women equal rights to economic resources, as well as access to ownership and control over land and other forms of property, financial services, inheritance and natural resources, in accordance with national laws.

There is a clear willingness under the SDGs to go 'beyond the add-women-and-stir approach' to aim at gender-transformational changes through the necessary policy and legal reforms at the national level. Although the targets above as demonstrated can easily fit into a gender justice grid, it remains to be seen if these efforts at the national level will be i) adequately implemented through the necessary allocation of resources, ii) effectively monitored and iii) followed by a holistic approach to gender justice rather than a fragmented approach to the different targets. These dimensions at the implementation level are key to ultimately achieving transformational changes through a nexus between representation, recognition and redistribution. Suffice it to say that at this stage, at least on paper, an ambitious 'reappearance' of gender equality in international policy frameworks has been signalled. This is especially exemplified by a clear visibility of contentious themes such as violence against women, sexual and reproductive health and rights and redistribution of powers and resources that were consistently watered down in past policy frameworks. It remains to be seen whether there will be a clear and adequate political will at the national level for the effective implementation and monitoring of SDG 5.

Other very relevant SDGs to the attainment of SDG5 are:

> SDGs Goal 8. Promote sustained, inclusive and sustainable economic growth, full and productive employment and decent work for all
> Target 8.5: By 2030, achieve full and productive employment and decent work for all women and men, including for young people and persons with disabilities, and equal pay for work of equal value
>
> SDGs Goal 1. End poverty in all its forms everywhere
> Target 1.2 By 2030, reduce at least by half the proportion of men, women and children of all ages living in poverty in all its dimensions according to national definitions

The issue of youth employment on the African continent in particular but also in Europe and globally is key to the reduction of inequalities and to poverty globally. SDG 1 and SDG 8 are thus the cornerstones of SDG 5 in IDA. If efforts on SDGs 1, 5 and 8 could be implemented at the national level in a coherent and gender-sensitive direction, then the possible outcomes ought to be nothing less than gender-transformative.

In conclusion and based on the analysis above, up to 2005 the concept of gender equality at the international policy level was the subject of a steady decline from its early revolutionary aspirations, to a gradual weakening in its interpretation, to an almost complete evaporation in the principal international policy frameworks. The politics of compromises on consensual definitions and interpretations of gender equality at the international policy level provided a fertile ground for the erosion of the concept.

The significance of identity politics in drawing the boundaries of gender equality

The examples in the section above clearly show the gradual political weakening of the meaning and interpretations of gender equality. This section explores the underpinning factors that have contributed to the conceptual weakening of gender equality in the World Conferences on Women. Moreover, the section seeks to draw patterns of correlation with the underpinning ideological trends that have contributed to the weakening of the concept of gender equality at the international legislative level.

If there was little political force left to counter neoliberalism, there was also little political force left to counter conservative religious interpretations of gender equality bounding the concept to cultural identities and Third World differences. The section above discussed how mainstream Shari'a law interpretations led to several Member States entering reservations on fundamental articles of CEDAW relating to the very concept of non-discrimination and gender equality. This section considers how similar patterns of bounding gender equality under cultural and religious identities occurred with the Vatican's active lobbying at

UN conferences to challenge the interpretation and strength of the concept of gender equality.

Doris Buss, in her article on the Vatican and the Beijing Conference on Women,[108] provides a detailed illustration of the strategies utilised by the Vatican to bound the interpretation of gender equality under cultural identities:

> The tactic of the Vatican was to argue for a core of rights, at the centre of which are the right to freedom of religion. . . . By challenging what it perceives as the over reliance on rights rhetoric, the Vatican sees itself as standing outside the dominant international framework within which questions of social relations are discussed . . . the Vatican perceives itself as being at the margin of international human rights discourse challenging the views of mainstream thinking: white feminism and Western-centric governments.[109]

The Vatican therefore took a strategic opportunity to make a conceptual 'alliance' with certain feminist critiques,[110] analysed in Chapter 1 above. It positioned its mainstream dogma against white, Western, neo-imperialist and colonialist governments. This was intended to exploit the fracture which polarised feminist schools of thought into perceived oppressive white Western heterosexual middle-class feminism on one hand and oppressed Third World and other communitarian feminisms on the other.

By aligning itself with female victims of oppression through the eyes of Third Worldism, the Vatican could twist its position as anti-colonialist and ambassador of marginalised Third World women. Through this strategy, the Vatican succeeded in obliterating its own colonialist missionary and evangelising past in the Third World countries of Africa and Latin America. Beyond these immediate contradictions, most interesting is the way in which the Vatican found common theoretical grounds to align itself ideologically with certain Third Worldist feminist critiques.

Moreover, it is important to explore how these ideological underpinnings relate to the ideological principles upon which some Member States entered reservations to CEDAW on the grounds of incompatibility with Shari'a Law. The Vatican's interpretation of 'gender equality' is found in the notion of 'gender complementarity'. It ensures that a conservative model of the family structure is protected. Men are maintained in their role as breadwinners and decision-makers guaranteed by their overwhelming participation in society's public spheres and women's role is to 'complement' as mothers and wives (read: as (unremunerated) domestic workers responsible for child rearing within the private sphere).

As Doris Buss points out:

> The concept of 'complementarity' in the Vatican's interpretation of gender roles, relations and hierarchies signifies a sexual division of labour in which women's reproductive capacity means that they will 'inevitably' become mothers and wives.[111]

With this concept being the Vatican's preferred interpretation of gender equality, it rejects the possibility of men and women having equal power (interchangeable roles) and instead finds common affinities with both the concept of *Qawama*, as well as certain branches of Third Worldist feminism which advocate the notion of 'motherism'.[112] The common grounds with the principle of *Al-Hijab* is of course the implied confinement of women to their 'complementary' roles within the boundaries of the domestic and reproductive spheres.

In the context of developing countries, where inequalities – particularly gender inequalities relating to access and control of resources – are central to poverty, such views restrict women's access to alternative roles beyond the proposed non-remunerated domestic role. In these contexts, their chance of escaping the poverty cycle, let alone aspiring for self-emancipation, are effectively limited. As in those Shari'a interpretations which led to reservations on the concept of non-discrimination in CEDAW, the Vatican finds it difficult to promote equality in resource and power sharing between women and men. 'Whereas it considers women and men to being of equal "dignity" in all areas of life, it cannot concede equality of roles and functions'.[113]

Thus, through the strategy of identity politics, the Vatican succeeded in up-keeping a phallocratic interpretation of gender roles and relations which clearly dismisses the principle of non-discrimination. Thus, the interpretation of 'women' as second-class citizens in 'need of protection', women in their traditional and 'complementary' roles as 'mothers' and/or 'fragile victims' but not as empowered equals and entirely free human beings are shared ideological values between Christianity and Islam. Arguably, such positions are not marginal or religion-specific. These are little more than patriarchal expressions of society which, in the proponents' views, ought not to be challenged by shifting the balance of powers in gender roles and relations. These expressions, if anything, represents the 'norm', the status quo of mainstream values which phallocratic societies in Europe, in the US and elsewhere have in common, rather than that of a cultural and identity-specific position in need of protection against Euro/Western-centric thinking.

In conclusion, this section demonstrates that using the identity politics strategy valorising cultural/religious differences was indeed an ingenious strategy to shrink the interpretation of gender equality down to a justification of gender inequalities. The analysis thus shows that religious and cultural oppositions to gender equality in IDA share common ideological grounds and are thus *political*, given their common objective in protecting patriarchal structures. Therefore, they ought to be analysed and challenged as such, rather than considered as static components of identities whose differences need further valorisation and are worthy of inclusion in international legal frameworks and policies on an 'equal footing' with other standpoints and perspectives. It is this misguided process of 'inclusion' which took place during international negotiations which has ultimately weakened the concept of gender equality at the highest strategic level, at the international law and policy level.

Consequently, it is argued that this weakened concept of gender equality ultimately leaves the existing structures of oppression intact. Instead of challenging patriarchal interpretations of gender equality, it served to protect them as legitimate and justifiable within the hegemonic trend of identity politics.

Conclusion

In conclusion, a holistic understanding of the boundaries circumventing women's freedom and women's human rights is only possible through an analysis which does not confine itself to identity politics in one particular cultural or religious context disconnected as it were from similar socio-cultural practices existing in other contexts. Rather, comparing underlying ideologies across cultures is crucial to avoid using cultural and religious differences as justification for maintaining gender inequalities, violations of women's human rights and injustices facing women.

This is particularly relevant to capture the deeper and political understanding of the broader implications and underpinning ideologies informing the reservation process of some Member States to CEDAW. The reservations put forward to Articles 1 and 2 of CEDAW are not a mere technical compromise at the international law level. Rather, they show the extent to which, by following the politics of identity, gender equality and basic women's human rights are overshadowed to the point of being 'opted out' of the only international legal instrument which is supposed to defend them. It is thus demonstrated that the compromise in question clearly amounts to a defeat of the very purpose of the Convention. The analysis demonstrates that identity politics and apparent cultural differences were prioritised when defining both the content and the adherence process to CEDAW. However, the analysis also shows that 'cultural differences' are 'different' in appearance only. As argued, the expression of such seemingly culturally grounded resistance shares underpinning ideologies which have in common those patriarchal structures which allow phallocratic dogma to become respectable under the (false) guise of the culturally distinct.

Thus, anxiety surrounding the possible exclusion of gender discriminatory Member States from CEDAW on the grounds of 'cultural differences' and religious perspectives resulted in the gender equality concept being overshadowed. The strategy of compromises was intended to result in the inclusion of the largest number of countries irrespective of differences surrounding their degree of commitment to the essence of the Convention. By following an inclusionary strategy beyond the point of compromise and ultimately silencing fundamental notions such as violence against women, CEDAW was effectively weakened.

In contrast, the Maputo Protocol of 2003 demonstrates that all the arguments brought forward to legitimise the omission of violence against women in CEDAW and its reservation procedures are seriously questionable at best and invalid at worst. This leads to the conclusion that identity politics was prioritised over fundamental women's human rights, both regarding the content of CEDAW and in the reservation process surrounding its adherence. It can be concluded that a universalist analytical grid is useful to uncover the common ideological patterns in patriarchal societies which consider both the struggle against violence against women and gender equality difficult concepts to commit to.

Based on the analysis of the second section of the chapter, the concept of gender equality at the IDA international policy level has been the subject of a steady decline up to 2005, from its gradually weakened interpretation to its discarding.

At the international policy level, the section explores some of the common underlying reasons for the weakening of gender equality and thus the weakening of its potential impact in international conferences and policy platforms. The analysis shows that during UN international conferences, the Vatican, in its role as observer, tended to support initiatives which protected women in their traditional and complementary role as mothers and/or 'victims' but not initiatives which empowered women above or beyond their different complementary role with men in society. Likewise, as the analysis at the international law level demonstrates with the process of reservation to CEDAW, Shari'a law contradicts any understanding of women being as equal in rights or in any way superior to men.

The Vatican's dogma and Shari'a law thus find common ground in their rejection of gender equality in international legal frameworks and policy-making processes. However, after closer examination it becomes apparent that such positions are not merely isolated cultural stances or religion-specific. Rather, it is demonstrated that these are basic patriarchal visions of society which according to their proponents ought not to be challenged by shifting gender roles and power relations. Thus, the analysis demonstrates that using the exclusionary argument based on cultural/religious differences can be utilised as a strategic move to effectively weaken gender equality by leaving the existing structures of oppression intact. Thus, protecting traditional patriarchal interpretations of gender equality can fit well with the hegemonic ideological trend of identity politics.

In conclusion, the analysis above shows that whilst the change of focus in the interpretation of gender equality from its original revolutionary perspective was useful to neoliberal macro-economists' vision of IDA when formulating the MDGs and the Paris Declaration on Aid Effectiveness, it was similarly useful to conservative religious institutions in protecting traditional gender hierarchies. Arguably, this change in focus dovetailed with the identity politics focus underpinning the framing of gender equality, as discussed in chapter 1. This has become particularly problematic in the context of IDA as it falls short of providing an adequate international legislative and policy framework with which to address the socio-economic injustices faced by women living in poverty in developing countries.

Notes

1 Convention on the Elimination of All Forms of Discrimination Against Women (adopted 18 December 1979, entered into force 3 September 1981) (1980) 1249 UNTS 13, reprinted in 19 ILM 33 (CEDAW) <www.un.org/womenwatch/daw/cedaw/text/econvention.htm>.

2 Protocol to the African Charter on Human and Peoples' Rights on the Rights of Women in Africa (adopted 11 July 2003, entered into force 25 November 2005)

(2003) CAB/LEG/66.6/Rev 1(the Protocol on the Rights of Women in Africa) art 1(J) <www.africa-union.org/home/Welcome.htm.>

3 The main World Conferences on Women have been selected to represent a purposeful example of relevant policy framework underpinning the concept of gender equality at international level. These are: 'First World Conference on Women held in Mexico City' (19 June to 2 July 1975) <www.un.org/womenwatch/daw/beijing/mexico.html>; 'Second World Conference on Women held in Copenhagen' (14 to 30 July 1980) <www.un.org/womenwatch/daw/beijing/copenhagen.html>; 'Third World Conference on Women held in Nairobi' (15 to 26 June 1985) <www.un.org/womenwatch/daw/beijing/nairobi.html>; 'Fourth World Conference on Women held in Beijing' (4 to 15 September 1995); <www.un.org/womenwatch/daw/beijing/fwcwn.html>.

4 United Nations Millennium Declaration, UNGA Res 55/2 (8 September 2000) UN Doc A/55/L.2 <www.un.org/millennium/declaration/ares552e.htm> accessed 10 February 2011.

5 OECD, 'The Paris Declaration on Aid Effectiveness 2005 and the Accra Agenda for Action 2008 (OECD 2005/2008). <www.oecd.org/document/19/0,3746,en_2649_3236398_43554003_1_1_1_1,00.html>.

6 A Cornwall, E Harrison and A Whitehead, *Feminisms in Development: Contradictions, Contestations and Challenges* (Zed Books 2007) 15.

7 The international legislative level is understood hereby to include a purposeful example of key and relevant international and regional conventions providing the legal framework to the concept of gender equality in IDA, mainly CEDAW and the Protocol on the Rights of Women in Africa.

8 For the full list of reservations country per country and reservations principles see <www.un.org/womenwatch/daw/cedaw/reservations.htm>.

9 Reservations to Article 2 or Article 16 of CEDAW on the grounds of incompatibility with Shari'a law were entered by Bahrain, Bangladesh, Egypt, Iraq, Kuwait, Libyan Arab Jamahiriya, Malaysia, Maldives, Morocco, Oman, Saudi Arabia, Singapore, Syrian Arab Republic and United Arab Emirates. See <www.un.org/womenwatch/daw/cedaw/reservations-country.htm>.

10 Violence against women was not included in the main text of CEDAW but was only included as discrimination against women in General Recommendation N.19 made by the Committee on the Elimination of Discrimination against Women only. Recommendation N.19 was adopted at the 11th Session of the Committee on the Elimination of Discrimination against Women in 1992. See <www.un.org/womenwatch/daw/cedaw/recommendations/recomm.htm>.

11 See for instance: C T Mohanty, 'Under Western Eyes: Feminist Scholarship and Colonial Discourses' in Mohanty, Russo and Torres (eds), *Third World Women and the Politics of Feminism* (Indiana University Press 1991) 51–80; R Kapur, 'The Tragedy of Victimization Rhetoric: Resurrecting the "Native" Subject in International/Postcolonial Feminist Legal Politics' (2002) 15 *Harvard Human Rights Journal* 2.

12 The term 'devolution' is used here to show that gender equality, instead of evolving, has peaked in the mid-1990s and has recorded a steady decline since within the significant and influent policy framework at the international level.

13 UNGA Res 58/314 (16 July 2004) A/RES/58/314).

14 Complementarity is understood as maintaining traditional division of female and male gender role to uphold forms of patriarchal societal structures.

15 See CEDAW.

16 Ibid.

17 As is further discussed in Chapters 3 and 4.

18 For general discussions on reservations see: R Higgins, 'Introduction' in JP Gardner (ed), *Human Rights as General Norms and a State's Right to Opt Out: Reservations and Objections to Human Rights Conventions* (British Institute of International Comparative Law 1996) xix.

19 See <www.un.org/womenwatch/daw/cedaw/reservations-country.htm> accessed 18 February 2011.
20 Ibid.
21 Specifically on the universality of participation see: C Redwell, 'Universality or Integrity? Some Reflections on Reservations to General Multilateral Treaties' (1993) 64 *British Yearbook of International Law* 245.
22 See generally on the Vienna Convention: S Rosenne, *The Law of Treaties: A Guide to the Legislative History of the Vienna Convention* (Oceana Publications 1970).
23 Vienna Convention on the Law of Treaties (adopted 23 May 1969, entered force 27 January 1980) reprinted in 8 ILM 679.
24 R Higgins, 'Human Rights: Some Questions of Integrity' (1989) 52 *Michigan Law Review* 1; L Linzaad, *Reservations to UN Human Rights Treaties: Ratify and Ruin?* (Martinus Nijhoff 1995).
25 See CEDAW.
26 Ibid.
27 See: UN Doc HRI/GEN/2/Rev.1 (9 May 2001) (CEDAW/C/Rev.3, entitled Guidelines for preparation of reports by State Parties.
28 See reservations of the Republic of Maldives, which 'does not see itself, bound by any provisions of the Convention which obliges it to change its Constitution and laws in any manner'. See also reservations of Lesotho, Malaysia and Pakistan cited in H Charlesworth and C Chinkin, *The Boundaries of International Law: A Feminist Analysis* (Manchester University Press 2000) 105.
29 Ibid 107–108.
30 AA An-Na'im, 'Human Rights in the Muslim World' in H Steiner and P Alston (eds), *International Human Rights in Context: Law, Politics, Morals* (Oxford University Press 2000) 393–394.
31 Ibid.
32 If An-Na'im provides a factual interpretation of the verses, Djavann, further below offers an analysis as to the causes of the guardianship in question.
33 See also St Paul's Epistle to Timothy I, Chapter 2, Verses 9–14, Verse 12: 'But I suffer not a woman to teach, nor to usurp authority over the man, but to be in silence'.
34 See An-Na'im 393.
35 Whilst much of contemporary debates on the veil tend to focus on the length of the material, covering religious discrimination and in turn covering gender discrimination, the underlying principle as presented by An-Na'im here rarely seems to make the arena of public debates or attract media coverage. Yet far from the length of the piece of material, the problematic issue in relation to women's rights and freedom of movement seems to reside in the intention of its original theological source.
36 See global statistics on women in parliaments, <www.ipu.org/wmn-e/classif.htm>.
37 C Djavann, *Bas les Voiles!* (Gallimard 2003). See also V Teitelbaum, 'The European Veil Debate' (2000) 1 *Israel Journal of Foreign Affairs* 89–99; N Geerts, *Fichu voile!: Petit argumentaire féministe et antiraciste* (Luc Pire 2010). Further, '[I]f someone wears the uniform of Ku Klux Klan and says "I am sorry, I am wearing this uniform but did not quite make the link with the fact that it was racist." It seems reasonable to want to explain to that person that such outfit may be perceived as shocking (and oppressive, my addition) because it is politically, symbolically and historically charged. . . . What I dislike is when I am told this is not my concern. This vision is completely exotic and differentialist and consists in a refusal to see or understand the message that others are signaling within the public sphere, this attitude, is in my view, contrary to dialogue and contrary to antiracism'. (Evene.fr April 2010) Un Choix Réactionnaire? Interview Caroline Fourest.
38 Djavann 13–15. See also C Djavann, La Muette (Broché 2008); C Djavann, Comment peut-on être Français (Broché 2007); C Djavann, 'Que pense Allah de l'Europe?' (Broché 2004); C Djavann, 'Autoportrait de l'autre' (Poche 2009).
39 'In the Byzantine Empire, which included Sicily until the nineteenth century, head scarves were a sign of affluence for Christian and Jewish women. In larger cities these

were made of silk and often quite colourful. As a sign of modesty, a Christian woman entering a church, like a Jewish woman entering a synagogue, would cover her hair. The custom was one which the Christians inherited from Judaic tradition. Into the 1950s it was normal for Roman Catholic women to wear hats or even scarves in church, and today they are still expected to cover shoulders and arms (especially in the more important basilicas in southern Europe)'. ML Romano, 'Scarves, Veils and History' (2007) *Best of Sicily Magazine*.

40 See D Otto, 'A Post-Beijing Reflection on the Limitations and Potential of Human Rights Discourse for Women' (Transnational 1999) 3 *Women and International Human Rights Law* 115, 135; TE Higgins, 'By "Reason of their Sex": Feminist Theory, Postmodernism and Justice' (1995) 80 *Cornell Law Review* 1536; B Stark, 'Women and Globalization: The Failure and Postmodern Possibilities of International Law' (2000) 33 *Vanderbilt Journal of Transnational Law* 503.

41 The Convention on the Elimination of All Forms of Racial Discrimination (adopted 21 December 1965, entered into force 4 January 1969) (1965) 660 UNTS 195 <http://www2.ohchr.org/english/law/cerd.htm>.

42 See Charlesworth and Chinkin 108.

43 The Convention on the Elimination of All Forms of Racial Discrimination (n 285) Article 1: 'In this Convention, the term 'racial discrimination' shall mean any distinction, exclusion, restriction or preference based on race, colour, descent, or national or ethnic origin which has the purpose or effect of nullifying or impairing the recognition, enjoyment or exercise, on an equal footing, of human rights and fundamental freedoms in the political, economic, social, cultural or any other field of public life'.

44 The Vienna Convention.

45 The Convention on the Elimination of All Forms of Racial Discrimination (n 285) Article 5 stipulates that: 'In compliance with the fundamental obligations laid down in Article 2 of this Convention, States Parties undertake to prohibit and to eliminate racial discrimination in all its forms and to guarantee the right of everyone, without distinction as to race, colour, or national or ethnic origin, to equality before the law, notably in the enjoyment of the following rights: (a) The right to equal treatment before the tribunals and all other organs administering justice; (b) The right to security of person and protection by the State against violence or bodily harm, whether inflicted by government officials or by any individual group or institution; (c) Political rights, in particular the right to participate in elections-to vote and to stand for election on the basis of universal and equal suffrage, to take part in the Government as well as in the conduct of public affairs at any level and to have equal access to public service; (d) Other civil rights . . .; (e) Economic, social and cultural rights, in particular: (i) The rights to work, to free choice of employment, to just and favourable conditions of work, to protection against unemployment, to equal pay for equal work, to just and favourable remuneration; (ii) The right to form and join trade unions; (iii) The right to housing; (iv) The right to public health, medical care, social security and social services; (v) The right to education and training; (vi) The right to equal participation in cultural activities; (f) The right of access to any place or service intended for use by the general public, such as transport hotels, restaurants, cafes, theatres and parks'.

46 The Maputo Protocol art 1(J).

47 As further evidenced in Chapter 3.

48 Charlesworth and Chinkin 230 citing C Bunch, *Passionate Politics, Essays 1968–1986: Feminist Theory in Action* (St. Martin's Press 1987).

49 F Banda, *Women, Law and Human Rights: An African Perspective* (Hart Publishing 2005) 162.

50 UN Committee for the Elimination of All Forms of Discrimination Against Women (CEDAW Committee), 'General Recommendations No. 19 on Violence Against Women' (11th Session 1992) UN Doc A/47/38 para 6.

51 See The Inter-American Convention on the Prevention, Punishment and Eradication of Violence Against Women (signed 9 June 1994, entered into force 3 March 1995)

(1994) reprinted in 33 ILM 1534 <www.oas.org/juridico/english/treaties/a-61.html>; the Maputo Protocol on the Rights of Women in Africa art 1(J).

52 See The Committee of Ministers to Member States of the Council of Europe Recommendation Rec (2002)5 on the Protection of Women against Violence; The European Parliament Resolution on Female Genital Mutilation (200172035 (INI)); the European Parliament Resolution of 24 March 2009 on combating female genital mutilation in the EU (2008/2071 (INI)); the Declaration on the Elimination of Violence Against Women in the ASEAN Region (2004) <www.endvawnow.org/en/articles/584-regional-instruments.html>.

53 See K Roth, 'Domestic Violence as an International Human Rights Issue'; R Copelon, 'Intimate Terror: Understanding Domestic Violence as Torture'; and J Fitzpatrick, 'The Use of International Human Rights Norms to Combat Violence Against Women' in R Cook (ed), *Human Rights of Women: National and International Perspectives*, (University of Pennsylvania Press 1995) 326, 116, 532.

54 UNSC Res 1325 (31 October 2000) UN Doc S/RES/1325.

55 See Charlesworth and Chinkin 234.

56 Convention of Belém do Pará art 2.

57 The Protocol on the Rights of Women in Africa, art 1(J).

58 Convention of Belém do Pará.

59 The Maputo Protocol on the Rights of Women in Africa, (n 242) art 4(2) a.

60 Ibid art 5.

61 Ibid art 6.

62 Ibid art 14(1)(d).

63 See 'Report of the Committee on the Elimination of Discrimination Against Women' Fourth World Conference on Women (Beijing, 4–15 September 1995) UN Doc A/CONF.177/7.

64 Almost a year after the Protocol was adopted, only one Member State of the AU, The Comoros, had signed and ratified it. Twenty-eight Member States signed but were yet to ratify it as of 12 May 2004. A minimum of 14 further countries had to ratify the Protocol in order for it to come into force. On 26 October 2005, Togo became the 15th state to ratify the Protocol. As a result, it came into force on 25 November 2005, 30 days after the deposit of the fifteenth instrument of ratification. As of 16 July 2008, out of 53 African countries, 45 have signed the treaty and 24 have signed and ratified it.

65 'Africa: Entry into force of Protocol on the Rights of Women in Africa positive step towards ending discrimination' (Amnesty International Index: AFR 01/004/2005 (Public) News Service No 292, 28 October 2005) <www.ethiopianreview.com/archive/588109835108211102_ethiopia.htmlaccessed>.

66 The table is inspired by F Watkins 'Evaluation of DFID Development Assistance: Gender Equality and Women's Empowerment, DFID's Experience of Gender Mainstreaming: 1995 to 2004' (DFID December 2004), 9. The table was further expanded with information from UN data base on UN website <www.un.org/womenwatch/daw/daw/index.html>.

67 Ibid.

68 Ibid 8.

69 One hundred thirty-three Member State delegations gathered at the First World Women's Conference in Mexico 1975 and 113 of those were headed by women. Women also organised a parallel NGO Forum, the International Women's Year Tribune, which attracted approximately 4,000 participants. By the fourth World Women's Conference in Beijing 1995, there were 189 Member States Delegations and more than 5,000 representatives from 2,100 non-governmental organisations.

70 Charlesworth and Chinkin (n 272) 47. As an illustration, Charlesworth highlights the campaign for recognition of violence against women, a phenomenon which is prevalent in all countries, cultures and [socio-economic classes], as being a

[universal] violation of women's human rights and as an especially effective unifying force throughout the global conferences on diverse subjects of the 1990s.
71 'First World Conference on Women'.
72 'Report of the World Conference of the International Women's Year, Declaration of Mexico on the Equality of Women and Their Contribution to Development and Peace' (Mexico City 19 June – 2 July 1975) UN Doc E/CONF 66/34, 73.
73 Ibid. See also R Morgan (ed), *Sisterhood Is Global* (The Feminist Press at the City University of New York 1996).
74 'Report of the World Conference of the International Women's Year'.
75 Ibid.
76 See Chapter 1 above.
77 Report of the World Conference of the International Women's Year.
78 Usually combined with children's affairs, for instance in Tanzania and Uganda.
79 Within the United Nations system, in addition to the Division for the Advancement of Women, the Mexico City Conference led to the establishment of the International Research and Training Institute for the Advancement of Women (INSTRAW) and the United Nations Development Fund for Women (UNIFEM). They intended to provide the institutional framework for research, training and operational activities in the area of women and development.
80 'Second World Conference on Women'.
81 'The World Conference of the United Nations Decade for Women: Equality, Development, Peace Held in Copenhagen' (14–30 July 1980) culminated in UNGA Res 35/136 (11 December 1980) A/RES/34/158.
82 Ibid.
83 'Third World Conference on Women'.
84 'Nairobi Forward-Looking Strategies for the Advancement of Women' <www.un.org/womenwatch/confer/nfls/>.
85 'Beijing Declaration and Platform for Action' <www.un.org/womenwatch/daw/beijing/platform/> accessed 2 March 2011.
86 'Fourth World Conference on Women'.
87 'Beijing Declaration and Platform for Action'.
88 'Report of the Fourth World Conference on Women, Beijing Declaration and Platform for Action' (Beijing 4–15 September 1995) UN Doc A/CONF.177/20/Rev.1, 154 art 3.
89 As further evidenced in Chapters 3 and 4.
90 'Five-year Review of the implementation of the Beijing Declaration and Platform for Action' (Beijing + 5, General Assembly, 5–9 June 2000) <www.un.org/womenwatch/daw/followup/beijing+5.htm>.
91 Ten-year Review and Appraisal of the implementation of the Beijing Declaration and Platform for Action' (Beijing + 10) and the outcome of the 23rd special session of the General Assembly held during the 49th session of the CSW, from 28 February to 11 March 2005 <www.un.org/womenwatch/daw/Review/english/49sess.htm>. Beijing + 10's objective was a 'Review of the implementation of the Beijing Platform for Action and the outcome documents of the twenty-third special session of the General Assembly' and an assessment of the 'Current challenges and forward-looking strategies for the advancement and empowerment of women and girls'.
92 This was adopted by the General Assembly at its special session, in the Report of the Secretary-General, 'Implementation of the Outcome of the Fourth World Conference on Women and of the Special Century' (A/55/341).

ECOSOC, 'The Role of Employment and Work in Poverty Eradication: Empowerment and Advancement of Women' Res 2000/26 (28 July 2000); Session of the General Assembly, 'Women 2000: Gender Equality, Development and Peace in the Twenty-First Century' (A/55/341).
93 ECOSOC.

94 United Nations Millennium Declaration.
95 The Beijing 12 Critical Issues are enumerated as follows: 1) The persistent burden of poverty; 2) Unequal access to education; 3) Unequal access to health care; 4) Violence; 5) Armed conflicts; 6) Inequality in economic structures; 7) Inequality in the sharing of power; 8) Insufficient mechanisms; 9) Human rights violation; 10) Stereotyping in the media; 11) Environment; 12) The girl child. For further details on the content of each critical issues see <www.undp.org/mdg/reports.shtml>.
96 Millennium Development Goal 3: Promote gender equality and empower women. Target 3a: Eliminate gender disparity in primary and secondary education preferably by 2005, and at all levels by 2015. <www.undp.org/mdg/goal3.shtml>.
97 Millennium Development Goal 5: Improve maternal health. Target 5a: Reduce by three-quarters the maternal mortality ratio. Target 5b: achieve universal access to reproductive health. <www.un.org/millenniumgoals/maternal.shtml>.
98 OECD, 'The Paris Declaration and Accra Agenda'.
99 'The DAC guidelines for gender equality and women's empowerment' (1983) OECD/DAC.
100 JD Winship, 'A Summary of Gender Strategies of Multilateral Development Agencies and Selected Bilateral Donors, Development and Training' (September 2004) USAID Report.
101 'Concept and Approaches Linked to Gender Equality' (1998) OECD/ DAC Source Book 16.
102 'Gender Evaluation, Aid to Support Gender Equality, 1999–2003' (March 2005) OECD/DAC Report 1.
103 OECD, 'The Paris Declaration and the Accra Agenda'.
104 Ibid.
105 N Fraser, *Scales of Justice: Reimagining Political Space in a Globalizing World* (Columbia University Press 2009) 106.
106 Ibid 105.
107 See <https://sustainabledevelopment.un.org/sdgs>.
108 DE Buss, 'Robes, Relics and Rights: The Vatican and the Beijing Conference on Women' (1998) 7(3) *Social and Legal Studies* 3.
109 Costas Douzinas, 'Justice and Human Rights in Post-modernity' in C Gearty and A Tomkins (eds), *Understanding Human Rights* (Mansell 1996).
110 Examples of such feminist critiques are: A Bunting, 'Theorising Women's Cultural Diversity in Feminist International Human Rights Strategy' (1993) 20 *Journal of Law and Society* 6–22; N Duclos, 'Lessons of Difference: Feminist Theory and Cultural Diversity' (1990) 38 *Buffalo Law Review* 325–381; D Fuss, *Essentially Speaking: Feminism, Nature and Difference* (Routledge 1989); B Hooks, *Feminist Theory: From Margin to Centre* (South End Press 1984); C Mohanty, 'Introduction: Cartographies of Struggle' in CT Mohanty, A Russo and L Torres (eds), *Third World Women and the Politics of Feminism* (Indiana University Press 1991); E Spelman, *Inessential Woman: Problems of Exclusion in Feminist Thought* (Beacon Press 1988) 57.
111 See Buss.
112 As discussed in Chapter 1.
113 J Navarro-Valls, 'Report of the Holy See in preparation for the Fourth World Conference on Women', (1995) para 2 (a); 'To Promote Women's Equal Dignity' (6 September 1995) 36 *L'osservatore Romano* 2–4.

Part II

3 Variations on the politics of gender equality

This chapter analyses the varying political interpretations of gender equality through policy cases illustrating i) both neoliberal and social democratic trends amongst bilateral and multilateral donor policies and ii) the use of political ideologies in interpretations of gender equality at the country policy level.

Chapter 3 examines whether and how the changes in focus underpinning the concept of gender equality discussed in Chapter 1 have affected the interpretation of gender equality in donor policies[1] and recipient country policies.[2] As discussed in chapter 2, following four decades[3] of uneven struggle to recognise gender equality in international law and international policies, several multilateral[4] and bilateral[5] development agencies have formally and explicitly incorporated gender equality into their policies. They have done so either by formulating specific gender equality strategies[6] and/or by recognising gender equality as one of their priorities in their main development policy and strategy documents.

The first section does not purport to present an exhaustive catalogue of the latest multilateral and bilateral development agencies' policy documents. Rather, it offers an analysis of a selection of policies from some development agencies that are illustrative of political trends which have been critical during the last 20 years. The examples selected reflecting neoliberal perspectives such as those that can be found at the World Bank (WB)[7] and at the Department for International Development in the UK (DFID)[8] as well as socio-democratic perspectives that can be encountered in Scandinavian countries such as the Danish International Development Agency (Danida)[9] and the Swedish International Development Cooperation Agency (Sida).[10] The section illustrates how neoliberal[11] interpretations of gender equality can permeate the policies of agencies which have traditionally supported, on the contrary, more socialist interpretations[12] of gender equality in IDA.

The second section provides a critical analysis of recipient country policies. It examines how divergent political contexts in IDA recipient countries – from neoliberal to Marxist[13] – can interpret gender equality within a variety of policy instruments such as policies, strategies, political speeches and discourses. This section thus critically examines the variations on a theme of gender equality in different political and geographic contexts in the following examples: i) the case of abortion in Nicaragua and Third Worldist defences within the neoliberal[14] and neo-Sandinista[15] governments and the Catholic Church; ii) Yoweri Museveni's postcolonialist interpretation of gender equality within Uganda's neoliberal reforms;[16] and iii) a feminist vision beyond the politics of identity in Thomas Sankara's[17] speech on International Women's Day in 1987[18] in Burkina Faso.

These examples seek to illustrate some of the possible implications arising from the use of Third Worldist, neoliberal and Marxist focuses in the interpretations of gender equality at the national policy level.

Interpreting multilateral and bilateral themes

Following three decades of uneven struggle to recognise gender equality in international law and policies as discussed in Chapter 2, several multilateral and bilateral development agencies[19] formally and explicitly incorporated gender equality, either by formulating specific gender equality strategies and/or by recognising gender equality as one of their priorities in their main development policy and strategy documents.

The neoliberal spectacular wave

Nancy Fraser's expression 'neoliberalism's spectacular comeback', as noted in Chapter 1 to illustrate the 'unfortunate coincidence' with identity politics, was equally 'spectacular' in the context of IDA. The World Bank (WB) and the UK Department for International Development (DFID) present vivid illustrations of 'promoting economic liberalisation, privatisation and market mechanisms as instruments of growth and efficiency'.[20]

Both agencies have followed policies of concessional finance through budgetary support to:

> assist national governments to develop their own overall strategies for economic growth and poverty reduction through Sector Wide Approaches (SWAPs) and financing the cost of fiscal, governance and pro-poor reforms – such as privatising loss-making public sectors, cutting civil service, promoting decentralisation and anti-corruption measures.[21]

SWAPs, like general budget support, became the mantra of development at the millennium turn for many years. In practice, it was translated by the shift from project support to programme support using the rationale that rather than supporting isolated projects with individual 'country flags', recipient countries were expected to draw up their own Poverty Reduction Strategy Plans (PRSP). The PRSPs would then become the 'road map' for donors to collectively finance in a supposedly more harmonious and coordinated way, ideally resulting in a more effective and coherent aid package.

Mosse argues that:

> this 'pro-poor' poverty reduction strategy was adopted by DFID, under the heading: "Making globalisation work for the poor" and thus re-legitimising

> continuing donor emphasis on trade liberalisation, macro-economic stability and fiscal discipline overseen by the IMF, while mobilising new and increased aid resources.[22]

This rationale was further consolidated in the new development architecture under the term 'aid effectiveness' in the Paris Declaration,[23] as mentioned in Chapter 2, an international agreement that was endorsed in 2005 and to which the main recipient countries, donor agencies and organisations all committed to, to strengthen harmonisation, alignment and managing of aid for 'monitorable' results. This was reviewed and consolidated by the Accra Agenda for Action (AAA)[24] in 2008 during the 3rd High Level Forum on Aid Effectiveness to accelerate an effective use of IDA aimed, in principle, at the achievement of the MDGs by 2015.

From a practitioner's perspective, the lack of coordination and harmonisation of aid as well as its effectiveness is an undoubted flaw of IDA. However, whilst these aspects focus on technical means and propose a way to improve aid delivery at the operational level, they are by no means clear political visions for IDA. Such an 'engineer-like' architecture is at first sight devoid of political orientation and commitment, presented in a seemingly neutral technical language, while actually allowing the lead development agencies to implement neoliberal agenda more effectively and avoiding debating such political interpretation of IDA, as further discussed below.

According to Mosse and Lewis:

> The WB has been reframing its "adjustment lending" as "development policy lending" in what it describes as a major overhaul of the Bank's operational policy. This new WB framework unifies policies that applied to a whole range of instruments, including sectoral adjustment loans, structural adjustment loans and poverty reduction support credits.[25]

Consequently, and most importantly for the conceptual interpretation of gender equality, DFID and the WB (both using seemingly apolitical terminology) succeeded in reshaping IDA framework with their own priorities in mind. These failed to address social justice and the glaring inequalities within and across recipient countries.

Indeed, International Development Targets (IDTs),[26] the predecessors of the Millennium Development Goals (MDGs), themselves the predecessors of Sustainable Development Goals (SDGs), were instigated by DFID and agreed to by a series of UN conferences in the 1990s. They included a reduction by one-half of the proportion of people living in extreme poverty by 2015, universal primary education in all countries by 2015 and a reduction by two-thirds in infant and under-five mortality rates and by three-fourths in maternal mortality by 2015, according to DFID in 1997. The seemingly apolitical IDA terminology and technical buzzwords resembled the language of consumer products and commodities, such as 'access to rights' or 'justice delivery' and coincided with an unambiguous and yet political emphasis on trade liberalisation and macro-economic stability.

It is thus within this politicised framework that the apparently politically neutral WB's strategy for mainstreaming gender-responsive actions into its Development Assistance work was endorsed by the full Board of Executive Directors on 18 September 2001.[27] In this strategy, the WB pressed to make a 'business case for mainstreaming gender equality'. It stated that the primary pathways through which gender systems affect growth are: the productivity of labour and the efficiency of the economy, investments in human capital, especially girls' and women's education and health, investments in physical capital, especially women's access to capital or to the formal sector employment it creates and the functioning of markets and institutions and good governance in particular.[28] The WB gender policy research report *Engendering Development*[29] argues that gender inequality hinders development in terms of costs to well-being, productivity, growth, governance and further argues the case for economic development as being good for gender equality.[30] The WB report specifically highlights that discrimination can be reduced through competitive markets[31] and closely links gender equality with economic growth, supported by relevant macro-economic studies. In fairness there are also, some, albeit limited exceptions related to programmes on gender-based violence, women in post-conflict settings and women's power to influence at the decision-making level.[32] Overall, the WB thus translated gender equality as providing women with access to productive resources[33] and as one of the three main focuses for current and future strategies in private sector development.[34]

Translating the concept of gender equality must have posed a fundamental problem for the neoliberal macro-economists, without compromising the WB's fundamental political vision of the world, as exemplified through its structural reform programmes in Nicaragua and Peru. Unsurprisingly, in its definition of gender equality the WB does not explicitly mention social justice, wealth redistribution or power sharing. Instead, it focuses on the relevance of gender equality to economic development. The WB's interpretation of gender equality[35] thus legitimises the advancement of gender equality largely in so far as it makes economic sense, in order to retain it as relevant to its interpretation of development assistance.[36]

Another crucial element of the WB's gender policy[37] which carries a significant part of its neoliberal ideology is the gradual slippage from the term 'gender inequalities' into the term 'gender disparities'. The term 'disparities' used in the WB's gender policy document evokes the assumption that given the same chances and opportunities, a fair game can be played out amongst contestants – rich and poor, women and men. The underlying assumption is that through the establishment of a free market and the rule of law through the necessary justice reform programmes in which women and men would have equal rights, voices and opportunities, gender 'disparities' would be, de facto, addressed.

Arguably, interpreting 'inequalities' as 'disparities' does little more than uphold a system which protects a minority of men and women (but mostly men in developing countries) who already enjoy access to and control over, resources and power. Meanwhile, the majority of the population without or with less access and control over resources and power are relegated to the domestic sphere, as illustrated by Mansell, as follows:

> While wealth brings no obligation, poverty carries no claims or rights and this in turn legitimates a system in which, while all are equal before the law, the affluent are protected in their wealth and the poor in their poverty. And because those with wealth are successful and those without are unsuccessful in achieving the 'equally' desired goal (that is wealth), it makes sense to assume that our essential human nature is identical. And here, this leads to a vital feature of the rule of law, equality before the law.[38]

The interpretation of gender equality by the WB understood as equality within the market and before the law refers to 'formal equality', thus avoiding altogether challenging structural inequalities and power relations between women and men which are rooted in social injustices. Notions of social injustice clearly do not underlie the Bank's conception of economic 'development'. The WB's underpinning rationale in its work with gender equality as well as its potential influence on donor community and recipient aid countries can thus be summarised as follows:

> To promote economic development and attain the overarching poverty reduction goal – the global community must renew its attention to women's economic empowerment and increase investments in women. . . . Women's lack of economic empowerment imperils . . . growth and poverty reduction.[39]

If the reasoning behind this statement is taken to its logical conclusion, then gender inequalities are understood to be wrong in so far as they constitute a missed opportunity for economic production. Therefore, applying this rationale, women become an economic burden unless they are productive.

It takes little more than a journey through any Sub-Saharan African country to observe that, while constituting the majority and most active labour force, especially in the rural areas, women are at the same time the most heavily exploited. Their work is largely concerned with the domestic and in the productive but informal sectors of the economy. Yet the lion's share of the formal sector resources of the economy, such as land assets, are owned and controlled by a minority of men. By ignoring the glaring socio-political reality of women's secondary status, labour exploitation and class inequalities, which constitute the main barriers for women to access the formal sectors of the economy on an equal footing, the neoliberal analysis manages to turn the victims of exploitation into potential causes of the 'imperilment of economic growth'.

However paradoxical this perspective of IDA may be, the WB has gained ground in influencing the IDA policy agenda of several key aid agencies and has seen the number of its followers grow in recent years. The International Monetary Fund has been a long-standing ally of the WB at the multilateral level, as has DFID at the bilateral level (irrespective of whether the UK government of the time was Conservative or Labour – for its politics followed market liberalism in both cases). Together, they have been nurturing Global Development Policy targets as will be further explored below. More surprisingly, these perspectives have also gained ground in long-standing social democratic bilateral aid agencies in Scandinavian countries.

By the end of the 1990s, DFID's focus had shifted towards the WB-prioritised Millennium Development Goals (MDGs) and the associated country-level processes through Poverty Reduction Strategy Plans (PRSPs). Those committed to the 12 critical gender areas highlighted in the Beijing Platform for Action (PfA) raised concerns about the shrinking focus on gender equality in the Millennium Declaration. Between 2000 and 2015, the MDGs era, DFID's gender policy commitments have consequently narrowed down to cover essentially two social and uncontroversial sectors: health and education. As a result, in other important policy areas such as access to resources and inequalities in decision-making, DFID diminished its level of activity in mainstreaming gender issues.[40] An external evaluation of DFID 'gender equality and women's empowerment' undertaken between 2004 and 2006 raised much hope for improving DFID work on gender equality, a concept which, it was generally felt, had dropped off the main development policy agenda.[41] Following the evaluation, a gender equality action plan was drawn up, a gender leaflet produced and a largely 'gender-blind' White Paper 2006[42] was consequently introduced. The White Paper 2006[43] includes a 96-page long list of development commitments and only briefly mentions gender equality in a single, short statement as follows. Under the first chapter, and clearly aligned to the MDGs orientation, the UK government claimed that it would '[g]ive greater priority to our work in support of gender equality and women's rights'.

One could argue that whilst such a statement is limited, it does in principle translate a political willingness to actually give greater priority to gender equality. However, it could also be argued that this statement is merely rhetoric to counter any possible critique of gender blindness of the rest of the document and compromise DFID's thought world–leading position in forwarding gender equality. Neither the high-level foreword, nor the preface mentioned either gender equality or women's rights as being priorities. The White Paper's foreword, signed by the then Prime Minister Tony Blair in July 2006, stresses amongst other issues, the following points:

> This new White Paper on eliminating world poverty sets out how the UK will work with others to deliver on the promises we made last year. This will need an effort right across Government, to put our pledges into practice, to promote better governance across the world, to tackle the threat of climate change, and to create an international development system that is fit for purpose.

In short, the top priorities highlighted were i) good governance, ii) environment and iii) institutional reforms of the international development system understood in terms of aid effectiveness. These priorities reveal the UK government's understanding of the most effective response to poverty and thus its understanding of what development should be about. Furthermore, such prioritisation also sends a signal as to what is not included as a priority in poverty reduction strategies, namely social justice and structural inequalities, power relations and gender inequalities. These crucial aspects of development, which were very much present under Clare Short, the former Secretary of State for International Development, had gradually become at best secondary issues and, at worst, silenced as irrelevant. Tony Blair ends his foreword by stating that 'We are making real progress. There is no greater or more just cause facing us today'.

'Real progress' in IDA is thus considered from a governance and macro-economic perspective and, although there is no mention of social justice to be found throughout the White Paper, the short but crucial leap is made from development understood as social justice to development as defined in terms of economic growth and governance. This leap relies on the assumption that growth obtained at the macro level will naturally and eventually trickle down to the micro level to improve the lot of the poorest and (incidentally) that of women, without the need to specify and regulate any particular social justice targets or priorities. Blair's foreword precedes that of the Secretary of State for International Development at the time (Hilary Benn), an in-depth and impressive six-page preface presenting the White Paper's entirely gender-blind priorities with the exception of the then MDG 3 – which, as previously mentioned, deals with an uncontroversial interpretation of gender equality.[44]

However, DFID's gender equality action plan of 2006, insists that:

> At its heart, gender equality and women's empowerment is a political issue, needing a political response, and not a technical one. It means that the international community has to address the wider issues of promoting justice for everyone, tackling discrimination and upholding women's rights.[45]

However, despite its good intentions, DFID's gender equality action plan apparently did not manage to influence the very political instrument which frames the overall orientation and priority of UK development assistance: the White Paper itself.

DFID was thus left with a largely gender-blind development assistance policy instrument and a willing but not legally binding gender equality action plan[46] and related leaflet.

The section demonstrates that DFID and the WB shared much of the same core values, orientations and interpretations of development, and an agreement as to which themes ought to be prioritised. These priorities have had little to do with social justice and power relations or structural inequalities but were clearly aligned to a neoliberal and macro-economic understanding of poverty. The fundamental question is whether the underpinning political vision defining IDA's objectives is adequate to challenge and respond to the injustices and inequalities faced by women and girls.

Social democratic feminist and human rights resistance?

The Danish International Development Agency (Danida), like other Social Democratic Nordic bilateral development agencies, has been at the forefront of promoting gender equality in international development assistance since its first strategy for Women in Development was published in 1987.[47] The strategy of 1987 underlined 'the need to provide women with basic services and to recognize and promote women's key role as economic actors'.[48] Thus, both the welfare and the economic growth approach were linked in Danish assistance of 1980s.

The 1993 Danida Women in Development (WID) Policy, 'Women in Development, Towards the Year 2000', outlined a two-pronged approach: On the one hand, gender mainstreaming was defined as follows:

> integrating WID in all development efforts – gender mainstreaming means that women must be accorded a place in Aid on a par with that of men, in addition to women's interests in minor projects.[49]

Therefore, this essentially meant targeting participation in the mainstream sectors of development and the inclusion of small 'women's projects', which usually targeted violence against women or focused on micro-credits. On the other hand, the strategy of agenda setting was said to necessarily entail addressing the following:

> Women's perspective, sharpened by women's subordinate status, key position in the reproductive sphere, and lack of economic resources and political power, may provide a new understanding of old societal ills and bring forth a more humane social order. . . . The new agenda must aim at modifying the structures that generate and maintain inequality and exploitation . . . the prevailing sexual division of labour that prevents women from sharing fully in societal resources and power.[50]

This was the remnant of the original feminist intention towards redistribution. However, it was beginning to be overshadowed by:

> In view of the new emphasis on the market brought about by the [IMF and WB's] structural adjustment policy, its incongruity between (paid and unpaid) production and (paid and unpaid) reproduction is likely to be strengthened, unless counterbalanced by enhanced WID efforts within the traditional social fields of health, education, and employment etc.[51]

If anything, this further illustrated Danida's awareness of the pitfalls of an overwhelming focus on economic growth in IDA and its willingness, under the social democratic government, to 'counterbalance' the effects of liberal market economy through its WID policy with a political strategy for women in developing countries. However, such awareness did not survive the election of the liberal-conservative coalition government in 2002, or the sharp turn in the definition of gender equality[52] in the revised Danida strategy for gender equality in Danish development cooperation of 2004:

> Gender equality is: (i) Equality under the law, (ii) Equality of opportunity (including gender equality of rewards for work, and gender equality in access to human capital and other productive resources that enable opportunities) (iii) Equality in terms of political and economic influence (including the ability to influence and contribute to the overall Development process).

Danida's 2004 gender strategy opens with a quotation that sums up a substantive political shift in its interpretation of gender equality:

> Gender equality between men and women is neither social nor cultural cosmetics; rather it is an economic, political and democratic necessity.[53]

Whilst women's economic independence is a necessity and a pre-condition for emancipation and gender equality as a whole, this '*entrée en matière*' is nevertheless problematic for a number of reasons.

Firstly, it seems to imply a hierarchy in which economics and the neoliberal vision of democracy are viewed as primary, with social and cultural considerations being at best secondary or, at worst, irrelevant. Seen from a holistic interpretation, the quote could just as easily be rephrased as follows: 'Gender equality is neither number driven, nor is it neoliberal cosmetics, but is rather a social and political necessity'. However, Danida's original aspiration for a 'more humane social order', clearly expressed in the 1970s and 1980s, was no longer amongst its development priorities from 2004 to 2010.

The definition of gender equality which appears in the 2004 Danida gender strategy is presented as a quotation in inverted commas, but the source is not explicitly mentioned in the document. The definition was actually taken directly from the WB Policy document *Engendering Development*, in line with the conservative thinking of the Danish government at the time.[54] Consequently, gender equality was redefined following this change in political orientation, which effectively eclipsed the notion of redistribution and exploitation present in the former strategy.

Indeed, a turn in the political undercurrent, as Danish development policy once said to represent the

> continuation of domestic Danish welfare policies which put emphasis on income transfer as a central element in the redistribution between the rich and the poor. In that respect, the Danish aid policy has been understood as a 'doubling' of or as a transfer of Danish welfare (political) values onto the international scene. The strength of these values was an important explanation of the high degree of continuity which has characterised Danish development aid policy since the early 1970s.[55]

In a bid to address this issue, the revised gender strategy mentions the following compromise:

> The implementation of the strategy will demand changes to existing power structures, the status and roles of women and men. Therefore, working with gender equality will in many contexts be conflictual.[56]

The phrase 'changes to existing power structures' is all that resisted and survived from the original intention to address imbalances in power and resources allocation and distribution. Thus, after having developed one of the most cutting-edge and holistic WID strategies, Danida retreated behind a borrowed neoliberal interpretation of gender equality, as the strategy explicitly mentions whose standards of measurement were to be used:

> The WB's 'Doing Business' indicators – which describes the regulations for starting and running a business – will be applied in the Danish bilateral assistance in order to identify the precise obstacles to a favourable business climate in the respective Danish programme countries. The [WB] indicators provide a good starting point for a targeted Danish assistance, in which help to self-help is given, aimed at eliminating the concrete obstacles to generating economic growth.[57]

As previously pointed out, women's economic emancipation is arguably the key to their achieving independence and autonomy, as well as being an important part in addressing gender inequalities. However, solely targeting women's participation in the private sector as the 'new driving force of (economic growth and) development' within societies which are structurally predicated on social inequalities is bound to have limited effect in eradicating the social injustices women face.

In conclusion, both Danida and DFID had traded their previous and more socially inclined definition of gender equality with the WB's neoliberal interpretation of development and gender equality.

This begs the question as to whether any bilateral organisation managed to resist the 'spectacular neoliberal comeback' and the conceptual eclipses it brings with it, or even managed a return to more social justice perspective.

A clear return to social justice perspective is exemplified by Danida, Strategic Framework for Gender Equality, Rights and Diversity in 2014, under a new social democratic government which offered a multi-dimensional definition of gender equality encompassing equality in *Representation*, *Recognition* and *Redistribution*,[58] as follows:

> Gender equality refers to the equal rights, opportunities and influence of women and men, girls and boys in all aspects of life – political, civil, social, cultural and economic.
>
> It goes beyond parity in numbers, and while equality under law is a pre-condition, it contains a combination of quantitative and qualitative aspects.

> Firstly, it refers to *equal representation* and access to political influence, financial resources, land rights, legal aid and education. Secondly, gender equality involves *recognition* of gender-specific challenges and barriers faced by women, men, girls and boys. Thirdly, it involves *redistribution* of power and control over political and economic resources.
>
> In order to bring about *transformational change* and real gender equality outcomes, the human rights–based approach places strong emphasis on development engagements that contribute to bring about *redistribution*.
>
> Gender equality is not an issue of exclusive concern to women and girls but must equally *involve men and boys* if ingrained inequalities and discriminatory systems are to be effectively addressed.
>
> Categories of women and men, girls and boys are made up of complexities of power, class, age, religion, ethnicity, caste, gender identity and *sexual orientation* – in combination constituting individual human beings. Individuals are often restricted by stereotyped gender perceptions and expectations.

This constitutes no less than one of the most ambitious interpretation of gender equality, encapsulating both gender justice and a Human Rights Based Approach (HRBA) which together with SDG 5 should, in principle and if followed at programming level, offer the opportunity of achieving outcome-level results beyond numerical and quantitative cosmetics, towards transformative gender changes.

Currently, the 2014 Strategic Framework resisted the right-wing political turn of Denmark in the 2015 liberal-conservative coalition, which may be a hopeful sign that both Left and Right can no longer deny the importance of inscribing gender equality and development assistance at large not solely within a liberal economic growth paradigm regardless of the injustices and inequalities it tended to perpetrate, if not widen. HRBA, if anything, is the only 'universal' framework that guarantees a certain equity and basic dignified standard beyond cultural particularisms and political affiliations. The only framework that could ensure that human rights are not promoted on a selective basis, 'à la carte' as it were, but also include a focus on men towards gender equality and LGBTIQ. In Chapter 4, illustrative examples of its implementation at the programming level are included.

Since 1962, the overall goal for Swedish development assistance has been 'to improve the standard of living and quality of life of the poor people'.[59] An integrated Swedish development assistance agency called 'Sida' was created in 1995.[60] By the 1990s, beyond the overarching goal of poverty reduction, Sida had developed a total of six development objectives as follows:

> i) Economic growth (1978), ii) Social equality (1978), iii) Economic and political independence (1978), iv) Democratic development (1978), v) Sustainable use of natural resources and protection of the environment (1988) and vi) Equality between women and men (1996).[61]

Basic policy documents within the areas of poverty, democracy, gender equality and sustainable development were consequently developed in the years 1996–97.

Poverty reduction and development concepts were thus broadened to reflect an egalitarian stance.[62] The starting point for the formulation of these objectives has been multi-dimensional and based on the view that poverty must be challenged on a number of fronts – not solely on the economic level.

The priorities of the Swedish government for international development assistance could be summarised as follows:

> Every person has the right to live in dignity. The elimination of poverty in our world is the greatest moral, political and economic challenge faced by humanity, but is absolutely essential for peace, stability and sustainable development. A world where there is flagrant injustice will remain a world in which all of us lack security not only poor people but prosperous individuals and states as well. Reducing poverty and creating a fairer world is in everyone's interests . . . a world in which there is recognition of equal opportunities and rights for women and men alike.[63]

This interpretation of key concepts offered hope for many practitioners in the development field to implement and find appropriate methodologies to evaluate poverty reduction from a redistributive perspective. It also offered considerable hope to gender experts that gender equality was no longer considered a marginal issue in development assistance but figured high on the political agenda of one of the leading IDA bilateral agencies.

However, due to problems with Swedish government finances, the volume of development assistance was temporarily reduced in the latter part of the decade to a lowest level of 0.7% of GNP in 1999.[64] This coincided with what began to appear, from different evaluations of Sida's international assistance, as a lack of clarity in the relationship between the overall poverty goal and the six specific objectives:

> Specific objectives, which should have served as guidelines for the main goal, had instead been given far greater attention than the fundamental purpose and overriding goal.[65]

Sida missed an important opportunity for the implementation of its unique holistic and multi-dimensional interpretation of development and poverty reduction, as it could have included gender justice and redistribution, but chose to follow instead the neoliberal hegemonic trend.

As a result, 'the importance of particular specific objectives or sub-goals were underlined, and different specific objectives counterpoised to one another, for instance, growth versus equality between women and men'.[66] Nevertheless, the goal of gender equality was introduced as a response to the realisation that separate targeted projects or programme components for women alone were not proving to have the swift effect on development which had been hoped for. Gender mainstreaming was intended as a strategy which would enable gender equality to be dealt with alongside other policy issues such as the poverty goal and economic reforms – and not as a separate and marginal topic.

In practice and in many IDA agencies, this shift often led to the replacement of special central units and gender-focused functions at the institutional level and to the assumption that gender equality was inevitably going to trickle down from policy to programme and across the different policy objectives without need for specialised knowledge or specially allocated resources. This assumption in many ways contributed to the 'evaporation' of gender equality at the policy, programme and organisational level as it did not effectively allocate the adequate resources for implementation.[67]

In the late 1990s and early 2000s this coincided with the fact that development cooperation as a whole was increasingly moving from individual projects to process-focused support to sector-wide support and budget support. In addition, Sida could choose whether to opt to be a 'silent partner' in certain cases, partly financing an activity but leaving the main responsibility to another financier. This demanded that Sweden adapt its rules, routines, working methods and knowledge to new forms of collaboration by participating in informal consultation group for sector programme support with a number of nations, for instance, as well as in working groups in SPA (the WB programme for partnership with Africa, Strategic Partnership with Africa) and DAC (the OECD Development Assistance Committee) or further development of programme support and harmonisation of development assistance procedures. This led to an increased emphasis on partnership across donors and with the WB.

Nevertheless, Sida's recent definition of gender equality resisted the neoliberal wave as follows:

> Equal rights, responsibilities and opportunity for all individuals should not depend on whether they are born female or male. Gender equality is a matter of human rights and social justice for all.[68]

Although equal rights, responsibilities and opportunities were mentioned in Sida's definition of gender equality, these were positioned in 'parallel to' the concept of social justice for all. Consequently, women's empowerment was not omitted from Sida's gender policy document in 2005, but in contrast, was retained as a key concept and was defined as follows:

> Empowerment of women relates to the process of women gaining power and control over their own lives. It involves expansion of choices, and increased access to and control over resources, information and actions.

In its main policy document, Sida understands gender discrimination to be one of the main causes of poverty.[69] However and resisting purely neoliberal interpretations, it considers structural inequalities to be one of the 'five points of departure':

> Power structures are fundamental for working towards equality between women and men, girls and boys. Unequal power relations have created structural obstacles for women and girls in all spheres of society – political, economic, social, educational, cultural and religious – as well as for their full

> enjoyment of their productive, reproductive and sexual rights and roles. Sida should therefore consider and act upon unequal power relations between and among women and men, as well as the structural causes and frameworks of these power relations.[70]

At the same time, in putting gender equality within the human rights system, Sida provides one of the first examples of a bilateral agency taking a rights-based perspective in development.[71] The organisation explicitly grounded its work within a perspective in which:

> Gender equality is a key element of the human rights system established by the Universal Declaration of Human Rights in 1948. The Convention on the Elimination of All Forms of Discrimination against Women, defines what constitutes discrimination against women and sets an agenda for national action to end such discrimination.[72]

Thus, Sida at the time opted for a compromise at the policy level by keeping two traditionally opposed interpretations of gender equality – namely the neoliberal perspective focusing on rights and economic growth and the more holistic perspective focusing on social justice – while at the same time avoiding the use of the term 'redistribution'. It is not clear whether Sida is retaining both interpretations as part of its pragmatic approach or whether it is actually caught in a broader changing political landscape in IDA which leaves little alternative but to eventually harmonise and thus trade off core Left political values to follow the larger zeitgeist.

Since then, Sweden, having realised that i) systematic subordination of women and girls is still commonplace for countless women and girls all over the world, ii) new setbacks for gender equality at the global level constituted a barrier to women and girls' full enjoyment of their human rights, was amongst the first to develop a 'feminist foreign policy'.

> Sweden's Foreign Minister Ms. Wallstrom raised eyebrows, in 2014, by announcing that Swedish foreign policy would from that point forward be focused on feminist principles. Sweden's stance has become more visible with the rise of Mr. Trump; this summer, when the United States discontinued aid to family planning groups that provide abortions, Sweden offered to countervail the American policy by replacing any lost funds. Canada's new liberal government this adopted Ms. Wallstrom's idea, announcing a 'feminist international assistance program'.[73]

Sweden's feminist foreign policy implementation is based on an action plan 2015–2018 in which six objectives apply, namely:

1 Full enjoyment of human rights by all women and girls especially related to increasing impact of a gender perspective in international response to

migration and humanitarian emergencies including linkages between refugee migrations, human trafficking and prostitution. Furthermore, the principle of non-discrimination includes LGBTI;

2 Freedom from physical mental and sexual violence for all women and girls;
3 Participation of women and girls in preventing and resolving conflicts and post-conflict;
4 Political participation and influence of women and girls in all areas of society;
5 Full enjoyment of economic rights and empowerment of all women and girls;
6 Sexual and reproductive health and rights of women and girls.

Whilst it is still too early stages to assess the impact of the Swedish feminist foreign policy, re-appropriating and rehabilitating the term 'feminist' is in itself a courageous statement. Although, it is not mentioned what is meant by 'feminism', which political undercurrent of feminism is it referring to – a cross-cultural and rights-based feminism not shy to challenge cultural practices that are dismissive of women's rights or the politically correct feminism that accepts and respect cultural differences even if these place women in an inferior position or any other shades in between. Observing the objectives above, it is easily deducible that the focus is largely on *representation* and *recognition* as *redistribution* is not explicitly targeted. It can thus be assumed that gender justice is not specifically undercutting this otherwise bold and promising foreign policy title.

If anything, these cases seek to illustrate that a critical analysis of the politics behind the interpretation of 'development assistance' matters and can unveil intentions behind the interpretation of gender equality in IDA. Policy implementation, through dialogue and programming, remains subject to a coherent and genuine political will and action as well as an effective and consequent allocation of resources.

Interludes at the country policy level

This section critically examines the varying interpretations of gender equality at the country policy level in different political and geographic contexts such as: i) the case of abortion in Nicaragua's neoliberal[74] and neo-Sandinista[75] governments and the Roman Catholic Church; ii) Yoweri Museveni's politics[76] and gender inequalities in Uganda; and iii) Thomas Sankara's[77] speech on International Women's Day in 1987[78] in Burkina Faso. These examples seek to demonstrate the implication pertaining to the use of Third Worldist, neoliberal and Marxist focuses in the interpretations of gender equality at the country policy level.

The case of abortion in Nicaragua's and Third Worldist defences

The arrival in power in 1997 of President Arnoldo Aleman (1997–2002) was marked by a strengthening of neoliberalism and conservative ideology with regard to the general interpretation of the notion of equality and the concept of gender equality in particular. One indication of the government of Nicaragua's conservative political perspective on gender equality and women's rights was the fact that the choice of opening speaker of the 'Day of the Unborn Child', sponsored by the Catholic Church, was the new head of the National Women's Institute.[79]

The nomination of a conservative anti-abortion militant at the head of the national women's machinery signalled a toleration of 'gender equality and women's rights' and 'feminism' in so far as they did not interfere with the local cultural patriarchal definition of 'women and their (key) reproductive role'.

This perspective was then complemented in 2001 by key development goals for the government of Nicaragua (related mostly to poverty alleviation, macroeconomic stabilisation and modernisation of the public and private sectors) with only one statement of intent on gender equality, as follows:

> Alluding specifically to the Swedish objective of promoting equality of opportunity through development co-operation, emphasis has been placed on the strategic importance of activities which strengthen the productive capacity of women and in so doing improve their living standards and possibilities for participation in political life.[80]

Thus, gender equality was defined in terms of participation, in as far as it benefited economic growth, and representation and as a 'Swedish foreign' objective. Examples of this interpretation of gender equality were evident in Nicaragua as early as Beijing in 1995, where it contributed with a narrow economic interpretation of gender equality, also expressing strong reservations against paragraphs which could be perceived as legitimising homosexual relationships, or which supported a woman's right to abortion.

The neoliberal government led by President Aleman was clearly unwilling to address or even prioritise gender equality within its development priorities, only reluctantly including the concept when embedded in a strictly neoliberal interpretation and attributing this inclusion to 'foreign intervention' in the 'sovereign' national agenda (read: a form of neo-colonialism).

But while Sida's policy was considered too avant-garde and interventionist for the government of Nicaragua, it was very much in line with some Nicaraguan civil society's views and NGOs such as Ixchen,[81] which had provided support for illegal but safe abortions in both urban and rural areas, and braved the law to defend women against the death risk of unsafe abortion and violence throughout the country for the decades.

According to the CEDAW committee report of 2001,[82] Nicaragua had the highest fecundity rate of adolescents in Latin America, which was one of the highest in the world. Two out of three births took place in a risk situation, 11% of which were due to the fact that the mother was younger than 18 years of age.[83] Other statistics at the time showed the gravity of the situation, such as the fact that 10% of 15-year-old girls already had children and 46% of 19-year-olds had children. Only 11% of 15-to-19-year-old girls used any kind of contraception. Maternal mortality was consequently a considerable problem for women in Nicaragua.[84]

The Pan-American Health Organization estimated that there were 150 deaths for every 100,000 live births, but this situation was believed to be widely under-reported. These figures generally pointed to complications either during pregnancy or labour, or unsafe abortions. High maternal mortality rates were thus linked to both the large number of children per woman and high fertility rates in women aged under 19.[85]

During the years from 1996 to 2005 there was an average of 1,260 cases per year reported of sexual violence against women. There was a steady increase in the figures, from 1,100 cases of sexual violence per year in 1996 to just over 1,300 cases in 2005.[86]

Unsurprisingly, the government of Sweden announced in 2007[87] that it was suspending economic aid to Nicaragua because of its laws defending the unborn from abortion under any circumstances, including a ban on therapeutic abortions. More conservative and neoliberal aid agencies such as the WB continued doing business as usual in line with Aleman's conservative and narrow interpretation of gender equality.

With the end of Aleman's conservative neoliberal government, Daniel Ortega came into power in the footsteps of Latin America's Bolivarian Revolutionary leaders such as Hugo Chávez and Evo Morales.

Laura Mannen, a well-known Latin American solidarity activist, in an article entitled 'The government war on women's rights in Nicaragua' raised the following pertinent question:

> What has become of the revolutionary Nicaragua, which electrified the globe by overthrowing Dictator Anastasio Somoza and establishing a workers' and peasants' government in the 1980s?[88]

In her article she highlighted several critiques of the Marxist movement as follows:

> The Sandinistas did not fulfil their promises to the masses, and rather than advancing towards a promised socialism, they advocated a 'mixed economy' which included both state-run industries and profit-based enterprises. After the initial expropriation of Somoza family holdings, the Sandinistas slowed down land reforms and nationalization of vital industries.[89]

But most importantly, they were accused of promoting the following interpretation of a so-called Left egalitarian society:

> The Revolutionary front refused to recognize the national rights of indigenous communities along the Atlantic coast, demanding that they assimilate into Nicaraguan society and furthermore, female militants, who made up 30 percent of the Sandinista military forces, were told to postpone demands for equality in favour of building the new society.[90]

This revealed a betrayal of Left ideals in practice by an apparently Marxist movement. It also illustrated that both patriarchal and racist tendencies are by no means the monopoly of one particular political ideology. However, when the Left does not make these a priority, it is somehow more disappointing, as expectations turn into unfulfilled promises, particularly since Nicaragua had ratified CEDAW on 17 July 1980.

According to Mannen, using the arguments of feminist cultural relativists and identity politics weakened the claims of women's human rights feminist activists as further exemplified:

> This kind of political discourse illustrates how identity politics – whilst seemingly embracing the worthy goal of anti-imperialism – may turn feminist discourse against social justice and against the interests of women themselves. It also demonstrates that cultural relativism, in this case, is not so far removed from the views of nationalists and populist aspirations. Thus, Pro-Sandinista media have claimed that abortion rights are 'a flag raised by Nicaraguan pseudo-feminists with the intention of obtaining millions in foreign funds'[91] as well as accusing advocates for women's rights of being 'privileged imperialist pawns who are undermining the national culture'.[92]

This example shows the extent of the implication of the use of identity politics as a cultural shield against 'foreign scrutiny', whilst eclipsing social distributive justice and delegitimising the universality of women's human rights.

As Jocelyn E. Getgen argues in her article 'Reproductive Injustice: An Analysis of Nicaragua's Complete Abortion Ban',[93] in the first line of support towards the government political anti-abortion movement, the Roman Catholic Church was at the forefront, with the following legal outcome:

> Thus, Nicaragua's legislature voted to approve Law 603 and rescinded Article 165 of the Codigo Penal (Penal Code), eliminating the only exemptions to the country's general ban on abortion and criminalizing even the therapeutic use of the procedure for victims of rape or incest, or to save the health and life of the mother.[94]

Since the law was enacted, 'Nicaraguan women in need of therapeutic abortions have died because doctors were not allowed to provide necessary emergency obstetric care or other treatment'.[95] Thus, 'in October 2007, 80 women's deaths could be directly attributed to the new "killer law"'.[96]

Beyond the obvious violation of the fundamental women's right to live, this law constituted yet another obvious socio-economic injustice in practice:

> For the Nicaraguan rich women, a problematical pregnancy need not be a death sentence. You can fly to Miami or bribe a discreet private clinic in Managua. But in the wretchedly poor districts of the country, most young women do not have money. Their choice is either to go through with a

> pregnancy that may kill them or attempt a DIY termination that may kill them as well.[97]

The Inter-American Commission on Human Rights responded to Nicaragua's complete abortion ban by issuing an unprecedented statement declaring that: 'the Nicaraguan government's repeal of article 165 of the Penal Code endangers the protection of women's human rights'.[98]

In addition to this statement, the UN Committee on the Elimination of Discrimination against Women (CEDAW Committee) expressed its concerns regarding the ban and recommended that Nicaragua remove the criminal penalties imposed on women who obtain abortions and on doctors who provide them.[99] In contrast, Pope Benedict XVI affirmed the Catholic supporters' positions by:

> Reaffirming the Catholic Church's stance against abortion and calling on Catholic law makers around the world 'to introduce and support laws inspired by the values grounded in human nature'.[100]

Arguably, this is a striking example of how cultural relativism, identity politics and anti-imperialism can, at their worst, justify women's deaths. It also demonstrates how gender equality and women's rights can be interpreted in a manner which serves the conservative ideology of some, at the cost of women's lives which are, de facto, defined as being worth far less than that of an embryo.

In both supposedly diverse political scenarios of Aleman's neoliberal government and the neo-Sandinistas' government, in the best scenario on the basis of *representation*, gender equality is thus considered an issue at the margins of democratisation, a secondary matter that can wait, while in the worst scenario on the basis of identity politics and cultural relativism, it is rejected as an instrument of foreign interventionism, at all costs. Paradoxically, there is little if any denouncement by Third Worldists of the Vatican's interference in local abortion policy (be it in Nicaragua or elsewhere around the globe such as in the Philippines for example) as unacceptable foreign interventionism.

Yoweri Museveni's postcolonialist interpretation of gender equality

If Nicaragua ranked 124, amongst UNDP Human Development Index in 2009,[101] Uganda's ranking figured as 157 out of a total of 182 UN Member States in the same year.[102] Uganda was for a long time hailed as the 'donors' darling'. In particular, 'adjustment policies supported by the IMF and the WB characterised mainly by a concentrated focus on management of government expenditures, retrenchment, trade liberalisation and privatisation, formed much of the cornerstone ideology of the expanding economy'.[103]

Early in 2000, the WB, the IMF and other bilateral donors such as Denmark, the UK and Sweden proclaimed that 'Uganda was a success story, an example of a very poor country which had successfully carried out fundamental liberalisation of its economy through economic reforms'.[104]

Uganda had indeed implemented significant economic reforms, including

> a liberalization of the trade regime over the last decade and a half. This attracted foreign direct investment, mainly in manufacturing, and contributed to continued economic growth. Indeed, over the past six years, Uganda's real GDP had grown at around 6% per annum on average and was expected to continue growing at about 7% per year in the medium term.[105]

However, while macro-economic figures showed sustained growth, income inequalities were increasing.

> While Uganda's economy consistently registered an improved economic performance, with an average annual growth rate of about 6% since 1990/91, and an average annual increase in income per capita of 3.7% over past decades, the socio-economic advancement of the majority of Ugandans lagged well behind such percentages, particularly in the rural areas.[106]

One aspect which had particularly encouraged donors' funding was Uganda's progressive Constitution of 1995,[107] which contained a willingness to explicitly promote and protect women's human rights. The Bill of Rights is enshrined in Chapter 4 of the Constitution of Uganda 1995 and comprises 38 articles that cover both substantive human rights and their procedural enforcement. If women's participation in the spheres of political power was increasing in numbers,[108] so was the expectation that it would have eventually made a difference in the daily lives of Ugandan women.

In 1997, Ugandan women's movement organisations joined the Uganda Land Alliance (a civil society coalition) and conducted nationwide research on women's land ownership patterns.[109] Consequently, the amended clause on spousal co-ownership and land used for the daily sustenance of the family was tabled and passed before parliament on 25 June 1998 as follows:

> Where land is occupied as a home, where land is used, it should belong to both husband and wife. In a polygamous situation . . . where the wives work on the same piece of land, they shall hold the land jointly with their husband.[110]

The clause, albeit in its amended and watered-down form, was passed with unanimous vote in parliament.[111] However, when the Land Act in 2003 was published,

> to the astonishment of all, the Clause had mysteriously 'disappeared'. After months of research, and after official records justified the omission on the basis of 'procedural irregularities', President Yoweri Museveni eventually admitted that he had personally intervened and deleted the amendment himself, arguing that the Clause would more appropriately belong under the pending Domestic Relation Bill (DRB).[112]

In October 2002, President Yoweri Museveni wrote to Hon. Janet Mukwaya, Minister of Justice and Constitutional Affairs, a ten-page statement expressing his views on the Domestic Relation Bill.[113]

The president took personal responsibility for delaying the enactment of the family law when he caused the Ministry of Gender Affairs to withdraw the DRB under his administration 1996–2001. In essence, the president argued that in his view[114] the bill was:

> rather shallow and cannot address the issues of Ugandan society. I should warn the Ugandan population against the trends of copying Western ways of life which have caused enormous damage to humanity and thousands of broken families . . . the stampede for self-destruction by the human species by imbibing everything Western.[115]

Siding thus with identity politics, Third Worldist, anti-imperialist and cultural relativist theories, Museveni would have presented a powerful anti-neo-colonial argument were it not for the fact that Uganda inherited many of its general laws[116] from Britain in 1902.[117]

Besides the law of succession,[118] which was amended in 1972 during Idi Amin's regime, and the law relating to children,[119]which was amended and consolidated in 1996, as well as some specific legislations that allow for Polygamy, FGMs etc., the rest of Ugandan family law remained largely the same as it was at the date of reception in 1902.[120] However, the date of reception does not correspond to the date of inception. The inception of these particular family laws date back to the second half of the 19th century and would therefore necessarily base themselves in 19th-century British Victorian values, ideology, customs and traditions.[121] In other words, the DRB did not merely challenge Ugandan cultural traditions but the commonalities between contemporary Ugandan discriminatory customs and 19th-century (Western) conservative and discriminatory ideology. It is therefore this intersection which forms the moral and ideological basis of current Ugandan General Law and that of other Sub-Saharan countries[122] which the president was paradoxically trying to preserve at the time, in the name of anti-neo-colonialism.

The DRB was further purporting to recognise marital rape as an offence, which was not recognised under the Penal Code Act,[123] as the act of entering into marriage is taken as an irretrievable and unconditional consent to sexual intercourse, just as it was in colonial and postcolonial UK.[124] Interestingly, the DRB challenged the legal concept inherited from colonial times and long enshrined in the notion of title ownership of lands by landlords in Victorian England.[125] Arguably, far from challenging Ugandan traditions and customs from a supposedly Western perspective as postcolonial and cultural relativist critiques would have it, the DRB actually challenges imported colonial rules that happened to fit local traditional and patriarchal interests very well.

Thus, committing to gender equality when understood as participation and non-discrimination by ratifying CEDAW and adopting a new 'gender-sensitive' constitution, allowed heads of states to appear gender-sensitive on the international scene, and thus enabled them to attract donor funding without having to make drastic changes. In conclusion, this example illustrates the paradoxes in the use of Third Worldist and anti-neo-colonialist ideology to preserve what customary and colonial conservative ideologies have in common, namely patriarchal values and the maldistribution of resources.

Thomas Sankara's speech on International Women's Day

During an evaluation mission in July 2008 to Burkina Faso, the author asked one of the parliamentarians at the National Assembly in Ouagadougou why the portrait of Thomas Sankara was not displayed together with the rest of the leaders that preceded and succeeded him at the entrance of Burkina Faso's National Assembly. The author was told that only 'democratic' leaders had their portrait displayed on the wall the National Assembly.

Reports and testimonies from two students from the University of Perpignan, originating respectively from Gabon and Burkina Faso, and participating in the African youth forum, were collected in Jean Brial's research.[126] They provided a powerful (anonymous) account of how the so-called undemocratic leadership of Thomas Sankara was really felt to be:

> It was with pride that the student told the story of the radical and unique changes towards greater equality that took place under Thomas Sankara's regime, recalling poignant examples of ceilings imposed on Ministers' wages before their nomination, the relinquishment of their limousines for Renault 5 cars, motorbikes for police chief commissioners and Sankara's absolute integrity in hunting down corruption and gender inequalities even to the point of declaring 'a men's market day'. Supposedly on that day men were to be on market duty in order to sensitise them to the hardship of women's domestic chores, not to be taken for granted; remembering also the first school day's topic on apartheid and crimes against humanity and the week-ends spent in pioneering clubs to help build schools or health clinics. Like many others, the students thought that Sankara's death gave only more scope to corruption and nepotism. They mentioned the luxurious residence of president Blaise Compaoré in Ziniare, 40 km from Ouagadougou, and its hectares of surrounding private land filled with wild animals and in which lions were being fed with sheep – a handsome meal, that could have well benefitted the hungry neighbouring villages.[127]

Such anonymous testimonies have been corroborated by many interviews carried out with civil servants in 2004 and 2008, taxi drivers in the streets and key stakeholders focus group held in Ouagadougou and Tenkodogo.[128] During Thomas Sankara's short-lived political life, his rather 'democratic' achievements included pioneering measures for women's emancipation such as a legal banning of female genital mutilations and restricted polygamy.[129]

On the 8 March 1987, in the year Sankara was murdered, he delivered a long and memorable speech[130] on the liberation of women in which his understanding and appreciation of women's condition and interpretation of gender equality were exceptionally far-reaching.

Sankara understood and interpreted the concepts of gender inequalities and women's condition in Burkina Faso within the broader and more radical framework of power relations, exploitation and social injustices, translating these concepts with far more insight than some contemporary First and Third World feminists:

> In sum addressing gender equality in today's Burkinabe's society amounts to the abolition of the slave-like conditions in which women have been kept for thousands of years. It entails first of all, an understanding of how such system of slavery works, unravelling its true nature and all its subtleties, in order to succeed in devising actions that will ultimately set women free. . . . In other words, in order to win the common struggle shared by both women and men, it is important to acquire the knowledge of gender equality both at national and universal level and to understand how, today, Burkinabe women's struggle meets the universal struggle of all women, and ultimately, the fight for the entire rehabilitation of our continent. Consequently, women's condition is the crux of the human matter, here, there and everywhere. It is thus universal in nature.[131]

In his speech Sankara contextualised gender equality and women's condition within a universalist perspective. He further unequivocally interpreted gender inequality within the field of social justice and structural inequalities. Although he acknowledged that gender inequality may be expressed in different forms, he stressed that these are merely 'expressions of one fundamental inequality that remains unchanged in relation to men, confirmed and reconfirmed through times and geographies'.[132]

Thus, Sankara repositioned gender inequality and violation of women's human rights within a universal framework, whilst also consistently denouncing postcolonialism.

Furthermore, and against the hegemonic trends and beliefs of his own sociocultural context, it is without fear of being labelled radical or Western white feminist that he dared to define

> masculine stupidity as sexism or machismo, as a form of intellectual and moral void, a more or less conscious physical impotence . . . no matter how oppressed a man may be, he will find somebody to further oppress: his wife.[133]

Whilst defining women's emancipation as that which makes women responsible and autonomous – through productive activities and political struggles, Sankara's revolution, could simply not have taken place without the struggle for women's emancipation.

Sankara was furthermore not afraid to be serious about challenging traditions and socio-cultural norms that in his view:

> essentially existed to maintain oppression against women to the sole benefit of a 'churl' such as the institution of marriage and its cortege of oppressive traditions starting with dowry, virginity, domestic chores, domestic violence, polygamy, property title ownership often reserved for men, widows lack of inheritance rights and forceful marriage with the defunct brother, Female Genital Mutilations [134]

He indeed was one of the first to outlaw FGM, forced marriage and polygamy amongst others and promoting women's participation in the productive sphere. In short, his speech summed up the content of what could have been the targets of Uganda's DRB and what could have suited in many ways the objective of many countries' effective gender equality policy in Sub-Saharan Africa and beyond.

It is not without humour that Sankara encouraged women to free themselves from any unhappy marriage to join:

> a blossoming celibate – with or without children – given that women have sufficiently proven to the world, their unquestionable capacity for child rearing and family nursing, their unquestionable capacity to act responsibly without having to become the object men's subjection or tutorage.[135]

According to Sankara, marriage ought to be 'a choice that increases self-esteem, not a lottery!'[136] Once again, Sankara differed here from certain feminist critiques that have argued for 'womanism', 'motherism' or other kinds of compromises, by unambiguously advocating against oppressive misogynist cultural traditions, which in all fairness could clearly apply well beyond Burkina Faso and Sub-Saharan Africa as the Nicaraguan example above demonstrates.

It is clear from his speech that Sankara's social revolution could only be achieved when women would be entirely free and emancipated, as is further emphasised below:

> Never again may my eyes be cast upon a society; my steps ever take me again to a country in which half of its people are kept in silence. I hear the uproar of women's silence, I foresee their tempestuous rumble, I feel the fury of their revolt. I await the fecund eruption of their revolution, where power will be conquered from the womb of their oppression.[137]

This was Sankara's exceptional feminist dream and at the same time, it is impossible to have foreseen with any certainty whether he would have achieved it all had he not been murdered in October 1987. Surely though, his vision still defies biases in cultural relativist, anti-essentialist, Third Worldist and identity politics feminist thinking. He is a rare example of someone who was able to transcend these trends whilst still firmly remaining anti-neo-colonialist and positioning redistribution and universalism still as the overall goal of his politics. Sankara was defined as a revolutionary Marxist sometimes known as 'Africa's Che.'

Most interestingly, for the purpose of this study, is that one of the most radical and comprehensive interpretations of gender equality in the context of IDA comes from a young African man – albeit amongst the few exceptional African and world leaders – with a sufficiently self-critical mind to challenge two systems – not only the international community, with his early and visionary attacks on neo-colonial exploitation of African resources and the absurdity of the Third World debt,[138] but also on Burkina Faso's socio-cultural and traditional systems of oppression. This was not particularly easy, at a time in which Burkina Faso had barely won independence from the French and nationalism was dominating many minds and discourses. His critique, a feminist critique, was an extraordinary act of critique against his own culture and land which still remains unprecedented today, whether in Africa, Latin America, Asia, the Middle-East or Europe.

If parallels could be drawn with well-known 'revolutionary' leaders in Venezuela, Iran, the Occupied Palestinian Territories or Zimbabwe, for example, one obvious similarity would be the denunciation of imperialism and capitalism as the main sources of world's oppression. However, it is difficult to imagine any of them, like Sankara, challenging traditions, socio-cultural stereotypes, or indeed patriarchal power structures which benefit their own position, for women's emancipation and freedom from oppression. Least of all, it is difficult to imagine any of these leaders proclaiming a 'men's market day' before the world's cameras. On the contrary, the statistics and policies which most prominently characterise internal oppression against women in contemporary revolutionary and anti-imperialist-led countries is typically evidenced by the rate of violence against women, notably domestic violence, and any legislative and policy framework that has been put into place (or not) to address this most obvious form of internal oppression.

Following Thomas Sankara's death, Burkina Faso went through a period which is recognised as being less favourable for the promotion of women's emancipation, between 1987 and 1992. The theme had dropped off the political agenda due to the fact that alliances had been struck with conservative forces such as the Roman Catholic Church and traditional leaders – who had been challenged under Sankara – and members and activists of the ruling party.[139]

In conclusion, it appears that gender inequality as interpreted and described by Sankara still provides one of the most relevant and radical interpretations of gender equality in the field of IDA. Such a position poses a direct challenge to Third World feminists, as it demonstrates the possibility of being at once culturally self-critical, universalist whilst remaining firmly anti-neo-colonialist.

As an overall conclusion for the three examples above, one can claim that with the exception of a visionary man who was never allowed to live long enough to put his ideals fully into practice, neither neoliberalist, so-called Marxist revolutionary, nor anti-imperialist regimes seem to have addressed effectively the challenges of patriarchal power structures and internal oppression faced by women. From the theory to the practice, what still distinguishes Sankara from contemporary revolutionary leaders is both his self-critical eye, his adherence to a feminist radical perspective that also challenges contemporary hegemonic feminist thinking, and his independence from orthodoxies. In this sense, Sankara is a challenge to feminist culturalist theories that argue that women bring a different perspective by the mere fact of being women. Sankara in his speech, if anything, demonstrated a more radical feminist perspective clearly founded on gender justice (albeit useful perspective in the struggle against poverty and oppression) than most contemporary identity-driven feminists in the West and certainly more than the female parliamentarians in Burkina Faso in Blaise Compaoré's time.

Conclusion

This chapter thus illustrates the ways in which gender equality has been interpreted in donor policies and country policies.

The first section shows that DFID shares much of its core values, its orientations and interpretations of development, and the themes which ought to be prioritised, with the WB. These have little to do with social justice and the challenging of power relations or structural inequalities, but are clearly aligned to a neoliberal and macro-economic understanding of poverty. It is demonstrated that it is thus difficult to incorporate gender equality – together with its comprehensive and holistic approach – into a DFID and WB framework without changing gender equality's *raison d'être* quite fundamentally. The crucial question is thus not so much what the already defined IDA donor policies mean for women and girls (otherwise known as the 'add-women-and-stir' approach) but whether the political vision underlying these objectives is adequate to challenge and respond to the injustices and inequalities they face.

The contemporary situation in IDA exposes the ways in which gender equality has been skilfully diluted and fundamentally altered to suit the particular influential neoliberal orientations.

This chapter demonstrates that a critical analysis of the political interpretation of 'development assistance' matters and has crucial consequences for the definition and incorporation of gender equality in IDA. The chapter further shows that other bilateral donors at the forefront of mainstreaming gender equality and who have different political inclinations find it difficult to resist this trend. Their tendency at best is to opt for a compromise – an all-ideologies-inclusive strategy, and at worst, to simply trade their original social orientation for the prevailing neoliberal trend.

The second section offers a critical examination of the varying interpretations of gender equality at the policy level in different political and geographical contexts in the following examples.

The Nicaraguan example focusing on abortion is a striking example of how certain Third Worldist perspectives reviving cultural relativism and anti-imperialism can at best serve the interest of elite women and powerful clergymen and at worst justify women's deaths. It also shows how gender equality and women's rights can be interpreted in a manner that serves the conservative ideology of some, to the cost of women's lives that are, de facto, defined as being worth far less than that of an embryo. In the best scenario, gender equality is thus considered an issue at the margins of democratisation, a secondary matter that can wait, while in the worst scenario, it is rejected as representing foreign interventionism.

The example of Museveni's politics and gender inequalities in Uganda illustrates the paradoxes in the use of Third Worldist and postcolonialist ideology to preserve what customary and colonial conservative ideologies have in common, namely patriarchal values and the maldistribution of resources.

In the case of Thomas Sankara's speech on International Women's Day in 1987 in Burkina Faso, it is argued that gender inequality as interpreted and described by Sankara still provides the most relevant and radical interpretation and perspective in the field of IDA, despite being espoused many years ago, by a man. It poses a direct challenge to Third World feminists, as Sankara demonstrated the possibility of being at once culturally self-critical and universalist, whilst still upholding an anti-imperialist position. This example shows that Sankara was and still remains an exception, not only amongst contemporary elite African leaders and contemporary Marxist revolutionary leaders around the world, but within the Left and the hegemonic feminist identity politics itself.

The examples presented above thus demonstrate that with the exception of Sankara, neither neoliberalist, so-called Marxist revolutionary, nor anti-imperialist regimes seem to have effectively challenged the patriarchal power structures and injustices faced by women in IDA. Thus, from the findings regarding interpretations of gender equality at both the donor policy and the country policy level, the conclusions above outline the implications of overshadowing socio-economic and substantive justice for women in IDA.

Notes

1 Donor policies are overall frameworks that set the priorities and orientations for IDA of a given agency over a set period of time. They include, amongst others policy papers, strategy papers and action plans.

2 Country policies are national policy frameworks that set the priorities and orientations for poverty reduction. These include poverty strategy action plans, national and sector policy papers as well as orientation speeches.

3 The significant four decades in questions are defined from the 1970s and first World Conference on Women to 2010.

4 Examples of key multilateral IDA agencies are the UN, the WB and the EU.

5 Examples of key bilateral IDA agencies are Swedish International Development Cooperation Agency (Sida), Danish International Development Agency (Danida) and UK Department for International Development (DFID).

6 Gender equality strategies are overall frameworks that provide the definition of gender equality of a particular agency and set the guidelines for mainstreaming gender equality in the IDA sectors and programmes.

7 See <www.worldbank.org/>.

8 See <www.dfid.gov.uk/>.

9 See <www.um.dk/en>.

10 See <www.sida.se/English/>.

11 For a neoliberal interpretation of development see R Peet and E Hartwick, *Theories of Development: Contentions, Arguments, Alternatives* (2nd edn, The Guilford Press 2009)

87 citing J Sachs, *The Economic Transformation of Eastern Europe: The Case of Poland* (P K Seidman Foundation 1991).

12 By socialist interpretation of development it is meant: 'the breaking down the structures that fosters inequalities, reorienting production to meet the needs of the poor'. Peet with Hartwick 273.

13 Marxist interpretation of development is understood in this context as the realisation that: 'Development takes place in class societies in such a way that the material benefits derived from hard work and increased productivity are unequally distributed'. Ibid 16–17.

14 Nicaraguan neoliberal government refers to the period 1996–2001 led by President Arnoldo Alemán from the neoliberal right-wing party. For a chronology of Nicaraguan political history, see <www.monde-diplomatique.fr/2009/07/A/17457>.

15 Nicaraguan neo-Sandinista government refers to the current government of Daniel Ortega of the Sandinista National Liberation Front Party, elected in 2006.

16 For details on the neoliberal reforms of Yoweri Museveni, president of Uganda since 1986 from the National Resistance Movement (NRM) see <http://apeaceofconflict.com/2009/02/24/the-other-side-of-assistance-the-neoliberal-agenda-in-uganda/>.

17 For biographic details of Thomas Sankara, well-known anti-imperialist and Marxist revolutionary, who led the Burkinabe revolution of 4 August 1983 and led the country until 15 October 1987, date at which he was assassinated see <www.thomassankara.net/>.

18 International Women's Day is marked on the 8th of March of every year when women are celebrated for their achievements. The first women's day was celebrated in 1911, a rally was organised to campaign for women's right to vote, to work, hold public office and end discrimination, amongst other rights. For more details see <www.internationalwomensday.com/>.

19 For instance, at the multilateral level the WB, UNIFEM, UNHCR, UNICEF, UNDP, the EU and at the bilateral level Sida, Danida, DFID, NORAD, FINNIDA, CIDA and the Dutch Development Cooperation are also at times referred to as 'the Nordic +' groups which share a common vision of IDA.

20 D Mosse and D Lewis, *The Aid Effect* (Pluto Press 2005) 3.

21 Ibid.

22 Ibid.

23 OECD, 'The Paris Declaration and the Accra Agenda'.

24 Ibid.

25 Mosse and Lewis 29.

26 DFID International Development Targets (IDTs) were: 1) A reduction by half in the proportion of people living in extreme poverty by 2001; 2) Universal primary education in all countries by 2015; 3) Gender disparities in primary and secondary education removed by 2005; 4) A reduction by two-thirds in the mortality rates for infants and children under five and a reduction by three-quarters in maternal mortality by 2015; 5) Access through the primary health care system to reproductive health services for all individuals of appropriate ages as soon as possible and no later than 2015; 6) To implement national strategies for sustainable development in all countries by 2005, so as to ensure that current trends in the loss of environmental resources are effectively reversed at both global and national levels by 2015.

27 The WB, 'Integrating Gender into the WB's Work: A Strategy for Action' (The WB January 2002) <//web.worldbank.org/WBSITE/EXTERNAL/TOPICS/EXTGENDER/0,contentMDK:20167522~menuPK:489177~pagePK:148956~piPK:216618~theSitePK:336868,00.html>.

28 Ibid.

29 The WB Policy Research Report, *Engendering Development Through Gender Equality, Resources and Voice* (The WB 2001).

30 Ibid 181–203.

31 Ibid 196.
32 The WB, 'Improving Women's Lives: WB Actions Since Beijing' (The WB January 2005) 41.
33 Ibid 27.
34 Ibid 67.
35 The WB Policy Research Report, *Engendering Development* 73.
36 See sections related to 'The Business Case for Mainstreaming Gender: The Empirical Links of Gender to Poverty and Growth, Gender Equality and Growth, Gender and Poverty Reduction and Development Effectiveness' in The WB, 'Integrating Gender into the WB's Work: A Strategy for Action' (WB January 2002) 4–12.
37 The WB Policy Research Report, *Engendering Development*.
38 W Mansell, B Meteyard and A Thomson, *A Critical Introduction to Law* (3rd edn, Cavendish Publishing 2004) 145.
39 The WB, 'Gender Equality as Smart Economics: A WB Group Gender Action Plan for the Fiscal Years 2007–2010' (The WB September 2006) 2. <http://siteresources.worldbank.org/INTGENDER/Resources/GAPNov2.pdf>.
40 F Watkins, 'Evaluation of DFID Development Assistance: Gender Equality and Women's Empowerment, DFID's Experience of Gender Mainstreaming: 1995 to 2004' (DFID December 2004) 10.
41 Francis Watkins argues that i) 'The growing importance since 2000 of the Millennium Development Goals (MDGs) in DFID's work has narrowed the focus of Gender Equality Policy to social sectors, such as girls' education and maternal health, with relatively little attention being given to gender in areas such as economic opportunities and decision-making and ii) Overall commitments to Gender Equality objectives appear to have declined since a peak in 2000, but with considerable variations between country programmes. The reduction in commitments may be linked to decentralisation in DFID or to changes in Aid modalities'. Watkins, 'Evaluation of DFID Development Assistance'.
42 DFID, White Paper on International Development, 'Eliminating World Poverty: Making Governance Work for the Poor' (DFID July 2006). <http://webarchive.nationalarchives.gov.uk/+/www.dfid.gov.uk/Media-Room/News-Stories/2006/New-White-Paper-on-International-Development/>.
43 Ibid.
44 Ibid.
45 DFID, 'Gender Equality Action Plan' (DFID 2007–2009) 2 <www.dfid.gov.uk/pubs/files/gender-equality-plan-2007.pdf>.
46 The plan covers four areas which have more to do with form and systems than substance: i) results ii) building partnerships iii) using our resources and iv) planning for the future. Given the expected results, DFID anticipated the following: i) quality evidence and information available to and used by DFID and decision-makers ii) more accurate and comprehensive systems measuring practice on gender equality and to iii) promote accountability for gender equality and address reputational risk.
47 Danida, 'Women in Development: Danida's WID Policy Towards the Year 2000' (Denmark Ministry of Foreign Affairs 1993).
48 Ibid 7. See also E Boserup, *Women's Role in Economic Development* (Earthscan 1970).
49 Ibid 13. See also B Keller, A-L Klausen and S Mukasa, *The Challenge of Working with Gender: Experiences from Danish-Ugandan Development Cooperation* (Danida 2000).
50 Danida, 'Women in Development' 15.
51 Ibid 16. See also LA Richey, 'In Search of feminist Foreign Policy: Gender, Development, and State Identity' (June 2001) 36(2) *Cooperation and Conflict* 177.
52 Danida 'Gender Equality in Danish Development Cooperation, Strategy' (Denmark Ministry of Foreign Affairs Strategy 2004) 10 <http://amg.um.dk/en/menu/PoliciesAndStrategies/Cross-Cutting+Issues/GenderEquality/Strategy.htm>.
53 Ibid 2.

54 See G R Olsen and L Udsholt, *The Danish Aid Administration: Between Politics and Technical Rationality* (Copenhagen Centre for Development Research 1995) CDR Working Paper 1995 [95]12 <www.amazon.com/Danish-aid-administration-technical-rationality/dp/B0006F8UO2> accessed 10 February 2011: 'First, like it has been the case for other donors the WB has become an increasingly important international determinant of Danish Aid Policies. This is narrowly linked to the growing importance of the Bank in Development cooperation, particularly the poor African countries to whom Denmark has traditionally given priority in its Development cooperation'. See also P Mosley, J Harrigan and J Toye, *Aid and Power: The WB and Policy-Based Lending* (Routledge 1991) 3–61.
55 See Olsen and Udsholt, 'The Danish Aid Administration' (n 422); K E Svendsen, 'Danish Aid: Old Battles in Western Middle Powers and Global Poverty' in O Stokke (ed), (Scandinavian Institute of Africa Studies 1995) and K E Svendsen, *Social Development and International Development cooperation in Welfare, Development and Security: Three Danish Essays* (The Danish National Institute of Social Research 1989) 35–58.
56 'Gender Equality in Danish Development Cooperation' 11.
57 Ibid 9.
58 Denmark MFA, *Strategic Framework for Gender Equality, Rights and Diversity* (2014) 7.
59 Government Bill 1962 (Sweden) 100.
60 Sida was created by merging SIDA, BITS, Sweden Corp, SAREC and Sandö U-centrum international training and course centre. A sixth development objective was adopted in 1996.
61 Government Bill 15.
62 Parliamentary Committee of Inquiry into Sweden's Policy for Global Development, 'The Role of Development Assistance' (Globkom, the Committee on Sweden's Policy for Global Development 2002) 207–273. <www.sweden.gov.se/sb/d/574/a/93676>.
63 Ibid. See also H Malmqvist, 'Development Aid, Humanitarian Assistance and Emergency Releif' in 'Building Stability in Africa: Challenges for the New Millennium' 46 Monograph (February 2000).
64 Parliamentary Committee (n 431). Sweden development assistance ranked high with Sweden's aid volume as a proportion of gross national income (GNI) amounted to 0.98 per cent in 2008 and 1.03 per cent in 2006. <www.sweden.gov.se/sb/d/586/a/123522>.
65 Parliamentary Committee (n 431). See also the related DAC member peer review, OECD-DAC, 'Sweden (2000), Development Co-operation Review' (2000) <www.oecd.org/document/15/0,3746,en_2649_34603_1883855_1_1_1_1,00.html>.
66 Ibid.
67 See Sida, *Evaluation of Sida's Support to Development Co-operation for the Promotion of Gender Equality* (Sida Evaluations 2001); DFID, *Evaluation of DFID's Policy and Practice in Support of Gender Equality and Women's Empowerment* (DFID 2006).
68 Sida, *Gender Equality: Sida's Policy and Methods at a Glance, Key Steering Documents* (Sida 2005) 1.
69 Sida, *Policy Promoting Gender Equality in Development Co-operation 2005–2010* (Sida 2005) 4.
70 Ibid 6.
71 'According to the Swedish Policy for Global Development, a "rights perspective" and a "perspective of the poor" should influence all levels of interventions and work. The rights perspective includes human rights; the rights of the child; democracy; women's rights and equal opportunities for women and men'. Ibid 5.
72 Sida, *Gender Equality: Sida's Policy and Methods at a Glance* 1.
73 Ellen Barry 'Sweden's Proponent of 'Feminist Foreign Policy,' *Shaped by Abuse* (*The New York Times*, 17 November 2017).
74 See Nicaraguan neoliberal government.
75 See Nicaraguan neo-Sandinista government.
76 For details on the neoliberal reforms of Yoweri Museveni.

77 For biographic details of Thomas Sankara.
78 International Women's Day.
79 Ibid.
80 Ibid 12.
81 Ixchen was founded in 1989 with the aim of promoting sexual and reproductive health for women from a human rights and gender equality perspective. It receives funding from the governments of Switzerland, Norway, Holland and Denmark. There are 12 Ixchen locations throughout Nicaragua with a team of professional counsellors providing reproductive and general health care, sexual and reproductive health care, intervention and care for domestic violence victims both juridical and psychological support and educational activities that promotes women's rights, empowerment and domestic violence prevention. See Ixchen website <www.fsdinternational.org/node/view/192>.
82 UN Committee on the Elimination of Discrimination against Women, 'Consideration of reports submitted by states parties under Article 18 of the Convention on the Elimination of all Forms of Discrimination Against Women, Fifth periodic report of States parties, Nicaragua' (9 September 1999) CEDAW/C/NIC/5 <www.un.org/womenwatch/daw/cedaw/reports.htm#n>.
83 See PAHO, 'Nicaragua: Basic Country Health Profiles' (PAHO 1999). <www.paho.org/english/sha/profiles.htm>.
84 Ibid.
85 Ibid.
86 Ixchen, Centro de Mujeres and DFID, *No más vidas truncadas, Documentando delitos de violencia sexual contra niñas y adolescentes en cinco departamentos de Nicaragua* (Ixchen Centro de Mujeres and DFID 2006) 100.
87 'Sweden Suspends Economic Aid to Nicaragua for Not Allowing Abortion' *Catholic News Agency* (Managua, 29 August 2007) <www.Catholicnewsagency.com/news/sweden_suspends_economic_aid_to_nicaragua_for_not_allowing_abortion/>.
88 L Mannen, 'The Government War on Women's Rights in Nicaragua: Feminists Stand Up Against Anti-Abortion Crusade and Daniel Ortega's Rightward Turn' (February-March 2009) (30) 1 *Freedom Socialist* <www.socialism.com/drupal-6.8/?q=search/node/Laura%20Mannen> accessed 10 February 2011. On further details of Daniel Ortega's rape allegations on his stepdaughter, which to many Latin American feminists exemplify the non-credibility of Ortega's return as a Left and pro-feminist revolutionary leader, see T Rodgers, 'President Ortega vs. The Feminists' *Time* (16 October 2008) <www.time.com/time/world/article/0,8599,1850451,00.html>.
89 See Mannen.
90 Ibid. For a detailed portrait of the 'new' Daniel Ortega see P Davison, 'Daniel Ortega: Return of the Sandinista' *The Independent* (London, 8 November 2006) <www.independent.co.uk/news/world/americas/daniel-ortega-return-of-the-sandinista-423459.html>.
91 Ibid.
92 Ibid. See also M Molyneux, 'The Politics of Abortion in Nicaragua: Revolutionary Pragmatism or Feminism in the Realm of Necessity?' (May 1988) *Feminist Review* 29.
93 JE Getgen, 'Reproductive Injustice: An Analysis of Nicaragua's Complete Abortion Ban' (2008) 4 *International Law Journal* 144.
94 'Nicaragua Outlaws Abortion Even to Save a Woman's Life' *IPAS* (Chapel Hill October 2006) <http://ipas.org/library/news/news_items/Nicaragua_outlaws_abortion_even_to_save_a_woman's_life.as>. Before the repeal of Article 165, the Nicaraguan Criminal Code provided for therapeutic abortions and for legal purposes, called for three physicians and the consent of the spouse or nearest relative of the woman to intervene. See H Luz and M Reyes and others, 'Invoking Health and Human Rights to Ensure Access to Legal Abortion: The Case of a Nine-Year-Old Girl from Nicaragua' (2006) 9 *Health & Hum RTS* 62–66, cited in Getgen. See also D Lloyd, 'Nicaragua's

Abortion Ban Is Inhumane and Backward' *Politics Daily* (24 February 2010) <www.politicsdaily.com/2010/02/24/nicaraguas-abortion-ban-is-inhumane-and-backward/>.

95 IAR Lakshmanan, 'Nicaraguan Abortion Ban Called a Threat to Lives' *Boston Globe* (26 November 2006) A1. To the best of the author's knowledge, the total number of women who have died and the excess maternal mortality has not been officially reported. As of 27 November 2007, however, some reports claimed that 87 women had died since the complete abortion ban. 'Investigan denuncia a red de mujeres' *MSN* (27 November 2007), <http://latino.msn.com/noticias/articles/articlepage.aspx?cp-documentid=5429875>. Of these 87 women, 17 would have been saved had the abortion ban not existed and 12 others committed suicide, cited in Getgen. See also IPAS 'Analysing maternal deaths in Nicaragua' (26 June 2008) <www.ipas.org/Library/News/News_Items/Analyzing_maternal_deaths_in_Nicaragua.aspx>.

96 R Carroll, 'Killer Law: Special Report from Managua on Abortion' *The Guardian* (London, Monday 8 October 2007 and Friday 13 June 2008). See also UNHRC, 'Report on Violations of Women's Human Rights to Therapeutic Abortion and Emergency Medical Care, and of the Rights of women's Human Rights Defenders: In Response to the Second and Third Periodic Report' 94th Session (Geneva, 13–31 October 2008).

97 Ibid Caroll.

98 Centre for Reproductive Rights, 'Inter-American Commission Issues Landmark Statement Declaring Nicaragua's Abortion Ban Jeopardizes Women's Human Rights' (12 January 2006) <http://reproductiverights.org/en/press-room/inter-american-commission-issues-landmark-statement-declaring-nicaragua%E2%80%99s-abortion-ban-je>.

99 UN Committee for the Elimination of All Forms of Discrimination Against Women, 'Concluding Comments of the Committee on the Elimination of Discrimination Against Women: Nicaragua' (2 February 2007) UN Doc CEDAW/C/NIC/CO/6. See also UN Committee for the Elimination of All Forms of Discrimination Against Women, 'CEDAW Shadow Report: Nicaragua' (December 2006).

100 T Adeyemi and A Stevens, 'Nicaraguan Activists Press Abortion Legal Case' *Women's e-News* (16 March 2007) citing Pope Benedict XVI post-synodal apostolic exhortation: *sacramentum caritatis* of the Holy Father Benedict XVI to the bishops, clergy, consecrated persons and the lay faithful on the Eucharist as the source and summit of the church's life and mission § 83 (2007) <www.womensenews.org/article.cfm/dyn/aid/3099>, cited in Getgen. See also Letter from S A Canton to NC Cardinal, Minister of Foreign Affairs (10 November 2006) <http://reproductiverights.org/en/search/google/Nicaragua?query=Nicaragua&cx=013411022521635236165%3Aqnmyx__l41c&cof=FORID%3A11&sitesearch=#1030>; S Ertelt, 'Pope Benedict XVI Congratulates Nicaragua on Keeping Abortion Illegal' *LifeNews* (Washington, DC, 25 September 2007) <www.lifenews.com/2007/09/25/int-446/>.

101 UNDP, *Human Development Report* (UNDP 2009) 167. <http://hdr.undp.org/en/reports/global/hdr2009/>.

102 Ibid.

103 T Cargill, 'Uganda – Still the Donors' Darling' (December 2004) 60/12 *The World Today* 26–27; A Baffour, 'Behind Every "successful" Darling . . . there Is a WB (sorry) Donor' *New African* (London June 2001) <http://findarticles.com/p/articles/mi_qa5391/is_200106/ai_n21473476/>.

104 F Kuteesa, E Tumusiime-Mutebile, A Whitworth and T Williamson, *Uganda's Economic Reforms: Insider Accounts* (Oxford University Press 2010); H Ware, *Africa on a Global Stage* (Africa World Press 2005) 168.

105 WTO, 'Trade Policy Review (TPR) of Uganda' (Trade Policy Body of WTO, 19–21 December 2001) TPRB/182 <www.wto.org/english/tratop_e/tpr_e/tp182_e.htm>. See also 'A More Hopeful Continent, The Lion Kings? Africa Is Now One of the World's Fastest-Growing Regions' *The Economist* (New York, 6 January 2011) <www.economist.com/node/17853324>.

106 D Obot, 'A Fascinating Example of Successful Liberalisation' (Social Watch 2003) 166–167. <www.socwatch.org/node/10811> accessed 10 February 2011. See also SN Ssewanyana, 'Growth, Inequality, Cash Transfers and Poverty in Uganda: Country Study' (International Policy Centre for Inclusive Growth UNDP 2009) <www.ipc-undp.org/pub/IPCCountryStudy19.pdf>; N Ndebesa, 'The Inequalities Will Soon Breed Tragedy' *The New Vision* (Kampala, 21 December 2010) <http://allafrica.com/stories/201012220017.html>.

107 The Constitution of the Republic of Uganda (1995) <www.ugandaonlinelawlibrary.com/lawlib/constitution.asp>.

108 For a full historical account of the dramatic growth in a relatively short span of time of the Ugandan women's movement see AM Tripp, *Women & Politics in Uganda* (Fountain 2000).

109 See UWONET, 'Women and Land Rights in Uganda' (FES 1997): 'They highlighted the prevalence of widows being tragically forced off their homesteads by their husband's families. They also argued in favour of what became known as the spousal co-ownership amendment. This stated that without the wife's right to family property, husbands could not sell family land without the wife consenting or without gaining any financial benefit from the transaction. The lobbying of women's civil society organisations gained the support of some women MPs who championed the amendment in Parliament'.

110 Land Act 1998.

111 For a full account of how the land clause was conceived and courageously presented and tabled before parliament see M Matembe, *Gender, Politics and Constitution Making in Uganda* (Fountain Publishers 2002) 234–253.

112 See Tripp.

113 Response to President Yoweri Museveni's view on the reform of the Domestic Relations Bill by Hon. Sheila Kawamara Mishambi Member of East African Legislative Assembly (April 2003) <www.wougnet.org/Alerts/drbresponseSKM.html>.

114 Ibid.

115 The term 'Western' is presumably to be construed as referring to a combined European and American history into a sole socio-cultural concept and phenomenon.

116 General Law in Uganda as in other East and Southern Africa's jurisdiction is supposed to apply to all persons regardless of their ethnic origins and customary traditions.

117 Order in Council 1902 (Uganda).

118 The Succession (Amendment) Decree 1972 (Uganda).

119 Children Act 1996 (Uganda).

120 I Mulyagonja, 'Family Law Reform in Uganda: A Tale of Petty Issues, Bitterness and Crocodile Tears'(South African Constitutional Litigation and Legal Development Project Conference, Windhoek March 2001)

121 Domestic Relations Bill.

122 Ingrid Yngström argues that in Tanzania this was not always the case, as women used to be able to claim land from their families. But secondary rights became standard practice by the late 1950s when men began to 'assert greater control over land, by limiting land transfers made by lineage members to female family members'. See I Yngström, 'Women, Wives and Land Rights in Africa: Situating Gender Beyond the Household in the Debate over Land Policy and Changing Tenure Systems' (2002) 30(1) *Development Studies* 21, cited in SF Joireman, 'Applying Property Rights Theory to Africa: The Consequences of Formalizing Informal Land Rights' (Meeting of the International Society for New Institutional Economics, Wheaton College Boulder 2006).

123 The Penal Code Act 1950 (Uganda).

124 The marital rape exemption was abolished in England and Wales in 1991 by the Appellate Committee of the House of Lords, in the case of *R v R*.

125 See E Kharono, *Feminist Challenge to the Land Question: Options for Meaningful Action: A Concept Paper* (The African Gender Institute, University of Cape Town October 2010).

126 J Brial, 'L'assassinat de Thomas Sankara, Président du Burkina Faso, le 15 octobre 1987: Causes et Conséquences' (Mémoire de DEA, Université de Montpellier 2006).

127 Ibid.

128 Sida, 'Evaluation of the National Democratic Institutes' Programme on Strengthening Women's Participation in Political and Decentralisation Processes in Burkina Faso' (Sida, Evaluations 2008) 1–44; Danida, 'Draft Programme Formulation on Democratic Governance in Burkina Faso' (Ministry for Foreign Affairs Denmark 2004).

129 Sokari, 'African Revolutionaries: Remembering Maurice Bishop and Thomas Sankara' (19 October 2010) in *African History, History Is a Weapon* <www.blacklooks.org/2010/10/african-revolutionaries-remembering-mauice-bishop-and-thomas-sankara/>.

130 T Sankara, 'La libération de la femme: une exigence du future' (8 March 1987). Sankara delivered this speech on international women's day in a meeting in Ouagadougou, Burkina Faso. The full text is available in French <www.thomassankara.net>.

131 Sankara. See also Thomas Sankara, 'L'Homme Intègre' *Le monde Diplomatique* (Paris, 15 Octobre 2007).

132 Sankara. See the movement of women in black fighting against the impunity of the assassination of journalist and writer Robert Zongo <www.dailymotion.com/video/xej7dx_les-femmes-en-noir-du-burkina-faso_news>.

133 Sankara. See also B Jaffré, 'Thomas Sankara ou la dignité de l'Afrique' *Le Monde Diplomatique* (Paris, 15 Octobre 2007).

134 Sankara (n 519). See also A-C Robert, 'Président des Pauvres' (avril-mai 2007) 93 Manière de Voir; C Benabdessadok, 'Femmes et Révolution ou Comment Libérer la Moitié de la Société' (Décembre 1985) 20 *Revue Politique Africaine*.

135 Ibid. See also MS Kanse Lean, 'Le CNR et les femmes: de la difficulté de libérer la "moitié du ciel »' (Mars 1989) *Revue Politique Africaine*.

136 ibid. See MA Waters and MP Cartes *Thomas Sankara parle: La révolution au Burkina Faso de 1983–1987* (Edition Pathfinder 2007).

137 See Sankara. For details on Sankara's politics and coherence with his vision of women's liberation see B Jaffré, 'Biographie de Thomas Sankara: La patrie ou la Mort' (L' Harmattan 1997).

138 See Sankara's speech on Third World debt <www.thomassankara.net>.

139 B Bayili, *Religion, Droit et Pouvoir au Burkina Faso: Les Lyèlà du Burkina Faso* (Editions l'Harmattan 1998).

4 Universal nocturnes of injustices

The chapter begins by assessing whether it is possible to distinguish the universal from the particular in key examples of specific violations of women's human rights at the field level. In this way, the chapter seeks to challenge the prevailing assumptions of identity politics perspectives that have tended to promote anti-essentialism through multiculturalism,[1] resulting in the delegitimisation of universalism and with it the claim that women's rights are human rights.[2]

If asserting that there are both commonalities and differences in these violations across cultures would be stating the obvious, the first section examines whether it is possible to identify universal patterns whilst avoiding postcolonialist critiques. This section seeks to demonstrate that it is misguided to simply reject universalism altogether.[3] Rather, it is the nature of the approach utilised which needs to be challenged and refined.

Thus, the starting points for this chapter are women's human rights violations concerning violence against women and gender inequalities related to the unequal distribution of resources in Uganda. By extrapolating the related data in Uganda, this section attempts to identify commonalities with other neighbouring countries, regions and continents in order to uncover universal connections with similar patterns of violations of women's human rights and gender inequalities. The approach utilised thus explores the local contexts as a point of departure, as opposed to making abstract and 'ahistorical' generalisations.[4]

This chapter further seeks to show that violations of fundamental women's human rights and gender inequalities cannot be defined as if locked within the boundaries of cultural differences and identities. Such an approach ultimately risks the provision of justification and legitimisation of these very same inequalities and violations. In this context, the chapter discusses (mis)representation, (un)recognition and (mal)distribution of power and resources through concrete examples of IDA projects in countries from purposively different continents, respectively in Burkina Faso and Cambodia.

Transcending socio-cultural particularisms of women's human rights violations

In order to challenge a cultural relativist position, this section examines whether the universality of gender inequalities and women's human rights violations discussed in Chapter 1 can be substantiated. In order to do so, this section takes local realities and knowledge as its starting point, to highlight patterns of women human rights violations and gender inequalities across other countries and continents.

The starting point is thus women's human rights violations related to violence against women and gender inequalities related to the unequal distribution of resources in Uganda. By extrapolating such data from Uganda and Cambodia, this section seeks to identify commonalities with other neighbouring countries, regions and continents. The approach utilised takes a local context as a point of departure as opposed to abstract and 'ahistorical' generalisations.

Universal commonalities in all forms of violence against women

Under the *recognition* of specific forms of women's rights violations, a pre-condition to reach the following SDG 5 targets is to transcend socio-cultural boundaries that legitimise the profoundly illegitimate.

Target 5.2: Eliminate all forms of violence against all women and girls in the public and private spheres, including trafficking and sexual and other types of exploitation.

Target 5.3: Eliminate all harmful practices, such as child, early and forced marriage and female genital mutilation.

A most compelling photo-illustrated report[5] presents a sample of individual women's experiences in the miner community of Chorolque, situated at 5,052 metres above sea level in Bolivia. At this particular location temperatures can reach minus 20 degrees Celsius, where stone and ice cover the landscape inhabited by 5,000 miners. In this poverty-riddled context, violence against women is commonplace, as the following (anonymous) witness account testifies:

> When I came back from hospital with my newborn baby, I was a bit late at home at about 12:30 p.m. My husband shouted at me, 'Do you think you can just go in and out and about as you please?' he shouted and started to beat me. Later, I was about to serve him lunch, when he slapped me again to remind me that I made him wait for his lunch. I took the big spoon to defend myself, but he was stronger and took it off my hands and started to beat me all over with it. I tried to escape to the other room where the newborn baby was sleeping to ensure it would not wake up. And even then, he came after me again shouting at me: 'How dare you go out without having cooked for me first?' He kicked me in my stomach, I fell back on the glass wardrobe that broke on me, he continued to beat me saying I was just a stupid and a disobedient wife and that all this was my fault! Until today I cannot walk properly as a result.[6]

In a compelling book about violent crime perpetrated by women in Uganda, Lillian Tibatemwa-Ekirikubinza[7] presents the results of her research into the case histories of women who have committed violent crimes in the country. By outlining the precipitating factors leading up to their action, the author argues that in Ugandan society women are often left with few real choices for recourse to justice. This is the testimony of Karugaba, one such woman:

> He would abuse me as a bad cook and throw the food in my face. He used to say I was filthy dirty and that my bedroom stunk. He had even prevented me from sleeping in his bed. Together with my youngest child, I was permanently sleeping on a mattress on the floor of our bedroom, while my husband was using the bed. Before this event, he used to bring women in the house and I would have to leave my marital bed for him and his concubines.[8]

The third example occurred in Paris, on 12 January 2010 in the evening. Rayhana, aged 45, was walking home from the theatre.[9] Rayhana is a scriptwriter, actress and incidentally, a beautiful Algerian woman with long curly red hair. That evening, as on every evening that month, she played a part in the play which she had written herself and in which she tells the stories of veiled women, particularly the tragic story of a 16-year-old who is at risk of murder by her brother to save his 'honour', as she is pregnant outside marriage. Rayhana told the journalist the following story:

> As I was walking home after the play, two men started to shout at me, insulting me, by calling me a 'whore' and an 'infidel'. I accelerated my foot steps and lowered my head in silence, hoping they would leave. They continued to shout, 'Do you think we don't know who you are? We have warned you already about your play!' All of a sudden, I felt I was caught from behind and something which smelled like petrol was thrown in my face. As soon as I realised what it was, I could distinguish a lit cigarette approaching my face.[10]

Before her attackers succeeded in disfiguring her face, Rayhana managed to run away even though she could no longer see.

The three examples above relate events which took place in different cultures, within different religious contexts, at different times and locations. Reading these testimonies, one could choose to focus on the details which differentiate these three accounts and highlight the subtle nuances which do exist in these three events. However, for the purpose of challenging patriarchal systemic violence which subordinates women by essentially humiliating them in a sub-human status, how strategic or indeed useful would it be to focus on the detailed differences? Whose interests would it really serve to focus on the differences – the victims or the perpetrators whose actions would surely find a cultural 'explanation' anchored in these differences? Eclipsing the obvious commonalities in these accounts thus amounts to diluting the women's core defence, 'robbing' each of these accounts of a theoretical framework with the potential to de-isolate these individual situations and connect them to a broader and systemic understanding of such violations globally.

To illustrate this perspective further, violence against women in Uganda is taken as the point of departure below. Notwithstanding the importance of each and every form of violence against women in Uganda, one particular experience which combines domestic violence, marital rape and HIV/AIDS in Uganda was singled out in an entire Human Rights Watch report[11] as being one of the most lethal and yet common examples of abuse or combination of forms of abuse which women have faced within the domestic sphere.[12] In Uganda as elsewhere, intimate partner violence also includes marital rape and the inability to negotiate condom use to prevent HIV/AIDS infection. As in other countries in which women are largely or entirely financially dependent on their partner, the circle of domestic violence, marital rape and HIV/AIDS infection is often an inescapable spiral of breaches of fundamental women's human rights, leaving women with little alternative but to wait for death in silence, as illustrated in the testimony below

> He used to force me to have sex with him. He would beat me and slap me when I refused. I never used a condom with him. . . . When I got pregnant I went for a medical check-up. When I gave birth, and the child had passed away, they told me I was HIV-positive. I cried. The doctor told me 'Wipe your tears, the whole world is sick'.[13]

Based on 120 interviews conducted in Uganda from 2002 to 2003, the Human Rights Watch report establishes a systematic correlation between domestic violence, marital rape and HIV/AIDS infection. Many of the women interviewed by the Human Rights Watch team were afraid to introduce the subject of prophylactic protection with their husband for fear of being beaten, either for daring to suspect their husbands of having extramarital affairs, or because they might be accused of adultery[14] themselves. If they did raise the subject, violence and/or forced unprotected sex was typically the result. Thirty-four out of 50 women interviewed by the Human Rights Watch team confirmed that their husbands physically forced them to have sex without protection, commonly as a marital prerogative.[15]

Determining the extent of domestic violence in Uganda as elsewhere comes up against several methodological challenges. Whilst the number of workshop reports and research analyses on the issue are often illustrated with the strength of powerful personal accounts, they often lack statistical data at the regional and national levels to show the actual extent of the problem with accuracy. Evidence showing an increase in cases of domestic violence can be nevertheless found in specific reports, mini-surveys, media reports and articles addressing the issue as illustrated by the example here below.

At the time of the Human Rights Watch report, a community-based study on domestic violence in rural Uganda[16] showed that out of 5,109 women of reproductive age in the Rakai District of Uganda, 30% had experienced physical threats or physical abuse from their current partner. Analyses of risk factors highlight the pivotal role of male partners' alcohol consumption and HIV/AIDS infection in increasing the risk of male domestic violence against women. Some 70% of men and 90% of women interviewed regarded beating a man's wife or female partner as a justifiable part of husbands and wives' relations, especially when husbands have to remind wives that they are in charge.[17]

Regarding post-conflict and marginalised regions in Uganda such as Northern Uganda and Karamoja, this reveals that many communities appear to be in a state of latent conflict, with increasingly frequent manifestations of overt conflict in the form of clashes between communities and government officials, violent community disputes over boundaries or resources, or increased sexual and gender-based violence (SGBV) due to changing gender relations during and after the conflict amongst other examples.[18]

Beyond many legislative advances,[19] the Domestic Relations and Marriage and Divorce Bill, which has been tabled since the 1960s, represents the most important loophole in the legislative framework for the fulfilment of women's human rights and gender equality. SGBV, harmful traditional practices (HTPs) such as early and forced marriages are persisting, especially in rural areas, despite the constitutional provision on the minimum age for marriage and the legal prohibition on female genital mutilation (FGM).[20] Although there is no substantive provision on the right to health under Uganda's Bill of Rights, the Constitution provides for several rights that are determinants of health.[21]

Despite the annulment of the Anti-Homosexuality Act in 2014, discrimination against lesbians, gay, bisexual and transgender people and harassment and violence against them persist. This is as it were, a logical continuation to stereotypes that perpetuate discrimination against women, children, persons with disabilities, sexual minorities, ethnic minority groups, most-at-risk populations and people living with HIV.[22] During the UPR review 2016, concerns were raised that the government of Uganda had enacted several laws creating an increasingly hostile environment for civil society and human rights defenders.[23]

On a global level, the First World Report on Violence and Health back in 2002[24] echoed this by revealing the alarming extent of domestic violence worldwide. The report painted a global picture which showed that between 10% and 69% of women documented in 48 population-based surveys from around the world had reported being physically assaulted by an intimate male partner, this being one of the most fundamental and persistent violations of women's human rights.[25] According to the first report of such kind, physical violence in intimate relationships entailed common characteristics across the globe. It was often accompanied by psychological abuse and in a third to over one-half of cases, it also involved sexual violence. Partner violence also accounted for a significant number of deaths among women. Studies from a range of countries began to emerge showing that 40–70% of female murder victims were killed by their own husband or boyfriend, often during an ongoing abusive relationship.[26] Findings from the reported surveys began to demonstrate that sexual assault by intimate partners was neither rare nor unique to any continent, region, country, ethnic group or socio-economic and cultural background. Figures showing the percentage of women reporting sexual victimisation by an intimate partner in selected population-based surveys from 1989 to 2000 ranged from 7.5% to 42% in Durango, Mexico; 28.9% in Bangkok, Thailand; 23% in North London, UK; 25% in the Midlands province in Zimbabwe; 7.5% in Sweden and 7.7% in the US.[27]

Whereas domestic violence still often falls outside both formal legal systems and customary law, sexual and gender-based violence was at least recognised by the international community in the public international law domain as being a weapon of war and torture.[28] This included the use of torture and rape of detained women in conflict situations and crimes against humanity, including rape, sexual slavery, forced abortion or delivery, forced sterilisation and forced pregnancy. Rape was used as a tool of mass destruction during many armed conflicts in Liberia, Rwanda, Uganda and more recently in the DRC.[29] In some armed conflicts such as the Rwanda genocide in 1994 and 1992 in the Former Republic of Yugoslavia and Sierra Leone in 1999, rape has been used as a deliberate strategy to subvert community bonds and as a tool of 'ethnic cleansing'. During the 1994 genocide in Rwanda, approximately 500,000 women were raped, and an estimated 5,000 pregnancies resulted from those rapes.[30]

During the 1999 conflict in Sierra Leone, over 50% of women experienced some form of sexual violence, as this victim testifies:

> I was captured together with my husband, my three young children and other civilians as we were fleeing from the RUF when they entered Jaiweii. Two rebels asked to have sex with me but when I refused, they beat me with the butt of their guns. My legs were bruised and I lost my three front teeth. Then the two rebels raped me in front of my children and other civilians. Many other women were raped in public places. I also heard of a woman from Kalu village near Jaiweii being raped only one week after having given birth. The RUF stayed in Jaiweii village for four months and I was raped by three other wicked rebels throughout this period.[31]

In only five months of conflict in Bosnia in 1992, an estimated 20,000 to 50,000 women were raped.[32] Although quantitative statistics are sporadic with regard to the actual extent of women's human rights violations in the context of Northern Uganda conflict situation, an increasing number of reports and literature focus on experiences women face as a direct result of the conflict. Isis-Women's International cross-cultural exchange (Isis-WICCE) published a report on women's experiences of armed conflict situations in Uganda.[33] The report examined the effects of some of the longest-running civil conflicts in the history of Uganda, as specifically experienced by women and girls. The report provided details which are largely orally reported, about women's abduction and rape, forced marriages with member of rebel groups and of mutilations. Women who survived abductions by rebel forces reveal the further cruelty of government soldiers in tales of individual and gang rapes, forced prostitution, unwanted pregnancies and a life of extreme deprivation in IDP camps and supposedly 'protected villages'.[34]

Furthermore, the report detailed a plethora of war-related physical, mental and psychological disorders encountered in Awer, an IDP camp close to Gulu in Northern Uganda. Nearly all women interviewed had experienced at least one episode of torture and only a quarter of women survivors that experienced the subsequent effects, including infertility, chronic pelvic pain, sexual transmitted infections and vaginal tears, actually gained access to qualified health workers. The authors of the reports concluded that the war in Northern Uganda had debilitated the whole population living in the region.[35]

Based on the material examined above, it can be thus concluded that sexual and gender-based violence is a 'universal' violation of women's fundamental dignity and human rights across private, public and conflict-related spheres, as it is perpetrated in different countries, amidst different ethnic, religious and socio-economic backgrounds. However, one also has to conclude that there remains a major difficulty in recognising domestic violence as a 'universal' violation of women's rights and even, in some instances, as a simple crime. Far from being a Ugandan specificity, the notion of domestic violence, especially rape within marriage seems to be so structurally rooted as a husband's prerogative that the UN could only issue a resolution[36] denouncing rape in conflict situations, outside of the private/domestic sphere. Whilst making marital rape and domestic violence a 'crime' is a common battle that feminists across the globe have had to struggle for, its recognition, *tout court*, cannot and should not be confined to cultural specificities, falling thus into the 'culturally acceptable', as 'culturally different'.

Another example, which has been the object of much debate between cultural relativists and women's human rights activists, is female genital mutilation (FGM). FGM is the collective name given to a number of cultural practices which involve the partial or total cutting of female genitals for non-medical reasons.[37] FGM was performed for example in Uganda as early as infancy and as late as age 30 and most commonly, girls experience FC/FGM between 4 and 12 years of age. These cultural practices were perpetrated in light of traditional rituals by practitioners, were condoned and assisted by families, women and mothers themselves on the front line, religious groups and entire communities.[38] Female genital mutilations often result in harmful physical and psychological consequences. Although FGM is paradoxically undertaken as a symbolic celebration of entering 'womanhood', supposedly without conscious intention of inflicting harm, its damaging physical, sexual and psychological consequences make it first and foremost an act of violence against women and children.[39] Uganda is now amongst many nations, despite some cultural relativist critiques, which have enacted laws criminalising FGM.[40] If anything, FGM – whilst evidently a deeply culturally rooted practice – is still not confined solely within the boundaries of one particular culture. Rather, it is practiced in many countries and is supported by a common underlying rationale of men's control over female sexuality.[41]

In conclusion, the different categories of violence against women illustrated above show that the same types of violations of fundamental women's human rights are occurring across diverse spheres – private, public, conflict-related, cultural, ethnic, geographical, religious, historical and socio-economic. Thus, drawing universal connections across cultural identities is an approach which, objectively, is anything but Western, Eurocentric, top-down and neo-colonialist, but rather, uncovers common systemic patterns of injustices. Connecting problematics rooted in a given location to similar problematics in different socio-cultural contexts effectively de-isolates women's human rights violations from each other, to build a stronger foundation for much-needed solidarity worldwide and beyond the boundaries of one's own cultural specificities.

Universal common patterns of inequalities in the distribution of power and resources

Under *redistribution* of power and resources, a pre-condition to reach the following SDG 5 target:

> 5.a Undertake reforms to give women equal rights to economic resources, as well as access to ownership and control over land and other forms of property, financial services, inheritance and natural resources, in accordance with national laws

is to identify and address the inequitable patterns of distribution of power and resources across and within countries.

Taking Uganda as the same starting point as above, this section turns to women's unequal access and more importantly, unequal control over resources in formal economies, which is key to their lack of autonomy worldwide.

The political elite currently reflects the deep hierarchical and patrilineal structures of Ugandan society. Whilst it has effectively used the notion of gender equality and gender mainstreaming to win votes, it has done less to effectively respond to women's rights issues through equitable provision and redistribution of resources, social services and access to justice and effective protection against all forms of SGBV and harmful traditional practices,[42] as enumerated above.

The World Bank in a recent analysis[43] looks at the successes and risks of Uganda's growth and poverty reduction. The report highlights several elements that require the attention of policy makers. One element is the recent evolution of income inequality, which has increased significantly over the past years. Income inequality has increased among and within regions. Poverty in the North and East, for example, remains four times and eight times deeper, respectively than in the Central region. Gender inequality is higher in the lagging Northern and Eastern regions.[44] Another analysis[45] looks at the roots of this growth in inequality. During the past two decades Uganda witnessed remarkable increases in income inequality. The Gini coefficient increased from about 0.32 in 1990 to 0.48 in 2012. The increase in income inequality stood in total contrast to the high rates of GDP growth, which averaged about 7.5% per annum over the past two decades. Macro-economic stability coupled with liberalisation and/or market-based economics were promoted as policies that would effectively make Uganda realise high rates of GDP growth. The role of the state in the economy was rolled back through privatisation. Sectors that drove Uganda's economic growth were private sector services – especially banking, telecommunications, transport and wholesale trade and construction, which employ a relatively small proportion of the population (less than 15%). For example, between 2005 and 2009 the private service sector grew at an average rate of 8.8% compared to 1.3% for agriculture. This indicates that agriculture, from which about 70% of the population earns a living, grew at rates lower than the population growth rate. The low growth of agriculture compared to the relatively high growth rates of services and construction explains the increase in income inequality as measured by the Gini coefficient.[46]

Within this context of income inequality, women are in a central position as they play a key role in the agricultural production. In 2002 and with unfortunately little change in statistics today, while women were responsible for 60% of cash crop production and constituted 80% of the agricultural workforce, only 7% of registered landowners were actually women.[47] The statistics speak for themselves, and highlight the prominent position of gender inequalities within the broader economic inequalities. Such gender-based inequalities in land ownership significantly limit the opportunity women would otherwise have to independently guarantee basic elements of their livelihood.[48]

Women in Uganda, as in many other countries and continents, are, still, too often socialised with a view to a future which is

> synonymous to exploitable domestic life – essentially responsible for childbearing and rearing, caring for the sick and the elderly, serving the (usually male) head of household, cooking, subsistence farming, fetching and carrying water and fire woods, scrubbing cleaning and other household chores – as an almost inescapable destiny.[49]

Echoing this observation, evidence showing similar patterns of inequality in distribution of resources and the overwhelming participation of women in domestic chores has been gathered from more than 200 participants in the Danida Fellowship Training course on gender mainstreaming between 2006 and 2010. Participants in these intensive three-week courses came to Denmark from i) Latin America: Honduras, Nicaragua, Guatemala, Costa Rica and Bolivia; ii) Western Africa: Benin, Burkina Faso, Niger, Mali; iii) Eastern, Western and Southern Africa: Tanzania, Uganda, Kenya, Mozambique, Zambia and Ghana; and iv) Asia: Bangladesh, Cambodia, Vietnam, Bhutan and Nepal. At each training course, participants were asked to submit the same data over the division of labour, typical female and male gender roles country by country within both private and public sphere, in small working groups in order to present their findings.[50] Women's economic dependency obviously limits their choices and restricts their access to socio-economic rights, at best. At worst, in situations of general poverty, this confines women in a systemic subdued position in which domestic violence and abuse are allowed to thrive, thus impairing women's fundamental freedom and right to live a dignified and decent life.

Throughout all the differences in nuances in customary practices, an obvious common pattern across the three continents emerged: the overwhelming participation of women in domestic chores, child rearing and informal economies on the one hand, and the low participation of women in those decision-making processes which affect the development of their village, community, district and country on the other hand.[51] This trend is intensified in the rural areas, whilst some changes were clearly beginning to emerge in urban areas and within the different countries' elite having had access to secondary and tertiary education. This common pattern was largely followed by its reversal with regard to masculine gender roles, participation of men in domestic chores and child rearing ranging from low to non-existent, whilst their presence was overwhelmingly high regarding land ownership and decision-making from village, to district, to national levels and in formal economies. Nevertheless, changes in these gender stereotypes and male roles and masculinities were clearly emerging in the urban areas when both spouses were employed – at least with regard to child rearing.[52]

If by way of contrast, Cambodia presents in many ways a different country and continental cultural example, at the same time some patterns of similarities can also be distinguished. According to a World Bank report[53] Cambodia's economy grew by 7.8% on average per year during 2004–2014 and 7.0% in 2015, ranking among the 15 fastest-growing economies in the world. By the World Bank's reckoning, 56% live in 'vulnerable poverty' (below $2.60 a day), 20% live in the so-called middle class and just 3% are considered prosperous. But 'many people who have escaped poverty are still at high risk of falling back into poverty', said Neak Samsen, Poverty Analyst of the World Bank in Cambodia, in 2013. 'For example, the loss of just 1,200 riels (30 US cents) per day in income would throw an estimated three million Cambodians – 20 percent of the population – back into poverty, doubling the poverty rate to percent'. Furthermore, while economic growth has led to the development of roads, airports and the infrastructure needed for business, the infrastructure needed to lift millions out of poverty has not enjoyed such generous investment: in 2013, only 24% of Cambodians have access to electricity, 64% to clean water and 31% to sanitation.[54]

As in Uganda, while agriculture dominates 'income generation' in Cambodia, it accounted for just over 35% of the country's gross domestic product in 2012. This reflects low productivity, low returns to labour and low economic security.[55] Although actual national-level figures are not specified, women farmers are particularly constrained because of their very limited ownership of land.[56] Wage employment for women represents only a small share of women's paid work, at 30.1%. Women benefit less than men from wage work, with average monthly wages equal to less than 81% of men's earnings.

Thus, the apparent spectacular 'reduction in poverty' incidence at the macro level overshadows the fact that many households have moved only just above the poverty line and remain highly at risk. It is also important to note that a decline in the income poverty rate does not necessarily translate into improvements in well-being for women and girls in particular. Evidence of 'high rates of malnutrition and anemia among women and a high incidence of domestic violence are indicative of women's inferior position, disadvantaged access to control over resources, and unequal distribution of these'.[57]

Officially, like Uganda, Cambodia is a democratic state, with renewed human rights commitments anchored in the respective constitutions, poverty reduction strategies and national plans to follow SDGs. In practice, Hun Sen has acted as prime minister since 1985 – the same year as Museveni's rise to power after the overthrow of Obote. Both if anything, have so far, demonstrated little intention to concede power, surrounded by well-established systems of patronage and corruption.[58]

Land conflicts in Cambodia constitute some of the worst manifestations of these systems and the human rights abuses that are incurred as a result. Cambodia's rapid, unregulated and spectacular economic growth rests in part, upon the opacity of the land sector, as there is little public data available for state land boundaries, titled areas or agribusiness investment.[59]

Although the Strategy of Land Policy Framework states that

> It is recognized that for land policy to meet the needs of all Cambodians, it must be responsive to the needs of women. One main principle of such responsiveness is that land titling will continue to be available as joint ownership between husband and wife. Furthermore, the principle will be emphasized that women should be represented in the various commissions and committees, such as Cadastral Commission and in the Participatory Land Utilization and Planning (PLUP) procedures,

women's lack of decision-making power in the family also means that their interests and rights to own land will not be necessarily considered. Though Cambodian law officially states, 'all persons, individually or collectively, shall have the right to ownership', in practice women often do not have the ability to own land. Women can typically only own land with the approval of their husbands.[60] The land conflicts have exacerbated in a sense these pre-existing inequalities and as a result fuelled domestic violence.

Indeed, the relationship between land disputes, women's activism and domestic violence has been illustrated in several studies showing that violence against women and land grabbing were two of the most serious and widespread human rights abuses in Cambodia. For many of the women involved in land campaigns the two intersect: '[T]heir lives become marred by conflicts both in the public and private spheres . . . exposing the need for a genuine change of will and of policy by the Cambodian government on both issues of land and violence'.[61]

Aside the service provision and traditional 'development' sphere, the environment for NGOs is increasingly shrinking in Cambodia, in particular for NGOs involved in advocacy, civil rights and human rights, which are often perceived by the government as unwanted opposition, and their margin of action is thus being severely restrained. There is widespread concern from NGOs and other stakeholders on key issues relating to the increased violation of land rights and the restriction of fundamental human rights, such as the freedom of expression and freedom of assembly. As a result, human rights defenders were, for instance, continually and increasingly the target of threats and attacks in the run-up to the 2017 elections.[62] There have also been reports that protests have consistently been shut down and protesters detained without legal justification.[63] Consequently, the Special Rapporteur on the situation of human rights in Cambodia has continued to raise concerns regarding the situation of human rights defenders in relation to access to land. During its first Cycle of UPR in 2009, UPR reports stated that the land crisis in Cambodia was largely resulting from the government granting vast economic and other concessions to foreign and domestic companies and that many of the owners were high-ranking officials and financiers of the party and its election campaign in 2013.

Cambodia further accepted first-cycle UPR recommendations concerning forced eviction and lack of compensation and inadequate relocation of evictees. It noted that provisions in the Land Law grant ownership based on proof of possession of land for five years prior to the law coming into force. However, in practice the government often subsequently designated farmers who have occupied their land for years as 'newcomers' or 'illegal squatters', an argument that is still often used to evict the people without compensation.[64] In the second-cycle UPR reports in 2014, the authorities stated that they had registered 2,845,282 land titles for 500,000 families. Regarding evictions from the land, the government defended that

> certain people were not well informed and that the Government had had to take into consideration the interests and safety of the people and could not let the interests of the majority become a hostage to the interests of a minority.[65]

Yet UPR recommendations in 2014 did concern issues related to human rights defenders, the right of assembly, demonstrations and freedom of expression as well as human rights abuses and excessive use of force on the part of Cambodian authorities, amongst others related to land evictions. The CEDAW Committee remained concerned that women continued to face limited access to land and tenure security, being subjected to displacement and evictions due to large-scale land concessions and urban development. The CEDAW Committee was also concerned that relocation sites provided to victims of evictions frequently lack basic infrastructure and access to essential services such as water, sanitation and basic health care, affecting women disproportionately. CEDAW committee was further concerned that female human rights defenders who advocated for women's land rights were often subjected to intimidation and harassment by law enforcement personnel.[66]

Underpinning such women's human rights violations and gender inequalities are universal systemic patterns of exploitation pointing to an inequitable distribution of power and resources. It is thus argued that both violations of fundamental women's human rights and gender inequalities are universal forms of injustice faced by women across countries, regions and continents in development contexts.

Thomas Piketty in the World Inequality Report (2018)[67] highlights that

> income inequality varies greatly across world regions. In 2016, the share of total national income accounted for by just that nation's top 10% earners (top 10% income share) was 37% in Europe, 41% in China, 46% in Russia, 47% in US-Canada, and around 55% in sub-Saharan Africa, Brazil and India and in the middle east, the world's most unequal region, the top 10% capture 61% of national income.
>
> In recent decades, income inequality has increased in nearly all countries, but at different speeds, suggesting that institutions and policies matter in shaping inequality . . . since 1980, income inequality has increased rapidly in north America, China, India, and Russia. From a broad historical perspective, this increase in inequality marks the end of a post-war egalitarian regime which took different forms in these regions. . . . [I]n the Middle East, sub-Saharan Africa, and Brazil, income inequality has remained relatively stable, at extremely high levels. Having never gone through the post-war egalitarian regime, these regions set the world 'inequality frontier'. . . . The poorest half of the global population has seen its income grow significantly thanks to high growth in Asia (particularly in China and India). However, because of high and rising inequality within countries, the top 1% richest individuals in the world captured twice as much growth as the bottom 50% individuals since 1980.

Piketty and the research team explain that economic inequality is largely driven by unequal ownership of capital and that the combination of large privatisations and increasing income inequality within countries has fuelled the rise of wealth inequality among individuals – predicting further that in a future in which 'business as usual' continues, global inequality will further increase.

For SDG 1 'end poverty in all its forms everywhere' and SDG 10 'reduce inequality within and among countries' to succeed, the issue of global income inequalities and ultimately equitable growth and distribution of resources must be addressed as a pre-condition. Whereas on the one hand, global income inequalities need to be disaggregated by sex, on the other hand, gender inequalities need to be read in light of the country and global income inequalities.

As discussed in Chapter 2, the risk of confining gender inequalities to the boundaries of cultures is also that partial or fragmented solutions will be applied. Whilst it is important to ensure that a pre-defined vision of reality is not imposed from above in what could be characterised as top-down and possibly patronising approaches, imploding categories from within and extrapolating data across countries, regions and continents can, on the contrary, transcend cultural and identity boundaries, lifting problematics from their isolation into a more comprehensive, common and cross-cultural critical analysis.

In the context of violations of fundamental women's human rights and gender inequalities in IDA, the focus on commonalities responds much more towards the obvious need to search for effective responses, towards changes in gender justice, explored in the example of IDA programmes below.

(Mis)representation, (un)recognition and (mal)distribution

This section examines the implications of misrepresentation, unrecognition and maldistribution at the programme level. In order to do so, it provides a sample of selected IDA evaluations carried out by leading bilateral donors and NGOs, as follows: '(mis)Representation' and '(un)Recognition' is discussed in the context of women's political participation in Burkina Faso and (mal)distribution is discussed in the context of land rights disputes in Cambodia.

Women's political participation in Burkina Faso

The implications of focusing on *representation* are examined in the example of the Evaluation of Sida's Support to the National Democratic Institute for International Affairs (NDI) programme – 'Strengthening women's political participation in political and decentralisation processes in Burkina Faso 2005 to 2008'. The objective of this evaluation was to assess the programme against the OECD/DAC evaluation criteria, those being relevance, effectiveness, efficiency, impact and sustainability.[68]

The overall goal of the programme was 'to strengthen women's participation in Burkina Faso's political and decentralisation processes'.[69]

The programme had four immediate objectives[70] as follows: i) increase women's roles and responsibilities within political parties and local governments;[71] ii) strengthen women's ability to compete in elections and to serve as elected officials;[72] iii) enhance public understanding of democracy and its institutions;[73] iv) strengthen partner NGO's ability to play an effective role in promoting women's participation in politics and the decentralisation process.[74]

It was observed that the programme had a monitoring and evaluation system in place which could identify whether gender equality objectives had been effectively reached.

> Indeed, the objectives had been reached in accordance with the indicators specified in the original project document of 2005. However, the objectives and indicators tended to capture mainly quantitative results and activities undertaken rather than outcomes and qualitative changes achieved. Although the programme did set itself realistic targets in order to ensure their effective fulfilment, it was regrettable that important lessons learned, and qualitative effects were not captured or critically analysed in the analytical reports.[75]

With regard to the results and possible impacts of the programme, the substantive difference made by the programme at the political, legislative level could be identified as follows:

> a) a unanimously recognised improvement of intra-party's political dialogue, b) the clear understanding that the political participation of women could be a precious election asset, c) the advances of the 30% quota legislation for women and consequently, d) advances towards gender equality (at least in numbers) in political participation at national and local level.[76]

With regard to making a substantive contribution towards women's rights and gender inequalities amongst the poorest strata of the population, the programme made a difference by 'creating forums of discussion where citizens (or their representatives) could voice their concerns'.[77] However, the impact on the poorest was next to non-existent.

The main challenge is the assumption that by increasing the number of women, great societal causes such as the reduction of violence against women, gender inequalities and poverty stand a greater chance of being addressed. It is thus assumed that women are 'culturally' more likely than men to address social issues and injustices facing women. The evaluation demonstrated that if the individual commitment to address poverty, structural inequalities and gender inequalities is absent from the political vision of the women in question, results and impacts on the reduction of structural inequalities will thus remain non-existent:

> Without such individual (political) commitment, *substantive* and qualitative changes in Burkinabe's society towards the reduction of gender and structural inequalities are unlikely to occur.[78]

This was further demonstrated by the fact that during the course of the evaluation four women parliamentarians were interviewed, including the vice-chair of the Parliamentary National Assembly at the time. During the interview, it became apparent, from a ten-minute-silence when women MPs were asked about their understanding of their role as related to the reduction of poverty and social injustices, that there were no visible 'differences' between these women MPs and their male counterparts – except for the extensive jewelled looks and artificially whitened complexions.

This apparently anecdotal detail is a powerful and recurrent demonstration that merely focusing on increasing the number of women in parliaments will not, in and of itself, produce structural changes in society – whether or not it is maintained by some feminists that women are 'culturally' different.[79]

Thomas Sankara (albeit a man), faced with the same question might not have taken so long to provide a suitable answer for a country, ranking as one of the lowest in the world human development index.[80] The ranking, if anything, clearly indicates that poverty in Burkina Faso is all around and arguably ought to be the omnipresent preoccupation of parliamentarians. Thus, the apparent gender and poverty blindness of the women parliamentarians interviewed demonstrates that there is little connection between the world they are evolving in, their role as parliamentarians and the major problems faced by their constituents. In particular, there seemed to be little connection between their political visions and the potential 'difference' they were expected to make in – at least – improving the lot of 'women' (as the community they were, amongst others, supposed to represent the interests of) living in poverty and transforming the balance of power towards gender justice. Rather, based on the evaluation interviews, the main 'difference' they seem to have achieved in accessing such high position was a visible focus on the advancement of their personal status.

Thus, the study concluded that:

> Whereas non-discrimination and participation of women is an important and necessary concept in securing gender equality, what constitutes the linkage between non-discrimination and poverty reduction is a *substantive* focus, beyond the *quantitative* participation, on the reduction of structural inequalities and social justice for women and men.[81]

Thus, the reason provided for not addressing qualitative and substantive changes related to gender justice and redistribution is the assumption that only after quantitative progress in terms of participation is achieved can substantive issues in terms of redistribution and structural inequalities be addressed. Furthermore, it became clear from this programme that the extent to which gender equality is interpreted as redistribution essentially depends on how elected MPs from the elite tackle the issue of structural inequalities and to what extent they would be willing to share the power and resources which they might have long fought for themselves – whether women or men.

Seven years, later, and not without historical irony, the streets of Burkina Faso, led by its youth, set fire to the National Assembly in what was to become the 'first black spring'. The National Transition Council replaced the National Assembly following the uprising and distinguished itself by passing 140 pro–human rights laws in a record time of one year – in full *recognition* of specific women's human rights violations in the country. One of which was the Law on Prevention, repression and reparation of violence against women and girls, which was passed in 2015, and included a broad definition of physical, sexual, psychological and economic violence. It also *recognised* specific offences such as rape amongst intimate partners, forced and early marriage, sexual slavery, sexual torture, repudiation, women accused of witchcraft and sexual harassment at school and in the workplace. The law foresees the creation of special structures within the police, multidisciplinary day care centres with legal, psychosocial and medical services and a legal aid fund for the protection of victims. The law foresees funding of these services from Burkina Faso's state budget.[82]

Thus, gender transformational change at the macro level in the enactment of bold legislation on violence against women was driven by a multitude of factors including a strong and genuine political will much beyond lip service, joint pro–human and women's human rights forces in the country supported by international like-minded development allies. Although changing laws do not necessarily imply implementation, or even adherence by the population, or its ability to invoke the newly enacted rights and overcome the many persistent socio-cultural barriers, still it is a step ahead compared with mere *representation* of women MPs showing little concern, if any for the violations of human rights of their sisters in less fortunate positions.

Thus, when gender equality is overwhelmingly understood as centred on *representation*, the results cannot be expected to necessarily reach qualitative outcomes. On the one hand, it can be argued that the results achieved in equality as *representation* are 'first steps' towards gender equality and an achievement in its own right, compared with a previously gender-blind situation or a situation that excluded women from participating on a par with men. On the other hand, the risk is that these 'minimum standards' as they ought to be considered, become 'maximum standards' and are considered as the framework against which progress in gender equality is measured. Such an interpretation of gender equality significantly reduces the meaning of gender equality to numerical participation. The interpretation of gender equality solely as *representation* does not necessarily lead to the much-needed *recognition* of specific human rights violations unless clearly expressed by a genuine political will. This tends to isolate the meaning of 'gender equality' from a broader socio-economic analysis which arguably could have permitted a deeper insight as to the need to address inequalities in the *redistribution* of power and resources.

Reclaiming social justice in Cambodia

The implications of (mal)*distribution* are analysed in two pro–human rights but not specifically gender-targeted examples (contrary to the Burkina Faso example above) of projects led by Cambodian NGOs respectively: the Coalition of Cambodian Farmer Community (CCFC) and Equitable Cambodia (EC). Both organisations are technically and financially supported by DanChurch Aid (DCA) on land rights.[83]

Founded in 2011, CCFC is a membership organisation of over 17,000 farmers across 40 communities in eight provinces including Kandal, Takeo, Kampot, Sihanouk, Prey Veng, Svay Rieng, Kampong Thom and Preah Vihear. CCFC's mission is to empower rural communities to address land grabbing cases and forced evictions that are driven by financial investment initiatives developing factories, tourist resorts, etc.[84] Throughout its partnership with CCFC, DCA has provided general support to CCFC to work with a Human Rights Based Approach (HRBA), facilitation of networking and advocacy work as well as the protection of men and women human rights defenders.

CCFC's goal is to build the capacity of farmers, women and men, to organise themselves to claim their right to land. CCFC provides entire communities and their representatives with basic training on general human rights and specific laws such as the Land Law (2001) and the Cambodian Constitution, as well as in simple advocacy methods. Community Committee members are elected to leadership positions by other community members and are coached by CCFC over a long period of time. Sometimes months are spent living with the communities, thereby building solidarity and networks across different communities. The project is thus designed to assist farmers to organise themselves in locally based communities to raise awareness on how to use their basic rights. This is achieved by building capacity in terms of basic human rights, organising skills, community management, community leadership, land law and advocacy skill.

Moreover, CCFC also facilitates advocacy at the national level to include farmers' voices and concerns. CCFC has thus on many occasions attempted to engage and foster constructive dialogue between rights holders and duty bearers. Despite these attempts, CCFC like other NGOs working with human rights in Cambodia are perceived by duty bearers as political threats, capable of mobilising a significant number of demonstrators and exposing to the public the full extent of human rights violations and injustices. The reluctance to engage in constructive dialogue stems from the fact that these particular violations related to land evictions represent considerable economic interests. Therefore, personal threats were received by both leaders of CCFC and EC. Although citizens' mobilisation in Cambodia has shown to be powerful, effects and impact may remain limited due to the degree of individual repression on human rights defenders.

Many community members therefore saw little other option but to migrate to neighbouring Thailand and Vietnam, risking being further exposed to human rights violations such as human trafficking, women and children's labour and sexual exploitation and violence, etc. Thus, the linkages between migration and violations of human rights and right to land, livelihoods and decent standards of living are rather visible and have been the subject of concerns for many years especially in numerous CEDAW reports.

However, beyond the proposition to stay and engage in an often long-term and uncertain struggle to reclaim their land, there is little other option available. For those community members that have chosen to stay to engage in such social justice struggle through collective actions and to resist the temptation of authorities' and companies' luring and bribes, vulnerability and frustrations amongst the victims of land eviction are high. In the short term, livelihood standards may decrease unless livelihood measures are specifically included in the IDA support – which is what CCFC is putting in place especially for the community representatives, to lift both living standards and their morale. In particular, women land rights activists, as illustrated by a LICADHO study,[85] that are facing a concentration of challenges including double violation of their rights and violence both within the public and the private sphere and are in need of special support, as well as men activists suffering from depression as they have been abandoned by their families, which have been in turn worn out by the human and financial cost of human rights activism. This brings significant threat to the long-term sustainability of human rights activism focusing on equitable distribution of resources, given the livelihood conditions, political and economic pressure exercised on community members and their representatives. There were ample testimonies that these pressures exercised through various forms of economic and psychological violence have clearly led to depression, exhaustion and financial indebtedness. Within such a challenging environment and shrinking pro–human rights CSO space, the repeated attacks on human rights defenders have led to high risks of breaking down of human rights CSO leaders. Although courses on protection and security of human rights defenders are available, more ought to be done to care for and protect human rights defenders, especially those that are focusing on social justice through equitable distribution of resources as they are fundamental to the achievement of poverty reduction, SDG 1.

During the field mission, the following effects at the individual level could be retrieved: firstly, changes in awareness, knowledge, skills and behaviour of community members and secondly, changes in access to and control of resources, services and opportunities.

Following the human rights trainings, many farmers realised that they were no longer 'insignificant or invisible beings'. Becoming active citizens with rights had deeply changed their perspective and self-esteem. Community representatives felt they had gained new knowledge and were enabled to pass on that knowledge to their constituencies and other neighbouring communities. The skills which seem to have made a practical difference to community members' lives and allowed them to meaningfully engage in peaceful democratic process were the trainings on how to collect evidence to prove the legitimacy of land ownership as well as other practical skills imparted by other specialised partner NGOs such as safety protection during protests, conflict resolution skills to assist families in cases of domestic violence,[86] etc. Moving from being 'invisible and insignificant' to feeling that their fundamental rights were protected and cared for constituted a significant incentive to continue their struggles for human rights and justice despite exposure to clear threats and violence. Community solidarity thus accrued when they were faced with major threats targeting community division and fragmentation of civil society strategies often used by duty bearers such as local authorities and private investment companies alike. Following the training, community members could collectively engage and participate in demonstrations and protests as well as identify duty bearers. Several said that although the challenges they faced during protests and demonstrations were still tough, they no longer feared to voice their rights and reclaim justice.

A fortunate minority[87] actually recovered grabbed land following the intervention. According to CCFC's statistical data, the following figures provide some illustration of the extent to which land was recovered and the number of families affected.[88] For example, in the Kampot Province all 105 families recovered 100% of their 330 hectares of land back; in Sihanoukville province out of 11 communities four were in the process of land measurements but title deeds have yet to be delivered for 399 families and a total of 683.4 hectares of land; in Kandal Province the land conflict concerned 745 families over 480 hectares, out of which 235 hectares were successfully claimed back whilst the rest is still in the process of being negotiated with the relevant private investment company and cases are pending with the local authorities at provincial level. In the best cases, often the written title deed was still pending – sometimes in the hands of the works of student groups attached to the ruling party. Still, receiving a title deed was no absolute guarantee from counter title deeds which could be issued at any time by private investment companies and local authorities. This said, it can be assumed that communities that benefited from the training had built a greater capacity to mobilise and react in a united manner in the face of possible future risks. It is hoped that they will therefore become more resilient to unpredictable future land grabbing shocks.[89]

Regarding the cases of community members and community representatives who did accept and receive compensations in the form of cash, housing benefits and alternative non-farming land compensation, these had been usually inequitable. Even if 'unsatisfactory compensation' may be considered 'better than no compensation at all', in practice it meant a temporary variation of substantial decrease in living standards and access to livelihoods, under the poverty line. Entire families thus still struggled to seek alternative earnings; children often could no longer attend schools in order to support their families with work – often performed under child labour and sexual exploitative conditions – or to support the single parent as many marriages under such financial constraints, ended up breaking down.

This supports the argument for engaging a deeper reflection as to what constitute a so-called fair and equitable compensation for such human rights violations considering international standards. Whilst the principle of claiming for compensation is in line with international standards such as the UN human rights and business principle, the actual compensation is the subject of negotiations between the rights holders and duty bearers and could have little to do if anything with equity and social justice, unless these principles are clearly applied.

Seemingly, without a strong human rights organisation's support, it would be very difficult for rights holders in such an inequitable position of power and resources to stand a fair chance to claim their rights and protect their basic livelihoods.

At a systemic level, examples of effects are illustrated by: i) informal changes in traditional norms and hierarchical structures and ii) formal changes in policies, legislations and institutional/organisational arrangements.

Changes in the informal hierarchal structures at the village level frequently seemed to occur as community representatives are elected by community members and responsibilities allocated to various community members. This structure tended to supplant the politically appointed hierarchal and politicised structure in place with a more legitimate community representation. There were for example instances of politically appointed village chiefs who had been removed given their lack of involvement in the defence of community members' rights during the land evictions. Thus, it can be stated that the growing organisation's capacity to mobilise significant numbers of members has the effect of potentially shifting hierarchies and power structures.

As an example, rights holders began to be recognised and acknowledged by some duty bearers which seem to have become, at least in appearance, more inclined to peaceful dialogue and to 'listening to' farmers' concerns than before. Such attitudinal changes and responses of duty bearers at the local, provincial and national levels may well be a change of 'façade', but it is a change nevertheless in comparison to their previous tendency to ignore farmers all together and thus reducing them to non-existence. In at least one case, the National Assembly issued an intervention letter requiring the provincial authorities to approve a social land concession for 16 families.[90]

> While to date there have only been a few cases where communities have been successful, the fact that duty bearers are beginning to acknowledge some demands from communities is a sign of interest, even if done purely as a response to political pressure.[91]

Thus, many effects at the individual level have been achieved in this project and the main added value of applying HRBA within a justice framework is a contribution to (re)establishing social justice by focusing on redistribution of vital resources. Social justice in this case is essential to protect farmers from current and future human rights violations, not only to ensure their rights are fulfilled but are protected in a dignified and sustainable manner. The project further demonstrated a strengthened solidarity amongst the local communities jointly with like-minded international donors, showing, if anything, that fostering global and transnational solidarity beyond cultural divides is essential to human rights realisation.

The second example is a project led by Equitable Cambodia (EC), an NGO that 'promotes inclusive and equitable development to further the progressive realization of human rights in Cambodia through community organizing, legal empowerment and evidence-based advocacy'.[92] EC also focuses its work on advocacy for housing and land rights of communities affected by forced eviction through national and international advocacy, coalition-building across civil society and community organising. Like CCFC above, EC has also worked to build the capacity of communities and civil society stakeholders in their understanding of basic human rights and has written, developed and produced the actual training material.[93]

In this case, DCA supported the advocacy work of partners in the Sugar Case at the level of EU institutions. A briefing paper was prepared by Equitable Cambodia for the Special Rapporteur on the situation of human rights in Cambodia, Ms. Rhona Smith, in preparation for her mission to visit community members affected by sugar concessions in Oral and Thpong Districts, Kampong Speu Province, Cambodia on 16 October 2016 and summarises the facts of the case as follows: In February 2010 Phnom Penh Sugar Co. Ltd. (PPSC) received an Economic Land Concession (ELC) of approximately 9,000 hectares (ha) in Thpong District, Kampong Speu Province. The total size of the concessions grew to 23,000 ha, far above the 10,000-ha limit under Article 59 of Cambodian Land Law 2001. The PPSC concession encroached on the farmland and residential land of villagers from at least 18 villages and at least 1,000 households in Oral and Thpong Districts. Villagers from these districts were neither consulted nor included in the decision-making process regarding the evictions, and intimidation tactics were employed by local authorities and company staff to seize their land. In some cases, villagers' land was cleared without any prior notice.

Despite claims by PPSC that 'satisfactory compensations' had been awarded to the farmers, hundreds of families joined human rights civil society organisations to demand fair and just remedies for the harms they had suffered. In June 2016, community representatives from sugar concession–affected communities in Kampong Speu, Oddar Meanchey, Koh Kong and Preah Vihear Provinces submitted petitions to the Ministry of Land Management, Urban Planning and Construction, the Ministry of Environment, the Ministry of Agriculture and the National Assembly demanding a solution to their problems. On 6 October 2016, over 500 affected people gathered in front of the Trapaing Cho Commune Chief's office in Oral District, Kampong Speu to clarify that their land dispute was not solved, despite claims to the contrary by villagers working for the ruling party.

A clear challenge was that after communities had been filing complaints, there were some clear limitations in the use national courts. EC circumvented the issue by using multiple advocacy strategies of public process and pressuring companies. However, the key challenges for community members in this case were the pervasiveness of companies and authorities to break them down. Often the challenges also lied in identifying and anticipating their tactics, which could be, for example, the criminalisation of victims – using court systems to break victims down, threaten victims to be charged on defamation grounds. Other examples of strategies of fragmentation of communities and disempowerment of civil society's collective action by authorities were in terms of offering cash settlements, forced acceptance of underpaid jobs, offering individual housing or transports to minimise land claims to ultimately break down solidarity. The use of police and military force was not uncommon according to several testimonies, as well as many other examples such as: media manipulation tactics, delaying procedures on purpose to demoralise communities, using counter-demonstrations and networks to shut down rights-based protests and thereby dilute public adherence.

There are ample testimonies that these pressures actually constitute economic and psychological violence that have led to depression, exhaustion and financial indebtedness.[94] Within such a challenging environment and the national shrinking of CSO space, the repeated attacks on human rights defenders have led to high risks of exhaustion and breaking down of human rights CSO leaders as well.

Nevertheless, on a systemic level, examples of effects are illustrated by formal changes in policies, legislations and institutional/organisational arrangements.

Although there was a strong focus on strategic advocacy work throughout local, national, regional and international levels essentially to engage duty bearers'[95] responsibility vis-à-vis international human rights standards, the effects and impact remained nevertheless constrained by the strength and power of duty bearers' resistance to change, which reflected, if anything, the significance of economic interests at play overriding human rights standards and commitments to poverty reduction global goals.

In this case, EC's national and international advocacy campaign and lobbying was recognised by the EU as 'outstanding'. There had been a clear contribution to a second draft of agriculture and land management reform: cooperative law, civil society law. Amongst some of the most striking changes resulting from such contribution were the cancelling of ELC/moratorium on land concessions and the re-drawing of boundaries of existing land concessions. The high-level advocacy lobbying strategy targeting the EU and UK companies such as Tate & Lyle[96] for the sugar case has at least raised awareness overseas and led the EU and Cambodian government to develop terms of reference for an independent audit. The EU-supported audit of sugar concessions in Cambodia, which is a clear effect of EC and other NGOs' advocacy work, is still waiting for the TOR to be approved by the Cambodian government.

Indeed, EC and other NGOs, working under the banner of the Clean Sugar Campaign, have thus for years undertaken advocacy work to call upon the EU to conduct an independent, transparent and immediate investigation into allegations of serious and systematic violations of international human rights and labour law related to industrial sugar production in Cambodia by companies benefiting from 'Everything but Arms' preferential trade status. The Blood Sugar Campaign targets European and US sugar buyers and has triggered an EU investigation. The human rights investigations and reports thus expose other types of human rights violations, for examples, the illegal timber trade satisfying Chinese demand for luxury timber and the International Finance Corporation (IFC, part of the World Bank), IFC-funded rubber company, etc. In this way EC and other NGOs are effectively bringing to the public light human rights violations and social injustices that would normally be left invisible.

EC thus succeeded in effectively mapping and utilising different alliances and pressure points with a variety of international actors (either like-minded or adversarial) to gauge duty bearers' fierce resistance in Cambodia. Through its HRBA work, EC has demonstrated its strategic utilisation of a variety of mechanisms, from national and international court claims, to using judicial as well as non-judicial mechanisms such as the EU, ADB, IFC, OECD and the Thai Human Rights Commission to engage the responsibility of duty bearers in the fulfilment of their responsibilities, notably defence and protection of human rights.

Nevertheless, the success of the advocacy work remains ultimately dependent on the willingness of duty bearers (public authorities or private companies) to fulfil their obligations to respect and protect international human rights standards and engage their corporate social responsibility. It is also dependent in the cases of court claims on the independence and effectiveness of the justice system. Such HRBA advocacy work has had the effect of linking local stories to an international-level breach of human rights standards, thus adding considerable pressure and value to cases that would have otherwise remained invisible, and in effect, maximising their potential to obtain compensation or the return of the land.

Holding both legal and moral duty bearers to account exposes the extent to which they will try to negotiate their responsibility away, to not jeopardise their profits or marketing image, rather than providing an equitable compensation for the entire loss of livelihoods of the many communities. This, if anything, questions the idea of CSR and the assumption that compensation will be adequate and fair for the communities or indeed for women.

Thus, key focus on restoring social justice as redistribution of resources is explicitly and eloquently formulated in EC theory of social change. The combination of a social justice vision, engaging in different campaigning strategies and an HRBA strategic focus has thus been perceived as a potential threat by companies (whether Cambodian or Chinese) who are developing further tactics to either dismantle and divide communities, neutralise active human rights defenders and heads of such networks by filing defamation cases or by organising counter-demonstrations and networks with pro-government and Chinese-funded NGOs to split the civil society social movement. This, if anything, shows that such a combination of approaches is sufficiently effective to disturb those responsible for the massive human rights violations and attacks on basic livelihoods.

Choosing to combine a social justice vision of development focusing on redistribution and human rights is not an easy and comfortable road. As illustrated by these examples, the risks and challenges are significant, especially for human rights defenders on the front line. If anything, an equitable and justice-based development comes at a high price when hinging on such significant financial interests. This is indeed the path of the brave and the valiant.

Conclusion

As a general conclusion for this chapter, ignoring the universal and common elements at the heart of violations of women's human rights accounts whilst focusing solely on their cultural differences would essentially limit and weaken the consolidation of international political claims based on solidarity across cultures and continents. For if one sets such examples in their wider universal context, they have the potential to expose commonly shared human rights abuses, inequitable power relations and patriarchal behaviour. Instead, by viewing such examples through a sole stance of identity politics and cultural relativism, only a partial account is revealed. This effectively would exclude a deeper layer of analysis which identifies the common systemic and universal forms of injustices faced by women and men across the globe, resonating so tragically with one another.

This is further reinforced by the evidence related to women's human rights violations regarding violence against women and gender inequalities defined as the unequal distribution of resources in Uganda. This example demonstrates that by extrapolating the related data in Uganda, commonalities with other neighbouring countries, regions and continents can be identified, in order to uncover universal connections with similar patterns of human rights violations and inequalities. This further demonstrates that drawing universal patterns of connections across cultural identities as an approach does not have to be necessarily expressed in a Eurocentric, top-down and neo-colonialist manner, or indeed with such an enterprise in mind, but rather the opposite. This analysis shows that rather than projecting field data into 'ahistoricism', this method opens up the possibility of drawing analytical matrixes to uncover the patriarchal systems of oppression which sadly underpin the most common universal violations of human rights.

Thus, violations of fundamental human rights and gender inequalities cannot be fully defined in disconnection from one another, as if locked within the boundaries of cultural differences and identities, as this approach ultimately risks providing a justification and ultimate legitimacy for the perpetration of such injustices. The data collected from diverse socio-cultural settings show that underpinning human rights and women's human rights violations are universal systemic patterns of oppression, exploitation and inequitable distribution of power and resources.

Notes

1 See N Fraser, 'Multiculturalism, Anti-essentialism, and Radical Democracy: A Genealogy of Current Impasse in Feminist Theory' in N Fraser (ed), *Justice Interruptus: Critical Reflections on the "Postsocialist" Condition* (Routledge 1997) 173–188.

2 See C Bunch, 'Transforming Human Rights from a Feminist Perspective' in J Peters and A Wolper (eds), *Women's Rights Human Rights; International Feminist Perspectives* (Routledge 1995) 11.

3 See H Charlesworth and C Chinkin, *The Boundaries of International Law* (Manchester University Press 2004); H Charlesworth, 'Feminist Methods in International Law' (1999) 93 *American Journal of International Law* 379; PV Sellars, 'Individual' Liability for Collective Sexual Violence' in K Knop (ed), *Gender and Human Rights* (Oxford University Press 2004).

4 The term 'ahistorical' generalisation is cited as a purposefully counter example of the following premise: 'the application of the notion of women as a homogeneous category to women in the Third World colonizes and appropriates the pluralities of the simultaneous location of different groups of women in social class and ethnic frameworks; in so doing it robs them of their historical and political agency'. CT Mohanty, *Feminism without Borders: Decolonizing Theory, Practicing Solidarity* (Duke University Press 2003) 39.

5 P Lowe, *Fuego en el hielo. Mujeres mineras de Chorolque: Convierten el hielo en sopa y la piedra en pan* (Dirección de Medio Ambiente de la COMIBOL 2005) <http://incabook.com/products.php?B60231&osCsid=71dcfd7bd7afc0642ed19161c814bb15>.

6 Ibid 140–150.

7 L Tibatemwa-Ekirikubinza, *Women's Violent Crime in Uganda: More Sinned Against Than Sinning* (Fountain Publisher 1999).

8 Ibid 63.

9 'le petit théâtre des Métallos' in the 9th Arrondissement of Paris.

10 M Desnos, 'Rayana Agréssée: Une Femministe qui Dérange?' *Paris Match* (Paris, 15 January 2010) <www.pointdebasculecanada.ca/breve/2216-ecirctre-une-feministe-qui-derange-en-laquofranceraquo-des-laquohommesraquo-lui-ont-jete-de-lessence-et-un-megot-de-cigarette-laquoen-pleine-faceraquo.php>.

11 Human Rights Watch, 'Just Die Quietly: Domestic Violence and Women's Vulnerability to HIV in Uganda' (August 2003) Human Rights Watch Report 15 (15 A). <www.hrw.org/en/node/12290/section/9>.

12 On the violence in Uganda see: ABK Kasozi, *The Social Origins of Violence in Uganda 1964–1985* (Fountain Publisher 1994); CM Madrama Izama, *The Problem HIV/AIDS: A Discourse on Laws, Marriage and the Subordinate Status of Women in Uganda* (Uganda Law Books 1996).

13 Interview with Harriet Abwoli, Mulago, 9 January 2003 in Human Rights Watch, *Just Die Quietly*.
14 Under the Section 154 of the Penal Code Act 1950 adultery is punishable with imprisonment.
15 Human Rights Watch, 'Just Die Quietly' 23.
16 M A Koenig and others 'Domestic violence in Rural Uganda: Evidence from Community-Based Study' (2003) 81(1) *Bulletin of the World Health Organisation* 53–60 <www.who.int/bulletin/Koenig0103.pdf>.
17 Ibid.
18 For example, district, UWA, NFA.
19 Moreover, Affirmative Action in the Local Government Act (1997) provides for one-third women's representation at all local council levels. Other national legislation that promotes to some extent gender equality includes among others: the Land Act 1998, which partly protects women's land rights; the Local Government Act 1997; the Prevention of Trafficking in Persons Act 2009; the Domestic Violence Act 2010; the Prohibition of Female Genital Mutilation Act 2010 and the Equal Opportunities Commission Act 2007. In addition to laws, the government of Uganda has adopted several policies: the Gender Policy and National Equal Opportunities Policy, etc.
20 UNESC, Committee on Economic, Social and Cultural Rights, 'Concluding observations on the initial report of Uganda', 8 July 2015 E/C.12/UGA/CO/1, para. 26.
21 See UWONET et al., *Unfinished Business, the Women's Manifesto 2016–2021* (2015) 4.
22 UNHCR UPR submission (2015) 6.
23 UN UPR country team submission (2015) 4.
24 WHO, First World Report on Violence and Heath (WHO 2002) <www.who.int/violence_injury_prevention/violence/world_report/en/index.html>.
25 Ibid 89–100.
26 Ibid.
27 Ibid 100–103.
28 See UNSC Res 1325 (31 October 2000) UN Doc S/RES/1325.
29 See S Swiss and JE Giller, 'Rape as Crime of War: A Medical Perspective' (1993) 270(5) *Journal of the American Medical Association* 612–615; C McGreal, 'Hundreds of Thousands Raped in Congo Wars' *The Guardian* (London, 14 November 2006). <www.guardian.co.uk/world/2006/nov/14/congo.chrismcgreal>.
30 See statistics <www.survivors-fund.org.uk/resources/history/statistics.php>; Human Rights Watch, 'Struggling to Survive: Barriers to Justice for Rape Victims in Rwanda' (September 2004) Human Rights Watch Report 16 (10A). <www.hrw.org/en/node/11975/section/1>.
31 Human Rights Watch, 'We'll Kill You If You Cry: Sexual Violence in the Sierra Leone Conflict' (January 2003) Human Rights Watch Report 15 (1A) 31.
32 A Riding, 'Rape Is "a Weapon of War" in the Bosnian Genocide' European Inquiry' (9 January 1993) Ocala Star-Banner 50 (131) 127 <http://bosniagenocide.wordpress.com/2010/12/09/rape-is-a-weapon-of-war-in-the-bosnian-genocide-european-inquiry/>.
33 Isis-WICCE, 'Women's Experiences of Armed Conflict in Uganda: Gulu District 1986–1999' (July 2001) Isis-WICCE Report Part 1.
34 Ibid.
35 Isis-WICCE, 'Medical Interventional Study of War Affected Gulu District, Uganda' (July 2001) Isis-WICCE Report Part 2.
36 UNSC Res 1325(31 October 2000) UN Doc S/Res/1325(2000).
37 For illustrated definitions of the three main types of female circumcision: clitoridectomy, excision and infibulation, see O Koso-Thomas, *The Circumcision of Women: A Strategy for Eradication* (Zed Books 1987) 15–17.

38 A Rahman and N Toubia, *Female Genital Mutilation: A Guide to Laws and Policies Worldwide* (Zed Books 2000).
39 Ibid. See also on female genital mutilation Ayaan Hirsi Ali, *Infidel: My Life* (The Free Press 2007).
40 See Rahman and Toubia.
41 On the defence of female circumcision as a prevention of promiscuity: 'In many African communities it is believed that the clitoris, left intact, causes women to become over-sexed, to respond too readily to sexual approaches and may provoke them into making uncontrollable sexual demand on their husbands; and if their demand is not satisfied they may be driven to seek extra-marital sexual adventures'. O Koso-Thomas, *The Circumcision of Women: A Strategy for Eradication* (Zed Books 1987) 8.
42 See: UGMP, *Power Belongs to the People, the Citizens Manifesto, 2016–2021, Governing for Equal Opportunity and Shared Prosperity* (2015).
43 World Bank, *Uganda, Promoting Inclusive Growth* (February 2012).
44 Coffey, *Gender Equality in Uganda: A Situation Analysis and Scoping Report for the Gender Development Partners Group* (2014) 21.
45 L Bategeka, *Tackling Inequality in Uganda* (February 2013) <www.thebrokeronline.eu/Blogs/Inequality-debate/TacklingInequality-in-Uganda>.
46 Coffey, *Gender Equality in Uganda: A Situation Analysis and Scoping Report for the Gender Development Partners Group* (2014) 21.
47 S Tamale, 'Gender Trauma in Africa: Enhancing Women's Links to Resources' (Unpublished research 2002). <www.codesria.org/IMG/pdf/TAMALE.pdf>.
48 For African studies on women's land ownership see L Muthoni Wanyeki (ed), *Women and Land in Africa: Culture, Religion and Realizing Women's Rights* (Zed Books 2003).
49 Tamale, 'Gender Trauma in Africa'.
50 DFC, 'Danida Fellowship Courses on Gender Mainstreaming' (2006–2011). <www.dfcentre.com/?Programmes_%26amp%3B_Projects:Interdisciplinary_Courses>. The purpose of this series of training courses was to provide Danida programme staff with the conceptual and practical tools to improve implementation of the Danida gender equality strategy. Courses taught included international legal framework and women's rights, gender concepts and rights-based approaches. The courses were taught respectively in English, French and Spanish as participants came from Latin America, Eastern and Western Africa and Asia to Denmark.
51 Ibid.
52 DFC, 'Danida Fellowship Courses on Gender Mainstreaming'. See also BM Magubane, *African Sociology Towards a Critical Perspective: Collective Essays* (Africa World Press 2000).
53 World Bank, *International Development Association, International Finance corporation, Multilateral Investment Guarantee Agency, Country Engagement Note for the Kingdom of Cambodia for the Period FY2016–2017* (April 2016).
54 David Nathan, 'The Truth Behind Cambodia's Inequalities' *New Internationalist Magazine* (September 2014).
55 See Royal Government of Cambodia, Ministry of Women's Affairs. 2014. Country Gender Assessment 2014; ADB. 2014. Country Performance Assessment; and ADB. 2014.
56 About 31% of households headed by women had access to ploughs compared with 48% of those headed by men, and the gender gap was more than 23% in the plateau and mountain areas (Food and Agriculture Organization of the United Nations and Government of Cambodia, National Institute of Statistics and Ministry of Planning. 2010. National Gender Profile of Agricultural Households 2010. Report Based on the 2008 Cambodia Socio-Economic Survey. Phnom Penh.)
57 See Royal Government of Cambodia, Ministry of Planning. 2014. Annual Progress Report 2013: Achieving Cambodia's Millennium Development Goals. Phnom Penh.

World Health Organization. Global Health Observatory Data Repository. <www.who.int/countries/khm/en/>. 10 Royal Government of Cambodia, Ministry of Planning.

58 Canvas, Analysis of the situation in Cambodia (2015) 4.

59 As an example of such unclarity: 'a pre-election land titling push in 2012–14, thousands of university students were sent around the country to survey and title land to more than 600,000 land owners occupying state land. The government has promised that titling will continue in 2015 under the auspices of the Department of Land Management. But, a growing number of reports link Cambodia's land titling campaign with land grabbing and deforestation, particularly in indigenous communities. An alarming number of people whose land was surveyed by the student volunteers are still waiting for their land title. Seventy-four per cent of people whose land was surveyed between 2012 and 2014 are still waiting for at least one title according to nationwide reports from the NGO forum'.

60 ILC, Shadow Report on Women's Land Rights in Cambodia – Analysis of the status of compliance with CEDAW Articles 14, 15 and 16, August 2013.

61 LICADHO, 'Good Wives' Women Land Campaigners and the Impact of Human Rights Activism (2014).

62 The 2015 UN UPR submissions and outcomes document this.

63 Civic Freedom Monitor, Cambodia, November 2016 <www.icnl.org/research/monitor/cambodia.html>.

64 HRW, Report (2014) 2–3 A/HRC/WG.6/18/KHM/3.

65 A/HRC/WG.6/18/KHM/3.

66 CEDAW/C/KHM/CO/4–5.

67 F Alvaredo, L Chancel, T Piketty, E Saez, G Zucman, *World Inequality Report, Executive Summary* (World Inequality Lab 2018) 5–16.

68 Forti and Lamien Ouando (n 550) 3. For Sida's strategic objectives in Burkina Faso see also Sida, 'Strategy for Swedish Development Cooperation with Burkina Faso 2004–2006' (Sida 2004); Sida, 'Draft Country Report' (Sida 2007); NDI, 'Mid-Term Evaluation Report' (NDI February 2007); NDI, 'Semi-Annual Reports' (2006, 2007 and 2008).

69 Forti and Lamien Ouando 13.

70 Ibid.

71 See NDI, 'Rapport, Atelier national des Femmes cadres de partis politiques' (NDI Février 2008); Sida/NDI, NDI, 'Rapport Atelier de Formation des Femmes Maires, adjointes aux Maires et responsables des commissions permanentes' (NDI 2007).

72 NDI, 'Women's Political Participation in Burkina Faso' (Sida/NDI 2007); 'Le Manuel de la Candidate' (NDI/Sida 2007).

73 NDI, 'Rapport du Forum élues – population Kakologho' (NDI 2007).

74 NDI, 'Rapport du Forum National sur le Rôle et la Participation des Femmes à la vie politique' (NDI 2005); NDI, 'Rapport de Formations des Candidates aux élections législatives' (NDI 2007).

75 Ibid.

76 Forti and Lamien Ouando 31–33.

77 Ibid.

78 Ibid.

79 See C Gilligan, *In a Different Voice, Psychological Theory and Women's Development* (Harvard University Press 1982); IM Young, *Justice and the Politics of Difference* (Princeton University Press 1990).

80 UNDP, *Human Development Report* (UNDP 2008)145.

81 Forti and Lamien Ouando 25–27; See also NDI, 'Proposal for the program submitted by NDI to Sida' (NDI 2005) 6; Sida, 'Promoting Gender Equality in Development Cooperation: Policy' (Sida 2005–2010) 4–6; Sida, 'Gender Equality: Sida's Policy and Methods at a Glance: Steering Document' (Sida 2005) 1.

82 V Kristiansen and S Forti *Lessons Learned from Promoting Gender Equality in Danish Development Cooperation, Evaluation Study* (Danida 2016).
83 See S Forti, Documenting the effects of HRBA to Development, Cambodia Case Studies 3 & 4 Report (DCA April 2017).
84 DCA, Cambodia methodological paper in preparation of the field mission (November 2016).
85 LICADHO, 'Good Wives', Women Land Campaigners and the Impact of Human Rights Activism (November 2014).
86 Domestic violence refers here to violence between husband and wife and thus conflict resolution is sought to pacify family conflict as a whole rather than protecting women's rights or addressing violence against women specifically.
87 The clear majority of selected interviewees chosen to be interviewed by the partners were rights holders that had either not received compensation or received unsatisfactory reallocation, as the partners chose to show the team the most 'difficult' cases.
88 These statistics are derived from CCFC computer base data and could not be further verified, triangulated or documented.
89 DCA, Cambodia methodological paper in preparation of the field mission (November 2016).
90 Families did not accept the offer as it did not come with any commitment to develop infrastructure such as roads, water sources, etc. which they had access to on land they were forcefully evicted from.
91 DCA, Cambodia methodological paper in preparation of the field mission, (November 2016).
92 EC, Strategic plan 2016–2018 (2016).
93 DCA, Cambodia methodological paper in preparation of the field mission (November 2016).
94 For similar findings see also Equitable Cambodia, 'Report on Impacts of Sugar Concessions in O'Bat Moan village, Oddar Meanchey, Cambodia – O'Bat Moan Village Study', 4 December 2014.
95 EC has targeted a great variety of duty bearers such as public central and local authorities, international and regional organisations and the private sector at the local and international levels.
96 Following a mediation held in January 2015, the legal proceedings brought on behalf of 200 Cambodian villagers against Tate & Lyle Industries and T&L Sugars in the UK, and against the Koh Kong Sugar Industry Company Ltd. and Koh Kong Plantation Company Ltd. in Cambodia, have reached a tentative settlement. The precise terms of the settlement are still confidential (and were not accessible for this study) but include an allocation of 300 hectares of land for the villagers by the Koh Kong companies, still subject to approval by the Cambodian government.

Part III

5 Critical reframing of gender equality

Based on a summary of conclusions, Chapter 5 discusses a critical reframing of gender equality towards gender justice. The chapter thus focuses on the main elements which have particular significance for the transformation of the deep structures of inequality and injustice affecting women in the field of IDA and which need to be included in the process of reframing gender equality. These provide a challenge to a certain tendency to find consensus at all costs in conflicting theories[1] and propose instead to take the following stand. In light of Nancy Fraser's tri-dimensional matrix of justice,[2] the section proposes to refocus the interpretation of gender equality around the following: a clear political engagement with gender justice[3] through i) the notion of redistribution[4] and ii) the universality of violations of women's human rights.[5] The re-legitimisation of the universality of women's human rights violations[6] is further discussed in connection with the need for a common political engagement within a wider notion of social responsibility, as defined by Hannah Arendt.[7]

The last section of the chapter concludes with the limitations of this book and an outline of the key elements for further research. It is intended that this section will provide useful elements for decision-makers and practitioners, for their consideration when designing new strategic frameworks, policies and programmes to sharpen outcomes and impact on gender justice in IDA.

Summary of conclusions

The book has argued that the inadequacy of IDA's response to substantive socio-economic injustices affecting women living in poverty and deprivation has largely been due to a conceptual weakness in how gender equality is defined. This has coincided with shifts in feminist theory, as divergent schools of thought have promoted competing theories as to how gender equality is best understood or should be best interpreted. This has led to compromises being sought with those whose ideologies resist gender equality, or those who effectively limit the concept of gender equality to representation and recognition.

In particular, it has been the contention of this book that the interpretation of gender equality in IDA has changed and now reflects an insufficient focus on maldistribution and on the universal forms of violations of women's human rights. As a consequence, prevailing IDA discourse has insufficiently challenged the common patriarchal structures entrenching substantive injustices for women across societies and throughout the main levels of the IDA field. Furthermore, it is contended that such changes in focus form recurrent patterns across the main levels of the field of IDA. It is argued that analysing these ideological developments not only deepens our understanding of the weak response to gender inequalities and injustices in IDA at present, but possibly also informs a refocus of gender equality to more adequately address gender injustices and inequalities.

Chapter 1 has discussed how the focus of the theoretical framing underpinning the concept of gender equality changed and how key elements were displaced, dismissed, eclipsed and eroded. It argued that the main change of focus in theoretical framing was the eclipse of the notion of redistribution, which has taken place at various levels. Such misplacement has permeated the fundamental theoretical elements of the framework underpinning the concept of gender equality. The eclipse of the notion of distribution – whether accidental or not – is thus identified as crucial and recurrent within a variety of key elements forming the theoretical underpinning of the concept of gender equality, effectively denuding the concept of theoretical grounds with which to address socio-economic injustices for women within the field of IDA. The sidelining of redistribution was thus extended to the definition of IDA and to the definitions of WID and GAD.

Furthermore, the chapter showed that it ought to have become evident that an understanding of women's injustices and inequalities, viewed not in isolation but within broader visions of exploitation and subordination, would result in mutually enriching analyses and theoretical frameworks. Instead of an enriching and solidarity-based theoretical framework underpinning gender equality in IDA, critiques of cultural, religious and identity-related oppressions have prevailed under the guise of anti-essentialism, postcolonialism and in the name of multiculturalism. In practice, and as Fraser illustrated, Third World feminist critiques drifted towards a focus solely upon national identity and communanitarianism on the grounds of postcolonialist struggle, doing away with redistribution – which, paradoxically, was the very lens through which exploitations of all forms could be analysed.

The analysis thus challenged the justification upon which some theoretical perspectives argued that focusing on redistribution and universal women's human rights would have inevitably led to the much-apprehended material neo-colonialist threat of 'robbing women of their historical agency'. On the contrary, the chapter demonstrated that excluding redistribution and universalism leads to a weakening of the solidarity dimension, 'robbing women' of potential grounds for justice claims. This consequently challenged the grounds upon which redistribution and universalism were displaced, dismissed and eroded by the proponents of Third Worldist, anti-essentialist and difference feminisms.

The analysis further demonstrated that as shifts in power relations between North and South and East and West developed as new superpowers appeared, a sole intersectional identity politics analytical matrix could no longer be justified as the dominant analytical framework. Increasingly more relevant was the extent to which postcolonial ruling elites were willing to integrate redistribution and power sharing in their policies, addressing in other words South-South as well as North-South exploitation and inequalities.

In conclusion, the choice to date at the theory level has been an oscillation between either placing all dimensions on an equal footing, resulting in intersectional and multifocal analytical frameworks, or supplanting socio-economic analysis and universalism with local identities and cultural relativism. In either case, as a result and implication of this theoretical displacement, it has been increasingly difficult to frame the interpretation of gender equality within a contemporary theoretical framework which adequately addresses universal violations of women's human rights and systemic gender inequalities and injustices.

Chapter 2 concluded that a holistic understanding of visible and invisible veils limiting women's freedom and women's human rights is only possible to view through an analysis which does not confine itself to identity politics in one particular cultural or religious context disconnected, as it were, from similar socio-cultural practices existing in other contexts. Rather, comparing underlying ideologies across cultures was found to be crucial to avoid using cultural and religious differences as an alibi for justifying gender inequalities and injustices.

This has proven to be particularly relevant to capturing a deeper political understanding of the broader implications and underpinning ideologies informing the reservation process of some UN Member States to CEDAW. The reservations put forward to Articles 1 and 2 of CEDAW were not mere technical compromises at the international law level. Rather, they showed the extent to which, by following the politics of identity, gender equality and basic women's human rights had been overshadowed to the point of 'opting out' of the only international legal instrument purporting to provide adequate protection. It was thereby demonstrated that the compromise in question clearly amounted to a defeat of the very purpose of the Convention.

The analysis demonstrated that identity politics and apparent cultural differences had been prioritised when defining both the content and the adherence process to CEDAW. However, the analysis showed that 'cultural differences' were different in appearance only. As argued, the expression of such seemingly culturally grounded resistance shared similar underpinning ideologies which had much in common with those patriarchal structures allowing misogynist discourse to become respectable under the (false) guise of the culturally distinct.

Thus, anxiety surrounding the possible exclusion of gender-discriminatory Member States from CEDAW on the grounds of respect for 'cultural differences' and 'religious perspectives' resulted in substantive gender equality being diluted and overshadowed. The strategy of compromises was intended to result in the inclusion of the largest number of countries irrespective of differences surrounding their actual degree of commitment to the essence of the Convention. By following an inclusionary strategy beyond the point of compromise and ultimately silencing fundamental notions such as violence against women, CEDAW was effectively weakened.

Thus, a universalist analytical grid was proven to be useful to uncover the common ideological patterns in patriarchal societies which considered both the struggle against violence against women and gender equality difficult concepts to commit to when women are fundamentally considered as a secondary class of citizens with access to 'different' categories of rights.

Further, the chapter showed that the concept of gender equality at the international policy level has also been the subject of a steady decline from its gradually weakened interpretation to its discarding. It explored some of the common underlying reasons for the weakening of gender equality and thus the weakening of its potential impact in international conferences and policy platforms. It was demonstrated that there were basic patriarchal visions of society which, according to their proponents, ought not to be challenged by shifting gender roles and power relations. Thus, the analysis demonstrated that using the exclusionary argument based on cultural/religious differences was indeed a strategic move. Consequently, the analysis showed that this weakened concept of gender equality ultimately failed to address the injustices experienced by poor women in developing countries by leaving the existing structures of oppression mostly intact. It served instead as a protection of traditional patriarchal interpretations of gender equality as legitimate and justifiable within the hegemonic trend of identity politics.

In conclusion, the change in focus at the international legislative level affecting the interpretation of gender equality was characterised by a dilution of gender equality due to the privileging of inclusionary strategies to obtain a large number of ratifications and low-level consensus before the *political* and once-revolutionary focus and force of gender equality in IDA. The chapter further demonstrated that the focus in the interpretation of gender equality at the international policy level changed from its original revolutionary perspective to fit neoliberal interpretations of IDA and conservative religious institutions' focus on preserving traditional gender hierarchies. Arguably, this change in focus dovetailed with the identity politics focus underpinning the framing of gender equality, as discussed in Chapter 1. It was demonstrated that the main implication of such a change in focus was that the gender equality interpretation fell short of providing an adequate international legislative and policy framework with which to address the socio-economic injustices faced by women living in poverty in developing countries.

Chapter 3 illustrated the ways in which gender equality was interpreted at the national level, in donor policies and recipient country policies.

The chapter showed that DFID for some time had shared much of its core values, its orientations and interpretations of development, and the themes which ought to be prioritized, with the WB. These had little to do with social justice and the challenging of power relations or structural inequalities, but were clearly aligned to a neoliberal and macro-economic understanding of poverty. It is demonstrated that it was thus difficult to incorporate gender equality – together with its comprehensive and holistic approach – into for example a DFID and WB framework without altering gender equality's *raison d'être* quite fundamentally. The crucial question is thus not so much what the already defined IDA donor policies mean for women and girls (otherwise known as the 'add-women-and-stir' approach) but whether the political vision underlying these objectives is adequately bold to challenge and respond to the injustices and inequalities they face.

The contemporary situation in IDA exposes the ways in which gender equality has been skilfully diluted and fundamentally altered to suit particular influential neoliberal orientations. This chapter demonstrates that a critical analysis of the political interpretations of 'development assistance' matters and has crucial consequences for the definition and incorporation of gender equality in IDA. The chapter further shows that other bilateral donors at the forefront of mainstreaming gender equality and who have different political inclinations find it difficult to resist this trend. Their tendency at best is to opt for a compromise – an all-ideologies-inclusive strategy and at worst, to simply trade their original social orientation for the prevailing neoliberal trend.

The chapter offered a critical examination of the varying interpretations of gender equality at the policy level in different political and geographical contexts in the following examples.

The Nicaraguan example focusing on abortion is a striking example of how certain Third Worldist and postcolonialist perspectives reviving cultural relativism and anti-imperialism can at best serve the interest of elite women and powerful clergymen and at worst justify women's deaths within cultural identities legitimacies. It also showed how gender equality and women's rights can be interpreted in a manner that serves the interests of conservative ideologies of some, to the cost of women's lives that are, de facto, defined as being worth far less than that of an embryo. In the best scenario, gender equality is thus considered an issue at the margins of democratisation, a secondary matter that can wait, while in the worst scenario, it is rejected as representing foreign interventionism.

The example of Museveni's politics and gender inequalities in Uganda illustrates the paradoxes in the use of postcolonialist ideology to preserve what customary and colonial conservative ideologies have in common, namely patriarchal values, exploitation and the maldistribution of resources.

In the case of Thomas Sankara's speech on International Women's Day in 1987 in Burkina Faso, it is argued that gender inequality as interpreted and described by Sankara still provides the most relevant and radical interpretation and perspective in the field of IDA, despite being espoused many years ago, by a man. It poses a direct challenge, as Sankara demonstrated the possibility of being at once culturally self-critical and universalist, whilst still upholding an anti-imperialist position. This example shows that Sankara was and still remains an exception, not only amongst contemporary elite African leaders and contemporary Marxist revolutionary leaders around the world, but within the Left and the hegemonic feminist identity politics itself.

The examples presented above thus demonstrate that with the exception of Sankara, neither neoliberalist, so-called Marxist revolutionary, nor anti-imperialist regimes seem to have effectively challenged the patriarchal power structures and injustices faced by women in IDA. Thus, from the findings regarding interpretations of gender equality at both the donor policy and country policy levels, the conclusions above outline the implications of overshadowing socio-economic and substantive justice for women in IDA.

The change in focus thus affected the interpretation of gender equality at the national level, in the same manner as at donor level: the concept of gender equality was sufficiently malleable and weakened to fit any political agenda. The possible implications exemplified at the national policy level showed that with the exception of Sankara, neither neoliberalist, nor so-called Marxist revolutionary, nor anti-imperialist regimes seemed to have interpreted gender equality in a way that could effectively challenge the patriarchal power structures and injustices faced by women in IDA – clearly against their respective interests. Thus, from the conclusions outlined above, a recurrent pattern of overshadowing socio-economic and substantive justice for women at the policy level in IDA is largely identified, save where political engagement to the contrary is revealed.

Chapter 4 showed that ignoring the universal and common elements at the heart of violations of women's human rights accounts, whilst focusing solely on their cultural differences, would essentially limit and weaken the consolidation of international political claims based on solidarity across cultures and continents. For if one sets such examples in their wider universal context, they have the potential to expose commonly shared human rights abuses, inequitable power relations and patriarchal behaviour. Instead, by viewing such examples through a sole stance of identity politics and cultural relativism, only a partial account is revealed. This would effectively exclude a deeper layer of analysis which identifies the common systemic and universal forms of injustices faced by women and men across the globe, resonating so tragically with one another.

This is further reinforced by the evidence related to women's human rights violations regarding violence against women and gender inequalities defined as the unequal distribution of resources in Uganda. This example demonstrated that by extrapolating the related data in Uganda, commonalities with other neighbouring countries, regions and continents can be identified, in order to uncover universal connections with similar patterns of human rights violations and inequalities. This further showed that drawing universal patterns of connections across cultural identities as an approach does not have to be necessarily expressed in a Eurocentric, top-down and neo-colonialist manner, or indeed with such an enterprise in mind, but rather the opposite. This analysis showed that rather than projecting field data into 'ahistoricism', this method opened up the possibility of drawing analytical matrixes to uncover patriarchal systems of oppression which sadly underpin the most common universal violations of human rights.

Thus, the chapter showed, through field examples in Burkina Faso and Cambodia, that violations of fundamental human rights and gender inequalities cannot be fully defined in disconnection from one another, as if locked within the boundaries of cultural differences and identities, as this approach ultimately risks providing a justification and granting the ultimate legitimacy for the perpetration of such injustices. The data collected from diverse socio-cultural settings showed that underpinning human rights and women's human rights violations are universal systemic patterns of oppression, exploitation and inequitable distribution of power and resources.

In conclusion, the chapter demonstrated that at the programme and field levels too, the meaning of gender equality from systemic gender injustices at the field level, leads at best, to maintaining the status quo with regard to transformative changes in systemic injustices and at worst to the protection of elites' rights and empowerment.

On the one hand, it could be argued that the results achieved in representation and recognition were first steps towards gender equality and an achievement in themselves, compared with a previously gender-blind situation or a situation that excluded women from participating on a par with men. On the other hand, the main risk presented by some examples in the field clearly was that these 'minimum standards' as they ought to be considered became 'maximum standards' and the sole steps towards gender equality, thereby significantly reducing the meaning of gender equality to numerical performance. The overwhelming interpretation of gender equality as representation and recognition also entailed that connections to the broader level of structural inequalities at the national, regional and international levels were not made. This tended to isolate the programmes from broader socio-economic analysis which could have provided a deeper insight as to the relevance of the programme and its potential impact on the structural causes of gender inequalities.

Finally, the analysis of shifts in theories, policies and programmes showing the changes in focus and compromises in the interpretations of 'gender equality', analysed respectively in Chapters 1, 2, 3 and 4, uncovered the following common patterns: a consistent pattern of eclipse of the notion of redistribution leading to weakened and politically disengaged interpretation of gender equality. This in turned left the concept opened to political interpretation radically different from the original interpretation of gender equality (with some rare exceptions) which could effectively ignore substantive inequalities and injustices suffered by women in IDA and focus on quantitative issues of representation or anecdotal recognition of special women's needs. In parallel, the cultural relativist renaissance through the form of identity politics implied that gender injustices and inequalities suffered another layer of further isolation as commonalities across cultures and identities were no longer in focus or indeed legitimate and dismissed as postcolonialist – an argument that had particular resonance with political and religious entities with an interest in keeping women's conditions and status well within the boundaries of patriarchal rules and hierarchies.

Reframing gender equality as gender justice

As discussed above, under the dominant focus of 'representation' and 'recognition' in the interpretation of gender equality lie much of the same claims expressed by postcolonialists and Third Worldists such as Mohanty as well as difference feminists such as Young as follows:

> Sexual, ethnic, and national groups are often understood as entirely other and opposed, sharing no attributes with the defining group, locked in despised bodies and fixed natures.[8]

If anything, whilst such critiques of a monolithic definition of otherness may have their place in racist and homophobic contexts, this book has demonstrated the interest of breaking through the boundaries of identities and differences precisely not to confine the so-called other into the isolation of his or her condition and socio-cultural context. It was to the contrary argued for an urgent reconnection of the so-called other with our core humanity as the way forward towards addressing gender injustices, discrimination and inequalities.

As discussed throughout the book, the delegitimisation of universalism in women's human rights and the misplacement of distribution have had the following wider implications, as further evidenced in Siobhan Mullaly's conclusion:

> In recent years, feminism has had much to lose in abandoning its roots in a commitment to universalism, individual autonomy and human rights. The alternatives proposed do not provide the resources necessary to build a truly global feminism, global in the sense of addressing discrimination, inequalities (and injustices) in all its complex variety and monotonous similarity. . . . In recent years feminism's preoccupation with difference has meant that class politics and questions of economic injustices have been ignored. Yet, at both national and international levels, distributive injustices threaten the pursuit of justice. Extreme poverty persists throughout the world and income inequalities continue to grow in many countries, both rich and poor. Gender remains against this background, a significant factor of poverty and inequalities.[9]

The book argues for a clear rejection of cultural relativism as a possible justification, 'exotification' of the different 'other' and isolation of violations of women's human rights irrespective of where or when they take place.

Thus, from the example of interpretations of gender equality, it seems obvious that blind tolerance and inclusion regarding religious differences does not ensure an adequate response to inequalities and injustices faced by women, nor does it adequately challenge common patterns of patriarchy across the different religious and political contexts as evidenced in Chapters 3 and 4. Violence against women, whether occurring in the private or public sphere, must be unequivocally condemned in national legislation (as now targeted by the SDGs) and freedom from such violence must be recognised as being a full and integral part of core international human rights without any possible option for 'opting out'. Furthermore, reservations on the definition of equality between men and women ought to be inadmissible as it becomes clear that reservations, in spite of their claims, have little to do with cultural or religious differences and much more to do with patriarchal power structures which ought, if anything, to be questioned and challenged rather than protected and legitimised by cultural differentialists.

In the absence of quick fix to these basic problematics and the overwhelmingly few signs of a forthcoming renewed and cohered international feminist movement to effectively address them (illustrated by current anxieties as to the possible organisation of a fifth World Conference on Women for fear of losing the much-fought-for women's human rights *acquis*), the importance of a continued critical appraisal of identity politics in feminism could not be more emphasised.

In this context, Andrea Cornwall emphasises the need to re-politicise radical feminist engagement in development and also suggests that the 'most pressing task for feminist engagement with development in these troubled times, based on Kandiyoti's reflection is that of precisely finding an appropriate politics of solidarity'.[10] Rather than a politics based on further divides across cultures, individual differences and identities, the most pressing task is indeed to focus on how to address these.

In light of Nancy Fraser's tri-dimensional matrix of justice,[11] the section below proposes to refocus the interpretation of gender equality around the following: a clear political engagement with gender justice[12] through i) the notion of redistribution[13] and ii) the universality of violations of women's human rights.[14] The re-legitimisation of the universality of women's human rights violations[15] is further discussed in connection with the need for a joint and common political engagement within a broader notion of social responsibility, as defined by Hannah Arendt[16] – perhaps a renewed ground for cross-cultural solidarity. Finally, the section will discuss a key pre-condition pertaining to the critical refocus of gender equality on gender justice: the courage of a political engagement against the status quo.

Redistribution as the key orientation of a critical focus on gender justice

Nancy Fraser remains hopeful that the third phase of feminism will develop a three-dimensional politics, holding, in her view, tremendous promise for a third phase of feminist struggle. This era would simultaneously challenge linked injustices of maldistribution, misrecognition and misrepresentation. Fraser maintains the assumption that such a third phase would harmoniously balance and integrate those, arguably, fundamentally divergent concerns.

> Developing such a three-dimensional politics . . . could overcome the chief weaknesses of phase two (of feminist politics, my addition), by rebalancing the politics of recognition and the politics of redistribution . . . and could overcome the blind spot of both previous phases of feminist politics, by explicitly contesting the injustices of misframing. Above all, such a politics could permit us to pose, and eventually to answer, the key political question of our age: How can we integrate claims for redistribution, recognition, and representation so as to challenge the full range of gender injustices in a globalizing world?[17]

In her three-dimensional theoretical matrix, consisting of a nexus between recognition, representation and distribution, Fraser focuses on 'axes of injustices that are simultaneously cultural and socioeconomic'.[18] Her third way out of feminist divides is achieved by placing gender justice as the overall aim, focusing on 'the circumstances under which the politics of recognition can help support the politics of redistribution'.[19]

However, when the politics of recognition does not support the politics of redistribution, the result achieved may have little to do with gender justice. Whilst it is agreed that a new phase in feminism ought indeed to aim at gender justice, a choice as to which key 'elements' of gender justice should take the lead in pointing at the overall direction would need to be made. This is considered particularly in light of the critique that placing all key elements on an equal footing may not provide an adequate theoretical framing and response to the problematics at hand within the specific field of IDA.

It is sustained that given the key findings and conclusions above, it is evident that the overall focus of the tri-dimensional gender justice analytical matrix ought to be 'redistribution' for an impact on poverty reduction. It is further argued that whilst 'recognition' and 'representation' ought nonetheless to underpin gender equality and gender justice claims, they ought not be positioned on an equal footing with 'redistribution' if poverty reduction is maintained as the overall aim of IDA through the SDGs.

Repositioning 'redistribution' as the overall goal further implies that those living with more will necessarily have to re-learn to live with less. The solution for addressing gender inequalities from a redistributive justice perspective is disarmingly simple but at the same time next to impossible to achieve without international and national enforceable norms and political will. The underpinning focus of existing and future international norms and policies addressing gender inequalities need also to change from one of 'representation' towards substantive gender justice.

From a wider perspective, the key elements outlined above call for a broader change in political paradigm. Such a change in paradigm must come from and be firmly anchored within the Left to challenge hegemonic ideologies both within the Right and the Left itself, whilst at the same time emancipating terminology such as 'redistribution' from the ghost of the failed 'communist era'. 'Redistribution' is the Achilles' heel of poverty reduction. The end of the Cold War, together with the end of communism and the illusions of Marxist ideals, cannot be solely to blame for the silencing of the (sadly) still much relevant and contemporary notion of 'maldistribution' and increasing global inequality trends.

In conclusion, such a renewed focus ought to move the underpinning theoretical framework towards reasserting the political nature of the argument which must be made to achieve social and economic justice for women. It would do so by making the notion of gender equality move from apparent neutrality to becoming instead a bolder and politically charged concept which may be accepted or rejected but not open for compromises that pertain to avoid conflict whilst only weakening the meaning and scope of gender equality down to an innocuous term and as a result, a next to invisible impact in the field.

Reclaiming universal humanism in women's human rights

As Fraser acknowledges, the main pre-condition for achieving a would-be harmonious nexus in the three-dimensional gender justice matrix is an assumed universal perspective underlying fundamental human rights:

> In proposing to assess recognition claims from the standpoint of social equality, I assume that varieties of recognition politics that fail to respect human rights are unacceptable even if they promote social equality. . . . I assume that no identity politics is acceptable that fails to respect fundamental human rights, of the sort usually championed by left-wing liberals.[20]

In the context of IDA this very caveat constitutes a significant challenge in and of itself, as an unresolved debate. It has been argued in Chapter 1 that universalism has been delegitimised by the politics of identity, the subsequent revival of cultural relativism and with it, the very structures which support the universality of fundamental women's human rights. The significance of this caveat is such within the field of gender equality in IDA that it cannot be considered to be an assumption taken for granted.

Indeed, fundamental human rights 'of the sort usually championed by the Left wing' today is championing first and foremost antiracism and within it, a subdued exotification of the 'culturally different other'. This perspective that tends to reject any human rights critiques of the 'other' as culturally disrespectful, patronising and colonising has led to justifying for example FGMs or other demeaning practices on women that are clearly contrary to their fundamental rights and dignity as human beings.

In Flores d'Arcais' view, the works of Hannah Arendt provide

> a response and antidote to the almost obsessive anti-essentialism which has induced many hermeneutical philosophies to uncover the suspicious postcolonial-white-Christian-heterosexual-man beneath every universalism and every 'normativities'.[21] Instead, Arendt clearly shows that one cannot do without at least one form of universalism, and that is the opportunity for everyone to dare, the authenticity of existence within the equality of the public sphere. Thus, she argues that all human beings (*universalism!*) are entitled to this opportunity and all governments (*universalism!*) ought to respect the multiple rights that, de facto, constitute its primary justification.[22]

In this context, Flores D'Arcais describes a fundamental connection between human rights, individual choice and 'engagement' when he writes that:

> Human rights are not universal in the sense that they are intrinsically connected to human nature as such. They are on the contrary so disconnected from human nature, that mankind has lived through thousands of years

> violating them. Many hard-fought struggles had to be won, with generations of sacrifices to finally, making human rights, only temporarily acknowledged. Human rights are in fact, so uncertain, that their violations are occurring on a daily basis in our societies.[23]

On this basis, d'Arcais concludes that human rights are not that 'human' after all – meaning not inscribed in condescendingly defined Western human nature as it is assumed. Rather, they are *civil rights*, in that they do not depend on nature, nor do they descend from heavens. Human rights are rather and indeed a matter of choice of values upon which to base our short collective co-existence on earth and to relieve some of the inequitable and unjust overload some of us are carrying.

If women's human rights, too, do not depend on nature, then they must also be considered a matter of choice of values upon which to base our short common co-existence on earth. Without a chosen social and collective engagement and without political force, women's human rights and gender equality cannot be expected to become safe *acquis*. Universal women's human rights and gender equality are indeed a matter of choice of values in the actualisation of men and women's joint individual and collective *responsibility*. At the same time, the choice of such values ought not to be a limited privilege for a few, but indeed accessible to all – including the so-called exotic other – and especially those bearing the largest brunt of socio-economic and political injustices worldwide. It is in this sense that 'universalism' in women's human rights needs to be understood rather than as a presumed imperialist or neoliberal project.

Engaging 'collective responsibility' in Hannah Arendt's reflection entails the superiority of collective responsibility over personal identity claims and further provides the ethical grounds for a renewed universal responsibility of solidarity as follows:

> No moral, individual and personal, standards of conduct will ever be able to excuse us from collective *responsibility*. This vicarious responsibility for things we have not done, this taking upon ourselves the consequences for things we are entirely innocent of, is the price we pay for the fact that we live our lives not by ourselves but among our fellow men, and that the faculty of action, which, after all, is the political faculty *par excellence*, can be actualized only in one of the many and manifold forms of human community.[24]

Thus, to achieve transformative changes in gender justice, a critical refocus of gender equality in IDA must re-legitimise the universal form of humanism underpinning women's human rights and gender equality as a common global, individual and collective *responsibility*, in Arendt's sense. The collective notion of responsibility must thus be the underpinning politically engaged framework to a re-legitimised universal humanism and chosen common values of women's human rights and gender equality towards gender justice.

Possibly, in response to what may appear as a major deadlock within left feminist thought and as Anne Bottomley suggests, it is indeed necessary, more than ever before, to think: 'in Deleuzean terms, if we think more of feminism as a force, a movement of potentials, rather than an identity'.[25] If feminism ought indeed to be considered as a force which may result in impetus towards necessary changes in the context of development assistance, then the underpinning feminist theoretical framework must obviously be socially and collectively *responsible* and *engaged* in challenging social and cultural injustices.

Some years ago, Tracy Higgins warned that whereas the risk of coercion (e.g. definition of the problematics by one group over another) could not be fully eliminated, the risk of inaction was ever present. She further highlighted the inevitable dichotomy of either

> dismissing culturally distinct experience of women as false consciousness or ignoring pervasive limits on women's freedom under simple tolerance of cultural differences.[26]

If it is indeed the risk of inaction predicted by Higgins that seems to have prevailed as a result of the hegemonic focus on the politics of identity. Such foreseeable theoretical unfolding was clearly a misinterpretation of original feminist thinking and arguably did misplace the main purpose of feminism. As early as 1949, *The Second Sex* was published and became a landmark text[27] which arguably foresaw all subsequent trends in feminist thought, including difference feminism.[28] In her question 'What is a woman?' de Beauvoir was not looking for an immutable and static definition of womanhood in order to impose it as universal dogma over the 'other', even less to 'rob women of their agency' – but quite the contrary. The answers she provided echoed Sartre's answer to the question: What is a human being? in *Existentialism Is a Humanism.*[29] It is that choice, will and agency should precede the essence – even when and where that choice is severely more limited by hardships and challenging circumstances.

In her famous statement 'one is not born, but rather becomes, a woman', de Beauvoir emphasises that the choices and struggles to be set free from cultural, religious and ethnic stereotypes and limitations to one's freedom are the key elements that will ultimately define women as emancipated human beings, rather than second-class citizens. Clearly, in de Beauvoir's definition, women are not homogeneously encapsulated in their cultural, social, ethnic or religious background. Rather, their essence is defined by their own 'free' agency and their 'free will' to challenge their own environment, the deeply rooted stereotypes in which they are socialised, the unquestioned reality and 'normality' within formal and informal cultural norms and to be free to bring changes to one's own condition. The unequal and unjust conditions referred to by de Beauvoir are still contemporary more than half a century later, and given the problematics exposed in Chapter 4, are clearly not limited to the white, heterosexual French middle classes.

In de Beauvoir's view, becoming a woman meant a dynamic process of emancipation towards greater justice. It is in this sense that de Beauvoir, and some feminist theorists such as Charlesworth, carry the most useful theoretical framing for gender equality in IDA – within a visionary ability to distinguish the intrinsic universality in women's subordination and conditions across times, localities and cultures worldwide. Moreover, de Beauvoir, like the existentialist movement, places the responsibility for challenging these conditions with women themselves. De la Boëtie's *Discourse on Voluntary Servitude*,[30] written at the age of 18 in the mid-16th century remains no less contemporary today. Resonating in special ways against current dominant feminist trends and constituting perhaps one of the most pervasive challenges to the implementation of women's human rights, de la Boëtie develops the idea that it is an error to think that 'submission' is necessarily forced upon someone.

Whereas many arguments may be made about the varying degrees of freedom of choice available to women in different socio-economic and cultural conditions, the view that such an existentialist position is likely to 'rob women of their agency' – in Mohanty's terms – is clearly a misreading of the existentialist position as de facto postcolonialist. Thus, it could be deduced that the displacement of the legitimacy of fundamental women's human rights is partly based on a misreading of existentialism – justifying to some extent non-interventionism and the *status quo* in the face of violations of women's human rights.

The courage of a political engagement as a pre-condition

In this field, Bernard-Henry Levy offers some of the most thought-provoking arguments against contemporary indifference and the status quo that has been experienced most acutely in the field of international development assistance, certainly over the past two decades.

He argues that

> the concept of women's human rights ought to challenge the bleak outlook for all fields in which totalitarianism and patriarchy impose domination and oppression upon women – irrespective of whether these women may be perceived as willing victims or not.[31]

It should be possible to include an infinite range of diverse individual cultural situations by engaging socially and collectively in a recurrent critique of patriarchal and totalitarian patterns of social injustices – which remain a 'monotonous' common feature of women's realities, as illustrated in Chapter 4.

According to Levy, there are no satisfactory compromises between universalism and relativism from an ethical and politically engaged standpoint. Levy argues against the philosophy of the 'reasonable man', pacified, always preoccupied with finding consensuses at all costs, common senses and middle grounds. Such reasonableness has the key aim of reducing all conflicting theories to a lowest common denominator which, he argues, ends up not being much useful to either side and achieving little more than settling upon an insipid at best, and irrelevant at worst, middle ground:

> The philosophy that seeks to resolve once for all, all oppositions in conflicting stand points, and view them only as expression of misunderstanding and

> false dichotomies, which a good consensual debate and focus on interconnections has the duty to resolve . . . Kant used to define it as "sensus communis". In other words, "the right middle ground" . . . which he thought was nothing better than flat ideology, without aspirations or strengths, and which, after trying so hard to bring consensus between everyone, only end up embracing sheer emptiness.[32]

Thus, Levy contends that a crucial question that ought to be raised, rather than leading to compromise, is the challenge in which a particular theory is engaged with:

> Engaged intellectuals and philosophers do not remake the world neither do they save us all from the draughts of misfortune. They can merely seek to make living on earth, a little more bearable, merely relieving us a little of our burden. Wars and injustices are not thereby prevented but at least some of their (worst) victims are taken care of, thus ensuring that inhumanity does not have the very last word.[33]

If only feminist theories underpinning gender equality in the field of IDA could fulfil this role – a bold political engagement that ensured inhumanity would not have the last word, rather than seeking shallow compromises between relativism and universalism, there would be better scope for moving forward, well away from the current middle-ground position which makes transformative gender changes so difficult to reach.

This book has striven to demonstrate that there are non-ethnocentric violations of women's human rights and inequalities and that if anything, third wave feminism ought to be focusing on how to effectively address these. Indeed, focusing on differences is a matter of ideological choice, not an inevitability with which to compromise at any cost. Whilst being careful not to fall into messianic positivist interpretations of 'progress' (which is often a temptation in the field of IDA, but more in the name of a utopian bid to find solutions to the immensity of the problems at hand than a compelling postcolonial instinct), an unambiguous rejection of cultural relativism is urgently needed as a means of making one's social responsibility clear. Faced with the realities of women's human rights violations, there are no possible compromises on these issues, and to be lured by hegemonic trends of political correctness and tolerance for intolerant religious ideologies and so-called unsurmountable cultural differences is to protect and legitimise the unacceptable.

Some of the broader implications for not rejecting oppressive traditions, dogmas and theories is that not only neoliberalism, as Fraser argued, is succeeding in having egalitarian and social justice claims unattended and silenced, but worse, the extreme right across Europe is rapidly regaining ground[34] in re-appropriating the empty political space abandoned (and at times silenced) by the identity-politics-focused Left, but this time, with a genuine colonialist and racist project – such as the exclusion of foreigners from Europe using the defence of secularism and 'women's human rights' as an opportune, albeit paradoxical, alibi.[35]

This said, to reject oppressive traditions and cultural oppression, such as the few cases of women attempting to break free from the Mafia,[36] takes a certain degree of outstanding courage, a strong personal political will and sense of critical thinking to question one's own roots and cultural hierarchies and break free from the dominance of locally grounded feudalisms permeating one's family and deeply rooted in one's own mentality. In the case of the Mafia example, rare are the women that have had the courage to risk their lives not to submit any longer to the rules and ideologies of a minority. Likewise, with human rights defenders, journalists, writers, artists, bloggers and cartoonists that are refusing to be silent, submit to or silently support dominant rules and ideologies – be they totalitarian, religiously indoctrinated or dominant politically correct discourse which condone discrimination and human rights abuses under the guise of 'non-discrimination' – it takes some form of outstanding courage, something of a troublemaker and a beautiful mind, to question pre-established truths and hierarchies, often to be paid with one's life[37] – a minority of free thinkers in the midst of the mass of ideological followers or the mass of followers of virtual nothingness.

Much of today's development world is bedevilled by crimes against humanity, another terrain abandoned by the Left, in seldom publicised wars in places such as DR Congo, where violations of fundamental women's human rights, together with oppression and inequality, occur on a massive scale. The direct implications of silence and indifference can be quantified in death tolls and rape tolls in this instance. One may wonder indeed about left-wing feminists' astounding silence in the face of such massive women's rights violations, or when faced by the bravery of women Kurdish fighters, all occurring in non-postcolonialist struggles.[38]

Inevitably, it is fully recognised that a more profound legitimacy and power is awarded to these issues, when Kamel Daoud in one of his articles[39] invites us all to free ourselves from postcolonial reasoning and think beyond victimisation, in order to critically re-think both the West and the rest, both the North and the South in a mutually self-critical appraisal. He denounces postcolonial consciousness as developing a convenient fragmentation of humanity, of individual narcissistic victimisation. Thus, he denounces the impossibility for southern countries to free themselves from colonial history and re-invent their future as long as so little responsibility is taken for one's own conditions following half a century of independence. Defused across the left-wing intelligentsia and in particular within American academia, this school of thought allows for lopsided critiques, he argues: it allows us to talk about Western discrimination and racism towards migrants from the South but not the massive Sub-Saharan deportation from Algeria or from other so-called Arabic countries; it leads to considering as a violation of human rights the Mediterranean wall to Europe but not the wall between Algeria and Morocco, etc.

Daoud calls upon all of us to critically reassess the failures of our post-independencies and our enslavement to decolonising casts that have turned into predator casts. Such statement resonates well beyond Algeria, across northern Africa, Sub-Saharan Africa, the Middle East, Asia and Latin America. There is little mention of introspective critiques of intra-ethnic racism, misogyny, homophobia and other forms of culturally grounded discriminations. This failure is underpinning the reason why women's human rights have not adequately been addressed with stronger force, boldness and power in IDA. In this human rights enforcement or lack of enforcement game the West is certainly not innocent, but neither is the South, as Kamel Daoud highlights – a radicalised postcolonial ideology does not accept much nuances, and little self-critique for fear that these would exonerate colonial atrocities or sound as if the West is (still) patronising the rest. At the same time, there could be no better-crafted alibi: arguing that a given culture is 'not yet ready', half a century into independence to receive critiques by the 'West' not to abuse human rights. One may thus wonder, how many 'corrective rapes'[40] of lesbians so as to 'culturally straighten them up' should be silently ignored in post-apartheid South Africa whilst assigned to observe a 'culturally sensitive and non-colonialist' position. This, as many other examples in this book, show the kind of absurdity that risks being reached in reality.

Like with the example Thomas Sankara, it did take a man from the South to firmly and unambiguously condemn FGMs before feminist academics from the West and governments would follow in criminalising the practice. It took once again a man from the South to pronounce the following words which hegemonic feminist trends have somehow lost along the way:

> In the south, women's body belong to all, except to women themselves . . . it is a public space, a kind of dispossession at birth . . . imprisoning a woman is imprisoning oneself as a man, it is imprisoning life itself and together with it, our desire for the world that is badly in need of repairing.[41] . . . where women are hidden, buried, ignored or made invisible, it simply means that we are burying ourselves and together with it, life and humanity itself.[42]

In the South – and as still not fully addressed in the North and in the West – undermining women's human rights is undermining what unites us most deeply with men, our inner sense of humanity. Thus, for these reasons, a collective and political 'engagement' towards substantive gender justice must be reclaimed as the appropriate focus of gender equality within IDA.

Conclusion

On the basis of the summary of conclusions presented in the sections above, the key elements of a refocus of gender equality are envisaged as follows.

The first element of a refocus in the interpretation of gender equality is a (re) legitimisation of universality based on the awareness, in the Arendtian sense, of universal collective sense of social responsibility. A re-appropriation of a universalist perspective is the basis upon which gender equality in IDA can legitimately impact on injustices and inequalities facing women – for those that choose the challenging path of claiming gender justice.

It seems that such an adequate framing for such an element can be, for the main part, found in the past, notably in the original intentions of early feminists or in some hypothetical future in which current feminist theoretical divides – notably those discussed above – would be harmonized, as Fraser's third-phase feminism suggests. If finding agreement on the content of a possible third phase in feminism towards gender justice, in light of the deep political and theoretical divides discussed above, still seems a long way ahead, most important and urgent in the field of IDA is to reposition discarded key elements at the core of the meaning and focus of gender equality as relevant to IDA, in order to redirect its significance towards solidarity and gender justice.

The key pre-condition is the collective and political 'engagement' towards substantive and distributive socio-economic justice and universalism. The underlying intent behind some anti-essentialist critiques to serve the interests of so-called irretrievably different 'Third World' women and other excluded groups in the context of IDA seems to provide a justification for non-intervention at best and at worst grounds for the perpetration of culturally accepted violence, repressions, exploitations and other women's human rights abuses to continue in all impunity and with the silent consent of the dominant school of feminist thought.

Therefore, and as a pre-condition, in order for the concept of gender equality to be useful in addressing these social injustices across cultures, locations and ideologies, it needs to be reinterpreted and refocused to reach beyond self-contemplation on identities. Indeed, it needs to move towards a clear and unambiguous goal of redistribution as its overall orientation, based on an understanding of the universality of women's human rights violations and supported by a collective sense of political engagement and responsibility towards gender justice.

This begs the question of the whole point and orientation of feminism – was it not conceived to address and hopefully to bring some form of change in women's condition? The title of Charles Jenck's book[43] *Critical Modernism: Where Is Post-Modernism Going?* in the field of architecture could be fairly posed to post-modern feminism with its prevailing focus on identity politics. This book has striven to show that if anything, it is not going where it was intended: in addressing women's conditions and in particular, it is not relieving those living in poverty from carrying the overwhelming burden of gender injustices.

Whilst remaining realistic as to the potential of the claims made in this book to change the minds of a few, it ought to remain possible still to be free to challenge cultural, social, economic, political and religious ideologies where they clearly interfere with fundamental women's human rights, gender justice and the core of our humanity.

Orientations for further research on women's human rights in the humanitarian field through HRBA

This section concludes with the limitations of the book and presenting possible orientations for further research.

As indicated in the methodology, the research is based on purposive examples of gender evaluations undertaken in the IDA field rather than a comprehensive comparative analysis. Thus, the research takes a limited sample and attempts to identify common patterns and trends to support the book's discussions. Based on these analyses, whilst a change of paradigm is implicitly suggested, elaborating the full content of it is beyond the scope of this book. Nevertheless, some further orientations and key elements are drawn in this chapter which might be useful to policy makers, donor officials, national programme officers and other practitioners alike to incorporate in their respective fields of work.

The implied suggested change of paradigm in this book would imply a rejection of a 'certain tendency'[44] that dismisses the idea of 'grand theories' as inadequate and at the same time aware that normativism occurs within dynamics (hence the term 'framing'). This implies that before embarking on a full re-conceptualising of an entirely new focus and paradigm underpinning gender equality – which is beyond the scope of the book – there is a need to first and foremost renew and re-legitimise relevant fundamental ideas (key elements) of gender justice. This is the reason why the book focuses on and is limited to these.

To broaden the field of IDA to the increasingly interlinked field of humanitarian aid, it is thus suggested that further research be undertaken as follows. In light of newly emerging and enduring conflicts worldwide, it is suggested that the analytical framework developed in this book be adapted to the humanitarian field, post-conflict and fragile country contexts.

It is suggested that the proposed further research is oriented at analysing how key ideological shifts which underpin the interpretation of gender equality have played out at theoretical, international legislative and policy levels, at the national and donor levels and programme level within the humanitarian field, in fragile states and post-conflict zones. The main approach would keep a critical perspective throughout the research and also be used as a relevant strategy to expose the reasons why certain interpretations of gender equality have been privileged over others, and to reveal the hegemonic ideologies underpinning the interpretation of gender equality related concepts in fragile states and post-conflict zones. As with the IDA field, the research will 'reconsider what is usually taken for granted and to question common assumptions about the meaning of'[45] gender equality in fragile states and post-conflict zones.

It is expected that a critical approach would equally lead to further reflection on issues such as the hegemonic ideologies underpinning the interpretations of the concept of gender equality, the interests at play underlying these ideological trends and the extent to which these have addressed (or not) inequalities and injustices faced by women living in poverty in fragile states and post-conflict zones. Thus, the same questions will constitute the central concern of this further research as follows: Is gender equality a means towards broader social changes and poverty reduction in fragile states and post-conflict zones? Is the interpretation of gender equality in the field of post-conflicts and fragile states, as neutral and apolitical as it is presumed to be, or has it also excluded key elements of substantive justice to the benefit of representation and equal participation in structurally unequal and unjust environments?

Through adopting a critical approach, further research will seek to uncover whether, like the interpretation of gender equality in IDA, the interpretation of gender equality has, over the years, changed to displace substantive distributive socio-economic justice for women as well as other key elements and pre-conditions such as the universality of women's human rights across culturally diverse local contexts.

This therefore may also involve systematically analysing the broad levels of the humanitarian field: the theory level, the international legislative and international policy level, the donor and national policy level and finally the programme and field level. It is by critically examining the changes in focus in the interpretations of gender equality throughout these different levels that one might, through the same analytical matrix employed in the field of IDA, identify common and recurring patterns of these phenomena in the humanitarian context. It is expected that a critical examination of these common and recurrent patterns will not merely challenge specific interpretations of gender equality, but at a deeper level, question the adequacy of the theoretical framework which underpins the concept of gender equality within the humanitarian field, in the selected fragile states and post-conflict zones in relation to gender justice.

Ultimately, it is anticipated that such a critique might be useful in formulating a re-envisioned focus underpinning gender equality in the humanitarian field. Such a focus should provide, through a renewed interpretation of gender equality in fragile states and post-conflict zones, a more adequate response to gender inequalities and injustices faced by women.

If the methodology and analysis developed in the context of this book is applied in the context of post-conflict countries, it might have as effect the broadening of programmes that have usually had a narrower scope, in order to integrate issues of gender justice that would centre around redistribution of power and resources. The post-conflict context provides both precarious conditions for targeting gender justice outcomes and at the same time a unique opportunity to rebuild a society anew, refocused on gender justice. The challenge is to identify and focus on commonalities across diverse cultures against the backdrop of a revival of cultural relativist approaches emphasising differences and the legitimisation of local customary practices.

The importance of the problem relates to the fact that although gender work in the humanitarian field has increasingly progressed towards greater visibility and has been increasingly considered by donors, national duty bearers and rights holders, the results and impacts yielded, safe from some exceptions, often fall short of addressing structural gender inequalities, substantive justice and qualitative changes. Rather, gender evaluations in the humanitarian field have demonstrated that most results achieved through a gender mainstreaming approach have largely focused on representation, essentially increasing the quantitative participation of women and on the recognition of their special needs (rather than rights).

To address this problem the analytical approach envisaged in this further research is as follows:

> A Human Rights-Based Approach (HRBA) to gender work in the humanitarian field will essentially entail an assessment of the level of integration of CEDAW and other relevant regional women's human rights instruments.

> These include both conventions and soft laws. The objective of using HRBA is to identify the extent to which women's human rights have been included and the extent to which interlinkages with humanitarian activities have been made. This approach will also reveal the extent to which opportunities have been missed by omitting women's human rights.

A HRBA emphasises the responsibility to protect, promote and fulfil human rights on states and the private sector as the main duty bearers, and as further highlighted in the SDGs. HRBA is evolving within the overall framework of international law that specifies obligations that are legally binding through the ratification of international treaties and covenants examined in Chapter 2 above and reflected in many of the SDG targets and indicators. Non-legally binding instruments and international development policy commitments such as SDGs are thus also used to hold duty bearers accountable to their expression of goodwill. Thus, a HRBA applied to gender work and within an SDG framework will focus on assessing the degree to which duty bearers' capacity to be accountable and fulfil their obligations has been strengthened, notably in relation to obligations specified in CEDAW (if ratified and save for possible reservations), in UN Security Council Resolution 1325[46] on women, peace and security and in UN Security Council Resolution 1820[47] condemning the use of sexual violence as a tool of war. On the rights holders side, the approach will focus on the extent to which women have been empowered and are willing to claim their rights, despite the many challenges they face, any changes at the individual level in terms of knowledge, behaviour and access to basic services but also identifying changes in terms of formal and informal normative systems that inform and perpetrates deeply rooted stereotypes and injustices.

It is thus hoped that this new research, by readapting the theoretical framework and analyses developed in this book, might have positive ripple effects and impacts in terms of deepening the understanding of gender equality of humanitarian practitioners working in increasingly challenging environments that are post-conflict zones and fragile states, so that they might gain the tools to influence changes on the ground. Ultimately, this research seeks to respond, in a simplified manner, to the complexities of working with gender equality in the humanitarian field whilst engaging all stakeholders to become actors in their own development, empowered by their capacity and fearlessness to claim gender justice and to be free to change their conditions.

Notes

1 See BH Lévy, *De la Guerre en Philosophie* (Grasset 2010) 41–47.

2 N Fraser, *Scales of Justice: Reimagining Political Space in a Globalizing World* (Columbia University Press 2009) 16–18.

3 Gender justice is understood within Nancy Fraser's three-dimensional theory of justice. Fraser's understanding of the notion of 'justice' moves beyond that of John Rawl, which can be understood as essentially 'egalitarian liberalist-nationalist denying that norms of egalitarian distributive justice may have any applicability at the

global or international level'. See J Rawl, *The Law of Peoples* (Harvard University Press 2001).

4 See Fraser 16.

5 Ibid.

6 Political engagement is meant in the sense employed by Bernard-Henry Levy. See Lévy, *De la Guerre*.

7 H Arendt, *Responsibility and Judgment* (Schocken Books 2003) 158.

8 Young, *Justice and the Politics of Difference* 260. In this statement Iris Marion Young attempts to redefine the theory of justice as dominated by the politics of difference, largely conceptualised through oppression and exclusion claims from the ethnic and sexual minorities in the US, projected onto the rest of the world.

9 S Mullaly, *Human Rights Law in Perspective, Gender, Culture and Human Rights: Reclaiming Universalism* (Hart Publishing 2006) 25, 223.

10 D Kandiyoti, 'Political Fiction Meets Gender Myth: Post-Conflict Reconstruction, "Democratisation" and Women's Rights' in A Cornwall, E Harrison and A Whitehead (eds), *Feminisms in Development: Contradictions, Contestations and Challenges* (Zed Books 2007) 15.

11 See Fraser.

12 See Fraser 16.

13 Ibid.

14 Ibid.

15 Political engagement is meant in the sense employed by Bernard-Henry Levy. See Lévy.

16 See Arendt 158.

17 See Fraser 115.

18 N Fraser, *Adding Insult to Injury: Nancy Fraser Debates Her Critics* (Verso 2008) 12.

19 Ibid.

20 Ibid 12–13.

21 See as one example: K Bedford, 'Loving to Straighten Out Development: Sexuality and 'Ethnodevelopment' in the WB's Ecuadorian Lending (2005) 13(3) *Feminist Legal Studies* 295–322.

22 P Flores D'arcais, 'Undici Tesi su Hannah Arendt' (2007) 1 *MicroMega* 97–98.

23 J Ratzinger and P Flores d'Arcais, 'Dio Esiste? un confronto su verità, fede, ateismo moderato da Gad Lerner' (2005) supplemento al 2 *di MicroMega, il fondaco di MicroMega* 40.

24 Arendt 158.

25 A Bottomley, 'Shock to Thought: An Encounter (of a Third Kind) with Legal Feminism' (2004) 12(1) *Feminist Legal Studies* 29–65.

26 T Higgins, 'Anti-Essentialism, Relativism and Human Rights' (1996) 19 *Harvard Women's Law Journal* 408.

27 S de Beauvoir, *Le Deuxième Sexe* (first published 1949, Collection Folio-Essais, Gallimard 1986).

28 See Gilligan, *In a different Voice*; Young, *Justice and the Politics of Difference*; R West, 'Jurisprudence and Gender' in K Barlett and R Kennedy (eds), *Feminist Legal Theory: Readings in Law and Gender* (Westview Press 1991) 201.

29 JP Sartre, *L'Existentialisme est un Humanisme* (first published 1946, Collection Folio-Essais, Gallimard 1996).

30 E De La Boétie, *Discours de la Servitude Volontaire* (1576).

31 See Lévy.

32 See Lévy 41–47.

33 See Lévy 105–106.

34 See JF Khan, 'Accusés, levez-vous!' *Marianne* (15 au 21 Janvier 2011).

35 Ibid.

36 See M Kahn and A Véron, *Des Femmes dans la Mafia: Madones ou Marraines?* (nouveau monde éditions 2015).
37 See S Forti, *External Evaluation of ICORN 2012–2016, Report* (Sida March 2018).
38 In his 'Critique of Pure Tolerance' Herbert Marcuse echoed precisely this point in 1969. See RP Wolff, Barrington Moore and H Marcuse, *A Critique of Pure Tolerance* (Beacon Press 1969).
39 K Daoud, 'Le discours de repentance de l'Occident est sclérosant- Il faut se libérer des explications post-coloniales et penser au-delà de la victimisation' *Le Point* (19 October 2017).
40 See Lydia Smith, 'Corrective Rape: The Homophobic Fallout of Post-Apartheid South Africa' *The Telegraph* (21 May 2015).
41 K Daoud, 'Enfermer la femme, c'est s'emprisoner soi-même' *L'entretiens par Stéphanie Antoine, France 24* (25 September 2017). See <www.youtube.com/watch?v=UQgyvrU0cdA>.
42 See K Daoud, 'La chasse aux corps amoureux' *Le Point* (14 September 2017).
43 C Jencks, *Critical Modernism: Where Is Post-Modernism Going?* (Wiley-Academy 2007).
44 According to Honneth: 'With the great exception of Jürgen Habermas – alongside whom Antonio Gramsci should perhaps be placed – for various reasons a certain tendency to anti-normativism has prevailed, which essentially prohibited from being endowed with normative expectations vis-à vis society. . . . If the adjective 'social' is to mean anything more than 'typically found in society,' social suffering and discontent possess a *normative* core'. A Honneth, 'Redistribution as Recognition: A Response to Nancy Fraser' in N Fraser and A Honneth (eds), *Redistribution or Recognition? A Political-Philosophical Exchange* (Verso 2003) 129.
45 Ibid.
46 See S/RES/1325 (2000) UNSCR 1325(2000).
47 See S/RES/1820 (2008) UNSCR 1820 (2008).

Bibliography

Books

An-Na'im AA, *Human Rights in Cross-Cultural Perspectives* (University of Pensylvania Press 1992)

———, 'Human Rights in the Muslim World' in Steiner H and Alston P (eds), *International Human Rights in Context: Law, Politics, Morals* (Oxford University Press 2000)

Apffel-Marglin F and Simon S, 'Feminist Orientalism and Development' in Harcourt W (eds), *Feminist Perspectives on Sustainable Development* (Zed Books 1994)

Arendt H, *Responsibility and Judgment* (Schocken Books 2003)

Batliwala S, 'The Meaning of Women's Empowerment: New Concepts from Action' in Sen G, Germain A and Chen L (eds), *Population Policies Reconsidered: Health Empowerment and Rights* (Harvard University Press 1994)

Bayili B, *Religion, Droit et Pouvoir au Burkina Faso: Les Lyèlà du Burkina Faso* (Editions l'Harmattan 1998)

Beauvoir de S, *Le Deuxième Sexe* (Coll. Folio-Essais, Gallimard 1986)

Boserup E, *Women's Role in Economic Development* (Earthscan 1970)

Branda F, *Women, Law and Human Rights: An African Perspective* (Hart Publishing 2005)

Brooks A, *Postfeminisms: Feminism, Cultural Theory and Cultural Forms* (Routledge 1997)

Bunch C, 'Passionate Politics Essays 1968–1986: Feminist Theory in Action' in Charlesworth H and Chinkin C (eds), *The Boundaries of International Law: A Feminist Analysis* (Manchester University Press 2000)

Carlsson H, Ehrenpreis M and Hughes J, *Improving Women's Lives: World Bank Actions Since Beijing*, World Bank Gender and Development Group (WB Publication January 2005)

Charlesworth H, 'What Are Women's International Human Rights?' in Cook R (ed), *Human Rights of Women: National and International Perspectives* (University of Pennsylvania Press 1994)

Charlesworth H and Chinkin C, *The Boundaries of International Law: A Feminist Analysis* (Manchester University Press 2000)

Collins Hills P, *Black Feminist Thought: Knowledge, Consciousness, and the Politics of Empowerment* (Routledge 2000)

Copelon R, 'Intimate Terror: Understanding Domestic Violence as Torture' in Cook R (ed), *Human Rights of Women: National and International Perspectives* (University of Pennsylvania Press 1995)

Cornwall A, Harrison E and Whitehead A, *Feminism in Development: Contradictions, Contestations and Challenges* (Zed Books 2007)

Costas D, 'Justice and Human Rights in Post-Modernity' in Gearty C and Tomkins A (eds), *Understanding Human Rights* (Mansell 1996)

Cotterel R, *The Sociology of Law: An Introduction* (2nd edn, Butterworths 1992) 5 citing Vago S, *Law and Society* (2nd edn, Prentice-Hall 1988)

Crew E and Harrison E, *Whose Development? An Ethnography of Aid* (Zed Books 2002) 25–48, 132–152

Dean J, *Solidarity of Strangers: Feminism After Identity Politics* (University of California Press 1996)

Dembour M-B, 'Following the Movement of a Pendulum: Between Universalism and Relativism' in Cowan J, Dembour M-B and Wilson R (eds), *Culture and Rights: Anthropological Perspectives* (Cambridge University Press 2001)

Dixon RB, *Seeing the Invisible Women Farmers in Africa: Improving Research and Data Collection* (University of California 1985)

Djavann C, *Bas les Voiles!* (Gallimard 2003)

———, *Que pense Allah de l'Europe?* (Broché 2004)

———, *Comment peut-on être Français ?* (Broché 2007)

———, *La Muette* (Broché 2008)

———, *Autoportrait de l'autre* (Poche 2009)

Fitzpatrick J, 'The Use of International Human Rights Norms to Combat Violence Against Women' in Cook R (ed), *Human Rights of Women: National and International Perspectives* (University of Pennsylvania Press 1995)

Fourest C, *La Tentation Obscurantiste* (Ed. Grasset 2005)

———, *La Dernière Utopie: Menaces sur L'Universalisme* (Grasset 2009)

———, *La Dernière Utopie: Menaces sur L'universalisme* (Grasset 2009) 57 citing Tamzali W, 'Féministes, je vous écris d'Alger' in *Libération* (Paris 14 Janvier 2004)

Fraser N, *Justice Interruptus: Critical Reflections on the "Postsocialist" Condition* (Routledge 1997)

———, 'Multiculturalism, Anti-Essentialism, and Radical Democracy: A Genealogy of Current Impasse in Feminist Theory' in Fraser N (ed), *Justice Interruptus: Critical Reflections on the "Postsocialist" Condition* (Routledge 1997)

———, *Adding Insult to Injury, Nancy Fraser Debates Her Critics* (Verso 2008)

———, *Scales of Justice: Reimagining Political Space in a Globalizing World* (Columbia University Press 2009)

Fraser N and Honneth A, *Redistribution or Recognition? A Political-Philosophical Exchange* (Verso 2003)

Fuss D, *Essentially Speaking: Feminism, Nature and Difference* (Routledge 1989)

Geerts N, *Fichu voile!: Petit argumentaire féministe et antiraciste* (Luc Pire 2010)

Gilligan C, *In a Different Voice, Psychological Theory and Women's Development* (Harvard University Press 1982)

Goetz AM, 'The Problem with Patronage: Constraints on Women's Political Effectiveness in Uganda' in Goetz AM and Hassim S (eds), *No Shortcuts to Power: African Women in Politics and Policy-Making* (Zed Books 2003)

Guy-Sheftall B (ed), *Words of Fire: An anthology of African-American Feminist Thought* (The New York Press 1995)

Higgins R, 'Introduction' in Gardner JP (ed), *Human Rights as General Norms and a State's Right to Opt Out: Reservations and Objections to Human Rights Conventions* (British Institute of International Comparative Law 1996) xix

Higgins T, 'Anti-Essentialism, Relativism and Human Rights' (1996) 19 *Harvard Women's Law Journal* in Steiner H and Alston P (eds), *International Human Rights in Context: Law Politics and Morals* (2nd edn, Oxford University Press 2000)

Hirsi Ali A, *Infidele: My Life* (The Free Press 2007)
Hooks B, *Feminist Theory: From Margin to Centre* (South End Press 1984)
Jaffré B, *Biographie de Thomas Sankara: La patrie ou la Mort* (L'Harmattan 1997)
Kabeer N, *Reversed Realities, Gender Hierarchies in Development Thought* (Verso 1994)
Kandiyoti D, 'Political Fiction Meets Gender Myth: Post-Conflict Reconstruction, "Democratisation" and Women's Rights' in Cornwall A, Harrison E and Whitehead A (eds), *Feminism in Development: Contradictions, Contestations and Challenges* (Zed Books 2007)
Kasosi ABK, *The Social Origin of Violence in Uganda* (Fountain University Press 1994)
Keller B, Forti S, Mikkelsen B, Possing S, Schoeman K, Serote RP, *Mainstreaming Gender Equality: Sida's Support for the Promotion of Gender Equality in Partner Countries, Country Report South Africa* (Sida 2001)
King EM and Mason AD, *Engendering Development Through Gender Equality, Resources and Voice*, A WB Policy Research Report (Oxford University Press January 2001)
Koso-Thomas O, *The Circumcision of Women: A Strategy for Eradication* (Zed Books 1987)
Kristeva J, 'Women Can Never Be Defined' in Marks E and de Courtivron I (eds), *New French Feminisms: An Anthology* (Schocken Books 1981)
Kuteesa F, Tumusiime-Mutebile E, Whitworth A and Williamson T, *Uganda's Economic Reforms, Insider Accounts* (Oxford University Press 2010)
Leeson PF and Minogue M (eds), *Perspectives on Development: Cross-Disciplinary Themes in Development Studies* (Manchester University Press 1988)
Lévy B et Sartre JP, *L'Éspoir Maintenant* (Verdier 1980)
Lévy B-H, *De la Guerre en Philosophie* (Ed Grasset 2010a)
———, *Pièces d'Identité* (Ed Grasset 2010b)
Lorde A, 'The Master's Tools Will Never Dismantle the Master's House' in Morroga C and Anzaldua G (eds), *The Bridge Called Me Back: Writings by Radical Women of Color* (Persaphone Press 1981) 98–101
Lykke N, *Feminist Studies: A Guide to Intersectionality Theory, Methodology and Writing* (Routledge 2010)
Lyotard J-F, *La Condition postmoderne: Rapport sur le savoir* (Les Éditions de Minuit 1979)
Macé E et Guénif-Souilams N, *Les Féministes et le Garçon Arabe* (Ed. de l'Aube 2004)
Magubane BM, *African Sociology Towards a Critical Perspective: Collective Essays* (Africa World Press 2000)
Mansell W, Meteyard B and Thomson A, *A Critical Introduction to Law* (Cavendish Publishing 2004)
Michael A, *Machines as the Measure of Men: Science, Technology and Ideologies of Western Dominance* (Cornell University Press 1989)
Mikkelsen B, *Methods for Development Work and Research: A New Guide for Practitioners* (2nd edn, Sage 2005) 312
Mohanty CT, Under Western Eyes: Feminist Scholarship and Colonial Discourse' in Mohanty CT, Russo A and Torres L (eds), *Third World Women and the Politics of Feminism* (Indiana University Press 1991a)
———, 'Introduction: Cartographies of Struggle' in Mohanty CT, Russo A and Torres L (eds), *Third World Women and the Politics of Feminism* (Indiana University Press 1991b)
———, 'Feminist Encounters: Locating the Politics of Experience' in Barett M and Philips A (eds), *Destabilising Theory: Contemporary Feminist Debates* (Stanford University Press 1992)
———, *Feminism Without Borders: Decolonising Theory, Practicing Solidarity* (Duke University Press 2003)

Morgan R (ed), *Sisterhood Is Global* (The Feminist Press at the City University of New York 1996)

Moser C, *Gender Planning and Development* (Routledge 1993)

Mosley P, Harrigan J and Toye J, *Aid and Power: The World Bank and Policy-Based Lending* (Routledge 1991)

Mosse D and Lewis D, *The Aid Effect* (Pluto Press 2005)

Mullaly S, *Human Rights Law in Perspective, Gender, Culture and Human Rights: Reclaiming Universalism* (Hart Publishing 2006)

Muthoni Wanyeki OL (ed), *Women and Land in Africa: Culture, Religion and Realizing Women's Rights* (Zed Books 2003)

Narayan U, *Dislocating Cultures: Identities, Traditions and Third – World Feminism* (Routledge 1997)

Okin SM, 'Feminism, Women's Human Rights and Cultural Differences' in Narayan U and Harding S (eds), *Decentering the Center: Philosophy for a Multicultural, Postcolonial, and Feminist World* (Indiana University Press 2000)

Peet R and Hartwick E, *Theories of Development: Contentions, Arguments, Alternatives* (2nd edn, The Guilford Press 2009) 87 citing Sachs J, *The Economic Transformation of Eastern Europe: The Case of Poland* (P K Seidman Foundation 1991)

———, *Theories of Development* (The Guilford Press 1999)

Peters J and Wolper A (eds), *Women's Rights Human Rights: International Feminist Perspectives* (Routledge 1995) 11–12

Rahman A and Toubia N, *Female Genital Mutilation: A Guide to Laws and Policies Worldwide* (Zed Books 2000)

Rai S, *The Gender Politics of Development* (Zed Books 2008)

Rawls J, *A Theory of Justice* (revised edn, Harvard University Press 1999)

Rosenne S, *The Law of Treaties: A Guide to the Legislative History of the Vienna Convention* (Oceana Publications 1970)

Sardar Ali S, 'Women's Rights, CEDAW and International Human Rights Debates: Towards Empowerment?' in Parpart J, Rai S and Staudt K (eds), *Rethinking Empowerment: Gender and Development in a Global/Local World* (Routledge 2002)

Sardar Z, 'Development and the Locations of Eurocentricism' in Munch R and O'Hearn D, *Critical Development Theory: Contribution to a New Paradigm* (Zed Books 1999)

Sartre JP, *L'existentialisme est un Humanisme* (Editions Nagel 1946)

Sellars PV, 'Individual' Liability for Collective Sexual Violence' in Knop K (ed), *Gender and Human Rights* (Oxford University Press 2004)

Sen A, *The Idea of Justice* (The Belknap Press of Harvard University Press 2009) 415 citing Hobbes T, *Leviathan* (first published 1651)

Spelman E, *Inessential Woman: Problems of Exclusion in Feminist Thought* (Beacon Press 1980)

Steiner H and Alston P, *International Human Rights in Context: Law Politics and Morals* (2nd edn, Oxford University Press 2000)

Steiner H, Alston P and Goodman G, 'Comment on the Universalist-Relativist Debate' in Steiner H, Alston P and Goodman R (eds), *International Human Rights in Context: Law, Politics, Morals* (3rd edn, Oxford University Press 2007)

Svendsen K E, *Social Development and International Development Cooperation in Welfare, Development and Security: Three Danish Essays* (The Danish National Institute of Social Research 1989)

Tamale S, *When Hens Begin to Crow, Gender and Parliamentary Politics in Uganda* (Fountain Publisher 1999)

Tibatemwa-Ekirikubinza L T, *Women's Violent Crime in Uganda: More Sinned Against Than Sinning* (Fountain Publisher 1999)

Tinker I, 'The Adverse Impact of Development on Women' in Tinker I and Bramson M (eds), *Women and Development* (Overseas Development Council 1976)

———, 'The Making of a Field: Advocates, Practitioners and Scholars' in Visvanathan N and others (eds), *The Women, Gender & Development Reader* (Zed Books 1997)

Tripp M, 'Conflicting Visions of Community and Citizenship: Women's Rights and Cultural Diversity in Uganda' in Molyneux M and Razavi S (eds), *Gender, Justice, Democracy and Rights* (Oxford University Press 2002)

Walker A, *In Search of Our Mother's Garden: Womanist Prose* (The Women's Press 1985)

Wanyeki LM (ed), *Women and Land in Africa: Culture, Religion and Realizing Women's Land Rights* (Zed Books 2003)

Ware H, *Africa on a Global Stage* (Africa World Press 2005)

Waters MA and Cartes MP, *Thomas Sankara parle: La révolution au Burkina Faso de 1983–1987* (Edition Pathfinder 2007)

Wolff RP, Barrington Moore J and Marcuse H, *A Critique of Pure Tolerance* (Beacon Press 1969)

Wood Sherif C, Harding S and Smith DE, *Feminism and Methodology*, Harding S (ed) (Open University Press 1987)

Young IM, *Justice and the Politics of Difference* (Princeton University Press 1990)

Young K, *Planning Development with Women* (St. Martin's Press1993)

———, 'Gender and Development' in Visvanathan N and others (eds), *The Women, Gender & Development Reader* (Zed Books 1997)

Young RJC, *Postcolonialism: A Very Short Introduction* (Oxford University Press 2003)

Journal articles

Abraham I, 'The Veil and the Closet: Islam and the Production of Queer Space' (2007) *Queer Space: Centers and Peripheries* UTS 1–4

Armstrong A and others, 'Uncovering Reality: Excavating Women's Rights in African Family Law' (1992) Working Paper N.7 Women and Law in Southern Africa

Arndt S, 'African Gender Trouble and African Womanism: An Interview with Chikwenye Ogunyemi and Wanjira Muthoni' (Spring 2000) *Signs: Journal of Women in Culture and Society* 253

Bedford K, 'Loving to Straighten Out Development: Sexuality and Ethnodevelopment in the World Bank's Ecuadorian Lending' (2005) 13(3) *Feminist Legal Studies* 295–322

Benabdessadok C, 'Femmes et Révolution ou Comment Libérer la Moitié de la Société' (Décembre 1985) 20 *Revue Politique Africaine*

Bottomley A, 'Shock to Thought: An Encounter (of a Third Kind) with Legal Feminism' (2004) 12(1) *Feminist Legal Studies* 29–65

Brems E, 'Enemies or Allies-Feminism and Cultural Relativism as Dissident Voices in Human Rights Discourse' (1997) 19(1) *Human Rights Quarterly* 136

Bunting A, 'Theorizing Women's Cultural Diversity in Feminist International Human Rights Strategy' (1993) 20 *Journal of Law and Society* 6

Buss D, 'Robes, Relics and Rights: The Vatican and the Beijing Conference on Women' (1998)7 *Social and Legal Studies* 3

Charlesworth H, 'Feminist Methods in International Law' (1999) 93 *American Journal of International Law* 379

Duclos N, 'Lessons of Difference: Feminist Theory and Cultural Diversity' (1990) 38 *Buffalo Law Review* 325–381

Duclos N and Charlesworth H, 'A Response to David Kennedy' (2002) 15 *Harvard Law Journal* 127

Dworkin R, 'What Is Equality? Part 2: Equality of Resources' (Fall 1981) 10(4) *Philosophy and Public Affairs* 283–345

E De La Boétie, Discours de la Servitude Volontaire (1576)

Eisenstein H, 'A Dangerous Liaison? Feminism and Corporate Globalization' *Science and Society* 69(3) cited in Fraser N, 'Feminism, Capitalism and the Cunning of History' (March–April 2009) 56 *New Left Review* 112

Engle K, 'Female Subjects of Public International Law: Human Rights and the Exotic Other Female' (1992) 26 *New England Law Review* 1509

Fenrich J and Higgens TE, 'Promise Unfulfilled: Law, Culture and Women's Inheritance Rights in Ghana' (2001) 25 *Fordham International Law Journal* 259

Flax J, 'Race/Gender and the Ethic of Difference' (1995) 23 (3) *Political Theory* 500

Flores D'arcais P, 'Undici Tesi su Hannah Arendt' (2007) 1 *MicroMega* 97–98

Fourest C, 'L'intégrisme est-il Queer?' (Automne 2005) 34 *ProChoix*

Fraser N and Bedford K, 'Social Rights and Gender Justice in the Neoliberal Moment: A Conversation About Welfare and Transnational Politics' (2008) 9(2) *Feminist Theory* 238

Getgen JE, 'Reproductive Injustice: An Analysis of Nicaragua's Complete Abortion Ban' (2008) 4 *International Law Journal* 144

Hellum A, 'Women's Human Rights and African Customary Law: Between Universalism and Relativism – Individualism and Communitarianism' (1999) 10(2) *The European Journal of Development Research* 102

Higgins R, 'Human Rights: Some Questions of Integrity' (1989) 52 *Michigan Law Review* 1

Higgins TE, 'By "Reason of their Sex": Feminist Theory, Postmodernism and Justice' (1995) 80 *Cornell Law Review* 1536

Kahn M and Véron A, *Des Femmes dans la Mafia: Madones ou Marraines?* (nouveau monde éditions 2015)

Kanse Lean MS, 'Le CNR et les femmes: de la difficulté de libérer la " moitié du ciel "' (Mars 1989) *Revue Politique Africaine*

Kapur R, 'A Love Song to Our Mongrel Selves: Hybridity, Sexuality and the Law' (1999) 8(3) *Social and Legal Studies* 353

Kennedy D, 'The International Human Rights Movement: Part of the Problem?' (2002) 15 *Harvard Human Rights Journal* 127

Koenig MA, Lutalo T, Zhao F, Nalugoda F, Wabwire-Mangen F, Kiwanuka N, Wagman J, Serwadda D, Wawer M and Gray R, 'Domestic Violence in Rural Uganda: Evidence from Community-Based Study' (2003) 81(1) *Bulletin of the World Health Organisation* 53–60

Malmqvist H, 'Development Aid, Humanitarian Assistance and Emergency Releif' in 'Building Stability in Africa: Challenges for the New Millennium' (February 2000) 46 Monograph

Mannen L, 'The Government War on Women's Rights in Nicaragua: Feminists Stand Up Against Anti-Abortion Crusade and Daniel Ortega's Rightward Turn' (February–March 2009) *Freedom Socialist* 30

Molyneux M, 'The Politics of Abortion in Nicaragua: Revolutionary Pragmatism or Feminism in the Realm of Necessity?' (May 1988) 29 *Feminist Review*

Moruzzi NC, 'A Problem with Headscarves: Complexity of Political and Social Identities' (1994) 22(4) *Political Theory* 653

Mutua M, 'Savages, Victims, and Saviors: The Metaphor of Human Rights' (2001) 42 *Harvard International Law Journal* 201

Navarro-Valls J, 'Report of the Holy See in preparation for the Fourth World Conference on Women' (1995) para 2 (a) 'To promote Women's Equal Dignity' (6 September 1995) 36 L'osservatore Romano 2–4

Otto D, 'A Post-Beijing Reflection on the Limitations and Potential of Human Rights Discourse for Women' (Transnational 1999) 3 *Women and International Human Rights Law* 115, 135

Rathgeber EM, 'WID, WAD, GAD: Trends in Research and Practice' (1990) *Journal of Developing Areas* 24

Redwell C, 'Universality or Integrity? Some Reflections on Reservations to General Multilateral Treaties' (1993) 64 *British Yearbook of International Law* 245

Richey LA, 'In Search of feminist Foreign Policy: Gender, Development, and State Identity' (June 2001) 36(2) *Cooperation and Conflict* 177

Riding A, 'Rape Is "a Weapon of War" in the Bosnian Genocide' (9 January 1993) 50(131) *European Inquiry Ocala Star-Banner* 127

Robert A-C, 'Président des Pauvres' (avril-mai 2007) 93 *Manière de Voir*

Sardar Z, 'Beyond Development: An Islamic Perspective' (1996) 8 *European Journal of Development Research* 2

Stark B, 'Women and Globalization: The Failure and Postmodern Possibilities of International Law' (2000) 33 *Vanderbilt Journal of Transnational Law* 503

Swiss S and Giller JE, 'Rape as Crime of War: A Medical Perspective' (1993) *Journal of the American Medical Association* 612–615

Tamale S, 'Law Reform and Women's Rights in Uganda' (2002) *East African Journal of Peace and Human Rights* 177

Tamir Y, 'Hands Off Clitoridectomy' (Summer 1996) 31 *Boston Review* 21

Teitelbaum V, 'The European Veil Debate' (2000) 1 *Israel Journal of Foreign Affairs* 89–99

Whitehead A, 'Some Preliminary Notes on the Subordination of Women' (1979) 10(3) *IDS Bulletin* 10

Willigen JV and Channa VC, 'Law Custom, and Crimes Against Women: The Problem of Dowry Death in India' (1991) 50(4) *Human Organisation the Society for Applied Anthropology*

Newspaper and magazine articles

Adeyemi T and Stevens A, 'Nicaraguan Activists Press Abortion Legal Case' *Women's e-News* (16 March 2007)

'Analysing Maternal Deaths in Nicaragua' *IPAS* (26 June 2008)

Baffour A, 'Behind Every "successful" Darling. . . . There Is a World Bank (sorry) Donor' *New African* (June 2001)

Boseley S, 'Nicaragua Refuses to Lift Abortion Ban' *The Guardian* (London, 11 June 2010)

Cargill T, 'Uganda – Still the Donors' Darling' *The World Today* 60(12) (December 2004) 26–27

Choura R, 'Killing for Honor – a Deadly Part of a Larger Trend' *Palestine Monitor* (2 August 2007)

Daoud K, 'Le discours de repentance de l'Occident est sclérosant- Il faut se libérer des explications post-coloniales et penser au-delà de la victimisation' *Le Point* (19 October 2017)

———, 'Enfermer la femme, c'est s'emprisoner soi-même' *L'entretiens par Stéphanie Antoine, France 24* (25 September 2017). <www.youtube.com/watch?v=UQgyvrU0cdA>
———, 'La chasse aux corps amoureux' *Le Point* (14 September 2017)
Desnos M, 'Rayana Agréssée: Une Féministe qui Dérange?' *Paris Match* (Paris, 15 January 2010)
Fox M 'Decision to Annul Section of Law on Violence Against Women' *Venezuelanalysis.com* (Caracas, 13 June 2006)
Jaffré B, 'Thomas Sankara ou la dignité de l'Afrique' *Le Monde Diplomatique* (Paris, 15 Octobre 2007)
Julliard J, 'Imprévisible Liberté' *Marianne* (Paris, 5–11 Février 2011)
Lloyd D, 'Nicaragua's Abortion Ban Is Inhumane and Backward' *Politics Daily* (24 February 2010)
Márquez H, 'Anti-Domestic Violence Campaign Targets Men' *IPS News* (Caracas September 2007)
McGreal C, 'Hundreds of Thousands Raped in Congo Wars' *The Guardian* (London, 14 November 2006)
'A More Hopeful Continent, The Lion Kings? Africa Is Now One of the World's Fastest-Growing Regions' *The Economist* (6 January 2011)
Ndebesa N, 'The Inequalities Will Soon Breed Tragedy' *The New Vision* (Kampala, 21 December 2010)
Romano ML, 'Scarves, Veils and History' *Best of Sicily Magazine* (undated)
Smith L, 'Corrective Rape: The Homophobic Fallout of Post-Apartheid South Africa' *The Telegraph* (21 May 2015)
Tebajjukiram M, 'Widow Inheritance to Be Banned in Uganda' *The New Vision* (Kampala, 22 November 2007)
'Thomas Sankara: L'Homme Intègre' *Le monde Diplomatique* (Paris, 15 Octobre 2007)
Wynter C and McIlroy J, 'Venezuela: Women Protest Domestic Violence' *Green Left* (November 1993)

Reports

World Bank

Carlsson H, Ehrenpreis M and Hughes J, 'Improving Women's Lives: World Bank Actions Since Beijing, World Bank Gender and Development Group' (World Bank January 2005)
King EM and Mason AD, 'Engendering Development Through Gender Equality, Resources and Voice: A WB Policy Research Report' (World Bank and Oxford University Press January 2001)
Mason C, Valdivieso S, Razzaz S, Blackden C, Fort L and Carlsson H, 'The Business Case for Mainstreaming Gender, The Empirical Links of Gender to Poverty and Growth, Gender Equality and Growth, Gender and Poverty Reduction and Development Effectiveness' in 'Integrating Gender into the World Bank's Work: A Strategy for Action' (World Bank Publication January 2002)
———, 'Integrating Gender into the World Bank's Work: A Strategy for Action' (World Bank January 2002)
World Bank, 'Gender Equality as Smart Economics: A World Bank Group Gender Action Plan for the Fiscal Years 2007–2010' (World Bank September 2006)

DFID

'Evaluation of DFID's Policy and Practice in Support of Gender Equality and Women's Empowerment' (DFID 2006)
Forti S and Ljungman CM, 'Evaluation of DFID's Policy and Practice in Support of Gender Equality and Women's Empowerment: Gender Equality Through Justice and Rights-Based Policies and Programmes' Thematic Study, Evaluation Report EV669 (DFID August 2006)
'Gender Equality Action Plan' (DFID 2007–2009)
'Gender Equality at the Heart of Development: Why the Role of Women Is Crucial to End World Poverty' (DFID 2007)
'Poverty Elimination and the Empowerment of Women: Strategies for Achieving the International Development Target' (DFID 2000)
Watkins F, 'Evaluation of DFID Development Assistance: Gender Equality and Women's Empowerment, DFID's Experience of Gender Mainstreaming: 1995 to 2004' (DFID December 2004)
'White Paper on International Development, Eliminating World Poverty, Making Governance Work for the Poor' (DFID July 2006)

Danida

'Commitment to Development Priorities of the Danish Government for Danish Development Assistance 2007–2011' (Ministry of Foreign Affairs of Denmark)
'Gender Equality in Danish Development Cooperation, Strategy' (Denmark Ministry of Foreign Affairs Strategy 2004)
'Programme Formulation on Democratic Governance in Burkina Faso' (Danida 2004)
'Strategic Framework on Gender Equality Rights and Diversity' (Ministry of Foreign Affairs 2014)
'Women in Development, Danida's WID Policy Towards the Year 2000' (Ministry of Foreign Affairs 1993)

Sida

'Evaluación de la cooperación de Suecia a Nicaragua en el área Democracia y Derechos Humanos (1997–2000)' (Informe Noviembre 2000)
'Evaluation of Sida's Support to Development Co-operation for the Promotion of Gender Equality' (Sida Evaluations 2001)
Forti S, 'External Evaluation of ICORN 2012–2016' (Sida, Evaluation Report March 2018)
Forti S, Lamien O, 'Evaluation of NDI's Programme on Strengthening Women's Participation in Political and Decentralisation Processes in Burkina Faso' (Sida, Evaluation Report July 2008)
NDI, 'Proposal for the Program Submitted by NDI to Sida' (Sida 2005a)
———, 'Rapport du Forum National sur le Rôle et la Participation des Femmes à la vie politique' (NDI 2005b)
———, 'Semi-Annual Reports' 2006, 2007 and 2008
———, 'Le Manuel de la Candidate' (NDI/Sida 2007)
———, 'Mid-Term Evaluation Report' (NDI February 2007)
———, 'Rapport Atelier de Formation des Femmes Maires, adjointes aux Maires et responsables des commissions permanentes' (NDI 2007)

———, 'Rapport, Atelier national des Femmes cadres de partis politiques' (NDI Février 2008)
———, 'Rapport de Formations des Candidates aux élections législatives' (NDI 2007)
———, 'Rapport du Forum élues – population Kakologho' (NDI 2007)
———, 'Women's Political Participation in Burkina Faso' (Sida/NDI 2007)
Sida, 'Strategy for Swedish Development Cooperation with Burkina Faso 2004–2006' (Sida 2004)
———, 'Gender Equality: Sida's Policy and Methods at a Glance, Key Steering Documents' (Sida 2005)
———, 'Policy Promoting Gender Equality in Development Co-operation 2005–2010' (Sida 2005)
———, 'Promoting Gender Equality in Development Cooperation: Policy' (2005–2010) 4–6
———, 'Draft Country Report' (Sida 2007)
———, 'Evaluation of the National Democratic Institutes Programme in Strengthening Women's Participation in Political and Decentralisation Processes in Burkina Faso' (Sida, Evaluations 2008) 1–44

Other bilateral IDA agencies

Winship JD, 'A Summary of Gender Strategies of Multilateral Development Agencies and Selected Bilateral Donors, Development and Training' (September 2004) USAID Report

OECD and EU

OECD, 'Concept and Approaches Linked to Gender Equality' (OECD/ DAC Source Book 1998) 16
OECD, 'Gender Evaluation, Aid to Support Gender Equality, 1999–2003' (OECD March 2005) 1
OECD, 'Gender Equality and Social Institutions in Venezuela' (SIGI 2007)
OECD-DAC, 'Sweden (2000), Development Co-operation Review' 'DAC Member Peer Review' (2000)

UN agencies reports

'A Comprehensive Policy Paper and Action Plan' (UNCHS 1996)
Development Fund for Women 2000 in DFID, 'Poverty Elimination and the Empowerment of Women, Strategies for Achieving International Development Targets' (September 2000)
IFRTD, 'Balancing the Load: Proceedings of the Asia and Africa Regional Seminars on Gender and Rural Transport' (IFRTD July 1999)
ILO, 'Trafficking in Women to Italy for Sexual Exploitation, Migration Information Programme' (IOM 1996)
———, 'Reducing Labour Exploitation of Children and Women: Combating Trafficking in the Greater Mekong Sub Region' Project Memo (ILO 2003–2008)
———, 'First Hand Knowledge, Voices Across the Mekong, Community Action Against Trafficking of Women and Children' A "Good Practice" Publication (ILO 2005)

———, 'Action Against Trafficking in Human Beings' (ILO 2008)
ILO/IPEC SE, 'Asia, Reducing Labour Exploitation of Children and Women: Combating Trafficking in the Greater Mekong Sub Region – ILO/IPEC SE Asia' (Phase I 1999–2002 / Phase 2 2003–2008)
———, 'Programa fortalecimiento de la ciudadanía de las mujeres en America latina y el Caribe' (PGU/IULA 2001)
'Las mujeres innovando la gestión de las ciudades FEMUM- PGU Cuadernos de 15 casos' (UN-HABITAT 1999–2000)
Lüdeking G and Williams C, 'Documenting the Work of the Community Development Programme in 60 Municipalities and Settlements of Bolivia, Costa Rica, Ecuador, Ghana, Sri Lanka, Uganda and Zambia (1986–1996)' (UNCHS/Institute of Social Studies Evaluation Research June 1999)
Sita M, 'Trafficking in Women and Children: Situation and Trends in African Countries' (UNAFRI May 2003)
Ssewanyana SN, 'Growth, Inequality, Cash Transfers and Poverty in Uganda: Country Study' (International Policy Centre for Inclusive Growth UNDP 2009)
UNCHS, 'Poverty, Participation, and Government Enablement, A Summary of the Findings, Lessons Learned and Recommendations of the UNCHS' (Institute of Social Studies Evaluation Research 1996–1998)
UNDP, 'Human Development Report' (UNDP 2009)
UNIFEM, 'Programme of Support for Integrated Actions in Gender and Race Equity in Brazil, UNIFEM' (2003–2008)
———, 'Progress of the World's Women 2000' UNIFEM Biennial Report (New York: United Nations
WHO, 'First World Report on Violence and Heath' (WHO 2002)

Other documents

Afzal S, 'To Estimate an Equation Explaining the Determinants of Dowry' (Iqra University September 2009)
Amnesty International, 'The Law Is There, Let's Use It: Ending Domestic Violence in Venezuela' (Amnesty International Report 2008)
Brial J, 'L'assassinat de Thomas Sankara, Président du Burkina Faso, le 15 octobre 1987: Causes et conséquences' (Mémoire de DEA, Thomassankara.net 2006)
'A Framework for Transforming Gender Relations in South Africa' (Commission on Gender Equality 2000)
'Global Database of Quotas for Women' (Institute for Democracy and Electoral Assistance IDEA, 19 February 2003)
Groots Kenya, 'WSSD Action Plan' (Groots Kenya 2002)
Hoffman MC, 'Nicaragua's First Lady Issues Scathing Denouncement of "False Feminism" That Supports Abortion and Opposes Family Values' (13 September 2008)
Human Rights Watch, 'We'll Kill You If You Cry: Sexual Violence in the Sierra Leone Conflict' (Human Rights Watch Report January 2003 15) (1A) 31
———, 'Just Die Quietly: Domestic Violence and Women's Vulnerability to HIV in Uganda, Human Rights Watch Report' (August 2003) 15 (15 A)
———, 'Struggling to Survive: Barriers to Justice for Rape Victims in Rwanda' (Human Rights Watch Report September 2004) 16 (10A)

———, 'Occupied Palestinian Territories, a Question of Security, Violence Against Women and Girls' (Human Rights Watch Report November 2006 18 N.7(E)) 3

IPAS, 'Nicaragua on the Verge of Banning Abortion' (IPAS 2006)

———, 'Nicaragua Outlaws Abortion Even to Save a Woman's Life' (IPAS October 2006)

Isis-WICCE, 'Women's Experiences of Armed Conflict in Uganda: Gulu District 1986–1999' (Isis-WICCE Report July 2001) Part 1

———, 'Medical Interventional Study of War Affected Gulu District, Uganda' (Isis-WICCE Report July 2001) Part 2

IXCHEN, Centro de Mujeres and DFID, 'No más vidas truncadas, Documentando delitos de violencia sexual contra niñas y adolescentes en cinco departamentos de Nicaragua' (IXCHEN, Centro de Mujeres and DFID publicación 2006)100

Joireman SF, 'Applying Property Rights Theory to Africa: The Consequences of Formalizing Informal Land Rights' (Meeting of the International Society for New Institutional Economics in Boulder, Colorado, Department of Politics and International Relations, Wheaton College 2006)

Kharono E, 'Feminist Challenge to the Land Question: Options for Meaningful Action: A Concept Paper' (The African Gender Institute, University of Cape Town 1998)

Lakshmanan IAR, 'Nicaraguan Abortion Ban Called a Threat to Lives' (Boston Globe, 26 November 2006) A1

Linzaad L, 'Reservations to UN Human Rights Treaties: Ratify and Ruin?' (Martinus Nijhoff 1995)

Lowe P, 'Fuego en el hielo. Mujeres mineras de Chorolque: Convierten el hielo en sopa y la piedra en pan' (Dirección de Medio Ambiente de la COMIBOL 2005)

Mulyagonja I, 'Family Law Reform in Uganda: A Tale of Petty Issues, Bitterness and Crocodile Tears' (South African Constitutional Litigation and Legal Development Project Conference 2001)

Narayan U, 'Informal Sector Work, Microcredit and Third World Women's "Empowerment": A Critical Perspective' (XXII World Congress of Philosophy of Law and Social Philosophy conference, Granada, Spain May 2005)

Obot D, 'A Fascinating Example of Successful Liberalisation' (Social Watch 2003)

Oloka-Onyango, 'Civil Society on the Barricades: The Role of Human Rights and Women's Organisations in the Formulation of the Bill of Rights of Uganda's 1995 Constitution' (Civil Society and Governance Programme, IDS 2000)

Olsen GR and Udsholt L, 'The Danish Aid Administration: Between Politics and Technical Rationality' (Copenhagen: Centre for Development Research, CDR Working Paper No. 95 1995)

Palestinian National Authority, 'Domestic Violence Survey 2005' (Palestinian Central Bureau of Statistics February 2006)

PWRDC, 'Annual Report, August 2007-December 2008' (PWRDC 2008)13

Sankara T, 'La libération de la femme: une exigence du future' (8 March 1987)

Svendsen KE, 'Social Development and International Development cooperation in Welfare, Development and Security: Three Danish Essays' (1989) The Danish National Institute of Social Research

Tamale S, 'Gender Trauma in Africa: Enhancing Women's Links to Resources' (2002) unpublished research

UWONET, 'Women and Land Rights in Uganda' (1997) FES

Walker A, 'A Fact Sheet on Women and Armed Conflict' (October 2003) IWTC Women's Global Net

Yngström I, 'Women, Wives and Land Rights in Africa: Situating Gender Beyond the Household in the Debate over Land Policy and Changing Tenure Systems' (2002) 30(1) *Development Studies* 21, cited in Joireman SF, 'Applying Property Rights Theory to Africa: The Consequences of Formalizing Informal Land Rights' (Meeting of the International Society for New Institutional Economics in Wheaton College Boulder Colorado 2006)

International and regional legislative instruments, UN resolutions and reports

CEDAW Committee, 'Progress Achieved in the Implementation of the Convention on the Elimination of All Forms of Discrimination Against Women' A/CONF177/7 (1980)

CEDAW Committee 'NGO Shadow Report: South Africa' (June 1998)

CEDAW 'NGO Shadow Report' (South Africa 'Report on Government's Implementation of CEDAW and the Beijing Platform for Action' Parliamentary Committee on the Improvement of the Quality of Life and Status of Women (November 1998)

CEDAW Committee, 'Concluding Comments of the Committee on the Elimination of Discrimination Against Women: Nicaragua' 17, U.N. Doc. CEDAW/C/NIC/CO/6 (2 February 2007)

Committee of Ministers to Member States of the Council of Europe Recommendation Rec (2002)5 on the Protection of Women Against Violence

Convention on the Elimination of All Forms of Discrimination Against Women (adopted 18 December 1979, entered into force 3 September 1981) (1980) 1249 UNTS 13, reprinted in 19 ILM 33 (CEDAW)

The Convention on the Elimination of All Forms of Racial Discrimination (adopted 21 December 1965, entered into force 4 January 1969) (1965) 660 UNTS 195

The Declaration on the Elimination of Violence Against Women in the ASEAN Region (2004)

ECOSOC, 'The Role of Employment and Work in Poverty Eradication: Empowerment and Advancement of Women' Res 2000/26 (28 July 2000)

European Parliament Resolution on Female Genital Mutilation (200172035 (INI))

European Parliament Resolution of 24 March 2009 on Combating Female Genital Mutilation in the EU (2008/2071 (INI))

The Inter-American Convention on the Prevention, Punishment and Eradication of Violence Against Women (signed 9 June 1994, entered into force 3 March 1995) (1994) reprinted in 33 ILM 1534

Protocol to the African Charter on Human and Peoples' Rights on the Rights of Women in Africa (adopted 11 July 2003, entered into force 25 November 2005) (2003) CAB/LEG/66.6/Rev1 (the Protocol on the Rights of Women in Africa) art 1(J)

Report of the Secretary-General, 'Implementation of the Outcome of the Fourth World Conference on Women' and of the Special Century' (A/55/341)

'Report on South Africa Government's Implementation of CEDAW and the Beijing Platform for Action' (Parliamentary Committee on the Improvement of the Quality of Life and Status of Women November 1998)

'Report of the World Conference of the International Women's Year, Declaration of Mexico on the Equality of Women and Their Contribution to Development and Peace' (Mexico City 19 June–2 July 1975) UN Doc E/CONF 66/34, 73

Resolution 1325 (2000) S/Res/1325(2000)
Resolution 1820 (2008) S/Res/1820 (2008)
Session of the General Assembly 'Women 2000: Gender Equality, Development and Peace in the Twenty-First Century' (A/55/341)
UN Committee for the Elimination of All Forms of Discrimination Against Women (CEDAW Committee), 'General Recommendations No. 19 on Violence Against Women' (11th Session 1992) UN Doc A/47/38 para 6
United Nations Millennium Declaration, UNGA Res 55/2 (8 September 2000) UN Doc A/55/L.2
United Nations Resolution Adopted by the General Assembly on 25 September 2015: Transforming our world: The 2030 Agenda for Sustainable Development, A/RES/70/1 (21 October 2015)
Vienna Convention on the Law of Treaties (adopted 23 May 1969, entered force 27 January 1980) reprinted in 8 ILM 679
'Zanzibar Declaration, Women of Africa for A Culture of Peace' (The Pan-African Women's Conference on a Culture of Peace, Zanzibar, 17–20 May 1999)

National legislative instruments

Constitution of Burkina Faso 1991
Constitution of the Republic of South Africa (1996) Chapter 2 Bill of Rights 7–39
Constitution of the Republic of Uganda 1995
Sweden, Government Bill 1962
Uganda, Children Act 1996
Uganda, Domestic Relations Bill 2003
Uganda, Land Act 1998
Uganda, Order in Council 1902
Uganda, The Penal Code Act 1950
Uganda, The Succession (Amendment) Decree 1972
UK, The Divorce Reform Act 1969

Index

For Product Safety Concerns and Information please contact our EU representative GPSR@taylorandfrancis.com Taylor & Francis Verlag GmbH, Kaufingerstraße 24, 80331 München, Germany

Batch number: 10725973

Printed by Printforce, the Netherlands